# More Than Words

*More Than Words* provides an introduction to both communication theory and practice. The authors cover the essential elements of communication, including communication between individuals and groups, in organizations and through mass media and new technologies. This new edition of the best-selling text has been fully revised and updated to take into account new developments in communication and media studies.

The third edition features case studies and assignments, and a new series of key questions helping students to understand central concepts in communication studies. It contains expanded sections on mass media and on practical communication and media skills, with guidance on listening skills, interpersonal and social skills, writing skills, leaflet design, as well as planning, scripting and producing audio and video material.

*More Than Words* is illustrated with new models and photographs and has checklist summaries for easy revision purposes. Clear and practical, it is an essential text for students of communication studies.

**Richard Dimbleby** is Principal of Bournemouth and Poole College of Further Education, and Chairman of Examiners for AEB's Communication Studies A-Level. **Graeme Burton** is a freelance author and lecturer, and was Senior Lecturer in Communication Studies at Filton College, Bristol. They are the authors of *Teaching Communication* (Routledge, 1990).

# More Than Words

**An introduction to communication**

**Third edition**

Richard Dimbleby
and
Graeme Burton

**London and New York**

First published 1985
by Methuen & Co. Ltd

Second edition first published 1992
by Routledge
11 New Fetter Lane, London EC4P 4EE

Third edition 1998

Simultaneously published in the USA and Canada
by Routledge
29 West 35th Street, New York, NY 10001

©1985, 1992, 1998 Richard Dimbleby and Graeme Burton

Typeset in Janson and Futura by Keystroke,
Jacaranda Lodge, Wolverhampton
Printed and bound in Great Britain by TJ International Ltd,
Padstow, Cornwall

*British Library Cataloguing in Publication Data*
A catalogue record for this book is available from
the British Library

*Library of Congress Cataloguing in Publication Data*
Dimbleby, Richard.
    More than words: an introduction to communication / Richard
  Dimbleby and Graeme Burton. – 3rd ed.
    Includes bibliographical references and index.
    1. Communication. I. Burton, Graeme. II. Title.
P90.D53     1998
302.2–dc21   97–38903

ISBN 0–415–17006–0 (hbk)
      0–415–17007–9 (pbk)

For our families

# Contents

# Figures and table

## Figures

## Table

# Preface

Just as toothpaste and mouthwash are really not the key to social success, nobody can give you a communication pill which will automatically transform you into a communication star.

Myers and Myers, *Dynamics of Human Communication*, 1985

## Why study communication?

If you're looking at this book we assume you're interested in knowing more about 'communication' and interested in learning how to communicate more effectively.

Whether we like it or not we spend every moment communicating. We depend on this activity in our personal, social and working lives. So it makes sense to find out *what* we're communicating, *how* we're communicating and *why* we're communicating.

We believe the study of communication is about:

**knowing** – what happens when people communicate with themselves and with each other;

**understanding** – how that knowledge can be used to explain and interpret the processes of communication in everyday life;

**skills** – using this knowledge and understanding to enable us to communicate more effectively.

## What is communication studies?

Many school and college courses now carry this label in some form. Increasingly people recognize that being an effective communicator is an asset.

In the past the art of effective communication (being able to express your ideas and opinions and understand other people's) was thought to be based on 'correct' uses of language.

However, communication studies goes beyond this to include 'appropriate' uses of both language and other forms of communication. These are studied to enable us to understand and deal with people.

Communication studies embraces the use and analysis of media technologies, e.g. information technology, video, films and audio materials.

The art of communicating is not a natural process or an ability we are born with. **We learn how to communicate.** Therefore we may study what we learn in order to use our knowledge more effectively.

**All communication involves the creation and exchange of meanings.** These meanings are represented through 'signs' and 'codes'. Communication studies is concerned with the business of making and understanding 'signs'.

**People seem to have a need to read meaning into all human actions.** Observing and understanding this process can lead us to be more aware of what we are doing when we are communicating.

## What this book offers

This book helps you to develop skills and techniques of communicating.

It describes theories about communication in order to understand why and how the processes of communication work.

Our aim has been to produce a readable book. We have simplified and abbreviated a good deal. We have not attempted to include discussion of all possible theories about communication. Readers who wish to follow up the ideas of this book with more factual detail and background information will find suggestions for further work at the end of each chapter and in the resource lists at the end of the book.

## How to use this book

The *general reader* may like to go from first to last page. Alternatively, you may prefer to dip into sections that particularly interest you. You may wish to use it as a source of reference.

The *teacher of communication* may want to use it as a course book and as a source of ideas and discussion, presentations and practical activities.

The *student* will find sections that provide an account of key concepts and understandings of communication, with examples and suggestions for your own practical work. On your own or in a group we hope you will gain ideas for analysing other people's communication and for creating your own communications.

All chapters will follow a similar pattern:

- brief summary of the whole chapter,
- a personal story attached to some sections,
- general concepts and ideas,
- particular examples, applications and cases,
- review of the main elements of the chapter,
- assignments to develop analytical and creative skills, with suggestions for further reading.

We hope that readers will explore the meanings of our illustrations as they relate to the sections and topics which follow them. In particular, these pictures may say something about people's values and views of others in terms of gender, age, status and occupation.

## Why another book about communication?

There are many books about communication. Some are about personal communication skills, some about the mass media, some about use of language, some about business communication. We have brought all of these topics together in one book to provide a general introduction.

Many of the available books are rather difficult to read because they contain a good deal of jargon and are aimed at graduate-level readers. We have tried to explain some of the jargon, to create a book that is accessible to people in the final years of school, to students at colleges and to any interested reader.

Richard Dimbleby
Graeme Burton
*January 1998*

# Acknowledgements

Now that we have reached our third edition we are pleased and humbled by the years that have passed, and by the numbers of colleagues, friends and students who have contributed to the ideas in this book, even if they don't realize it. Thank you to these people, past and present. Although it has become almost invidious to single out people for thanks, we have not forgotten Jackie Adams who laboured with the original typescript, nor Jane Armstrong of what was then Methuen for providing the original opportunity and support in creating this work.

We are grateful to our families for their continued support and patience and for helping make some of the photographs. Judy and Gill live with the pressures of book making – thank you. Nick Dimbleby has given us photographs and part of chapter 6 – thank you. And Leo has sacrificed valuable games time for humble word processing.

We are grateful to Shola Fagbemiro for allowing us to use her photograph. Also to the Engineering Industry Careers Service for figure 14. Also we gratefully give acknowledgements to the following for permission to reproduce their work: *The Independent on Sunday* for the illustration on page 122, Damage and Big Life records for that on page 216, and the Spice Girls for gracing our relatively unglamorous pages on page 154. Every effort has been made to trace copyright holders. Where this has not been possible we apologize to those concerned.

Not least, we offer our appreciation to Rebecca Barden, our editor at Routledge, and to her colleagues who have wrestled with our typescript, for making this possible and for pulling it all together. We hope that your faith is rewarded.

# Chapter 1

# What is communication?

One cannot not communicate.
Watzlawick, Beavin and Jackson, *Pragmatics of Human Communication*, 1968

This chapter provides a general introduction and background to the whole book by explaining four important aspects of communication:

1    How we experience communication, and how this experience can be analysed.
2    How communication serves our personal, social, economic, creative and play needs.
3    Ways of describing and explaining communication processes.

# 1 How do we experience communication?

### CATHY'S STORY

*Cathy was a bouncy kind of person. Even her hair, which caused her private despair, was springy and irrepressible. One of her friends had nicknamed her Tigger. Cathy wasn't sure if that was a compliment or not. But it didn't stop her being disgracefully cheerful in the morning. This one was no exception. Most of her friends were sitting at the table in the college canteen like a scene from* Return of the Zombies. *Cathy was punching buttons on the juke box and then chatting to the assistant on the till before she came bouncing back to the table. Tom was out of it anyway. You could hear his music even though it was coming through his headphones. Jacob had his head in his hands, but was not dying, only looking at a music mag. Sarah was reading a chapter for the next class, which she should have done a week ago. Cathy felt guilty at this, and pulled out her folder. She was looking at her notes, but not really concentrating. She had put in for entertainments officer in the union elections and this was very much on her mind. She wouldn't say anything to the others, but she really wanted to win the election. She had run her own poster campaign and had even made a tape for the college radio, with Jacob's help. Only the lecturer running the course had vetoed electioneering on the radio. Cathy glanced at her watch. She had just remembered that she wanted to photocopy something, and the class time was coming up. Tom waved his hand languidly as Cathy bounced out of the canteen.*

### ABOUT CATHY'S STORY

If you were asked to spot references to communication in this story, you would probably refer to objects that communicate: things like magazines or television are what many people immediately associate with the word 'communication'. In fact we also experience communication through other things such as talk and gestures. One could say that all such examples are, in one way or another, means of communication. See what you can find in the story, and see if you can guess what affects how the people in it communicate, or don't, as the case may be.

## 1.1 Means of communication

In this case, communication is defined in terms of the means by which it takes place. It seems that if we are talking about radio, or painting, for example, then we must be talking about communication. But this isn't good enough because it doesn't tell us how the means of communication is being used. It doesn't tell us why the communication is happening. In fact, it doesn't tell us a lot of things, all of which partly answer our main question, what is communication?

Still, we have to start somewhere, and it is useful to sort out how one describes the many means of communication that we use and experience. Not all of them are, strictly speaking, individual and separate forms. So we suggest that you use the following three terms:

(a) **Form of communication**
    **is a way of communicating such as speaking or writing or drawing.**
    Forms are distinct and separate from one another in so far as they have their own system for putting the message across. So, when marks are made on paper according to certain rules (such as those of grammar and spelling), then we create words and the 'form' of writing.

    As a generalization, many of what we would call 'forms' are ways of communicating which we control directly, such as non-verbal communication (gestures, facial expressions, etc.).

(b) **Medium of communication**
    **is a means of communicating which combines different forms.**
    A medium often involves the use of technology that is beyond the control of most of us. So, for example, a book is a medium which uses forms of communication such as words, pictures and drawings.

(c) **The media**
    **are those examples of mass communication which have come to be a distinct group of their own.**
    We are going to discuss these in chapter 5, and say something about what they have in common and how they communicate with us. Examples of these are radio, television, cinema, newspapers and magazines.

    These media are also distinctive in the way that they may include a number of forms of communication. For example, television offers words, pictures and music.

    Again, the term 'media' often identifies those means of communication which are based on technology that makes a bridge between the communicator and the receiver.

## Comment

**Some qualities of forms or media of communication are 'built in'.** So, something like speech is necessarily transient. There is no permanent record of what is said. A magazine, on the other hand, has the quality of storing what it communicates: there is a permanent record on the page and we can go back to the communication any time we want to.

**Some qualities of forms or media of communication are imposed.** For example, cartoons, whether in a newspaper or on television, would probably be described as funny, but they don't have to be. Serious cartoon films have been made. Commercial interests and film-makers have imposed a habit of using the medium in a particular way.

To take another example, we tend to think of radio as a broadcast medium. But this quality is also imposed, and is not a natural consequence of the technology of radio. Setting aside problems of crowded airwaves, there is no technical reason why radio should not be used by us for exchange of messages, as much as for transmission. Radio telephones are of course such a use, but we think of them as telephones not as a form of radio.

**All forms or media of communication extend the power of our senses.** All the communication that we give or receive must pass through our five senses, especially those of sight and hearing. This is true even when we use some piece of technology to aid our communication. A public address system extends the range of the human voice. A tape recording extends our ability to communicate over distances, or even through time. It can be carried from place to place and can be kept for many years. Computers are interesting because they are also extending human powers such as that of memory. A computer never forgets what it has been 'told', and can do the same job over and over again.

**Most means of communication are intentional.** That is to say, someone created them with the intention of communicating a message. This could include even unusual examples such as a church spire. It can be argued that this is intended to draw attention to the building, to its function and to a religion.

However, it is important to recognize that messages and meanings can also be understood in some cases where the means of communication is used unintentionally. For example, every day we deal with a flood of messages about our environment. Neighbours may not intend to tell us about their activity when they are using a lawnmower. But of course we do take a message about what they are doing and where they are from the sound of the lawnmower.

In chapter 2 we will see that this question of intention can be particularly important when understanding people's non-verbal messages. They may send these to us unintentionally.

## 1.2 Communication makes connections

In everyday experience we find that **communication is something which makes connections**.

The connections are made between one person and another, or between one group of people and another. Sometimes the connection is immediate, as when we talk face to face. Sometimes it is 'delayed', as when advertisers communicate with us through street posters. But still a connection is being made, mainly through what we have called forms or media.

What flows through the connection are the ideas, beliefs, opinions and pieces of information that are the material and the content of communication.

Our television set links us with the world at large through news programmes. Speech links us with each other.

But bear in mind the fact that being able to speak to someone doesn't mean that we can get across what we want to say. Having made the connection, we then have to learn how to use it to the best of our ability.

## 1.3 Communication is an activity

**We experience communication as an activity.**

It is something that we do, something that we make, and something that we work on when we receive it from others. In this sense, communication is not just about speech, but about speaking and listening; not just about photography, but about photographing and viewing photographs.

When we are talking to someone, we are actively engaged in making sense of what the other person is saying, as much as talking ourselves. For the same reason, it isn't true to say that watching television is passive. On the contrary, just as a group of people have been actively engaged in putting a programme together, so we are actively engaged in making sense of the programme.

## 1.4 Communication is learnt

**Communicating is something that we learn to do.**

In fact, we not only learn how to communicate, but we also use communication to learn how to communicate. This is what is happening in schools and colleges at the moment. It is what is happening as you read this book – we hope.

Our earliest experiences as babies include others talking and gesturing to us. We learn how to do the same thing, by practice and trial and error. There are some people who believe that we are born with some basic skills which help us learn how to talk and to understand what we see. Nevertheless, most of our communication skills must be learnt. An English baby, born in this country but brought up in Japan, will be Japanese, except in appearance. That is to say, that person will learn to communicate in the ways that a Japanese person does.

So, abilities such as talking or writing are not natural. They are taught us by parents, friends and school. And, as growing creatures, we want to learn at least some of these communication skills because we can see that they are useful. For example, to explain to others what we want.

The fact that we experience communication as something which we learn to do has important consequences for anyone studying the subject. It means that we should consider important questions such as why we learn, how we learn and what effect this has on us. Answers to these questions help explain other aspects of communication study, such as what effect television may have on us, or why we may have problems in communicating with others. So when we examine examples of communication in given situations, there is more to them than what is going on at the time. We must also examine what is behind the communication, what came before, what comes afterwards.

## 1.5 Categories of communication

**We can divide our experiences of communicating into four categories.**

These categories are loosely based on the numbers of people involved with the act of communication. They are a useful way of trying to define our field of study, like the terms 'form' and 'media'. Some forms or media belong more to one category than another, though there is no absolute rule. The remaining sections of this book are based on these categories.

(a)   **Intrapersonal communication is communication within and to the self.**

When we think, we are communicating within ourselves. We could be reflecting on the events of a day, or working out a problem in our heads. Arguments about how we think, for instance whether we use words or pictures when we think, have not been resolved.

We also talk to ourselves, and write diaries for ourselves. Again, the person making and receiving the communication is us.

(b)   **Interpersonal communication is communication between people.**

Usually this category is taken to refer to two people interacting face to face. There are 'odd' examples which could fall within this category, such as a telephone conversation. And it is worth remembering that face-to-face communication takes place in situations where there are more than two people present. Examples of familiar interpersonal situations are an interview, a salesperson talking to a client and a conversation between friends in a café. It is the fact of face-to-face contact and the emphasis on speech and non-verbal forms of communication which make such situations in this category distinctive.

(c)   **Group communication is communication within groups of people and by groups of people to others.**

In this case it is convenient to make two more divisions: small groups and large groups. Small groups behave differently from pairs. But they still interact face to face. More will be said about them in chapter 3. A family is a small group; so is a group of friends out for an evening together, or a committee meeting at work.

Large groups behave differently from small groups, not only because they are bigger, but because they are often brought together or come together for purposes that are rather different from those of small groups. Examples may include an audience at a concert and some kind of business organization or company. It is this last example that we will concentrate on in chapter 4.

**(d)   Mass communication is communication received by or used by large numbers of people.**

In making a definition based on numbers, we don't have to be specific. An open-air concert for a thousand people might reasonably be called mass communication. The point is that the numbers involved at any one time are much bigger than anything we would reasonably call a group. It is the fact of large numbers being involved that makes this category special, in terms of who is able to control the means of communication, and in terms of what its effect may be. This will be explored in chapter 5.

There are two kinds of examples to cite. The mass media form one subdivision, where obviously we are talking about large audiences. Apart from the examples already given, it is worth adding those such as the pop CD/cassette industry.

The telephone and postal systems are examples of the other kind of mass communication. There may not be large audiences for the kinds of communication which are sent out. But such systems are used on a large scale, by thousands of people at any one time. So they do fit this category on general grounds of number.

## 1.6  Communication is used

**We use communication in different ways** regardless of what means of communication are used in these ways. Examples of such uses are:

- to warn others (e.g. road safety signs or a warning shout)
- to inform others (e.g. teletext or a fact sheet)
- to explain something (e.g. a manual or the write-up for an experiment)
- to entertain (e.g. telling jokes or a film)
- to describe (e.g. a TV documentary or telling someone about a holiday)
- to persuade (e.g. a trailer for a radio programme or a poster for a charity)

These uses are talked about from a different angle, as functions of communication, in section 3.2 of this chapter.

## 1.7  Communication is culture

**How we communicate and what is 'said' through our communication helps define what is 'our culture'.**

Linguists have long argued that spoken languages, their words, say a lot about how a given set of people see the world. In the case of Hopi Indians it is literally the case that they have their way of seeing the world because they have a few words for colours which other people don't have. But culture is a very broad term for describing the beliefs of a people as represented through their arts, their religion, their social customs and so on. The point we would make is that one only knows art, religion, customs through acts of communication – therefore culture is communication and vice versa. And of course this means communication in the widest sense, it includes forms other than just words.

Cultures often have dominant symbols or icons, such as the turban for Sikhism or the tartan for Scottishness. But there is more to both these cultures than recognizable items of clothing. We suggest that you try making a list of verbal, visual and non-verbal communication for a culture of your choice, in order to work out what seems typical of that culture. Then you should try to describe what sort of beliefs and attitudes your list represents. In this way you will have worked out one example of how communication does define culture.

---

**What is it about different forms of communication that makes them useful in doing different jobs of communicating?**

Hint: think about reasons why you would choose to use video or would talk to someone face to face.

---

## 2 Why do we communicate?

SARAH'S STORY

*It was Friday night and a bad time for Sarah. The mirror was no help, so she took it off her wall. The darkening evening outside her window was cheerless, so she drew the curtains. She tripped over her sports bag as she turned away from the window, so she kicked it.*

*What would be the third thing to go wrong, she wondered. Last week she had lost her Saturday job. Not enough customers coming to the wine bar, he had said. Business is bad. Not so bad, she had found out, that he couldn't keep on the other part-timer. And we all know why he kept her on, thought Sarah darkly to herself.*

*And now she had broken up with Neil. She had to admit that they hadn't been getting along so well. But she hadn't expected him to actually break it up. It wouldn't have been so bad if it had been her idea. . . . So here she was looking at the wallpaper, bored as hell, and not feeling good about herself.*

*'Is there something wrong with me?' she wondered. 'I just couldn't stand him sulking every time I wanted to go off and do something different, maybe go out with some girl friends. Still, maybe I should have been more considerate. Maybe there's something about me that puts them off. After all, he's not the first to go.'*

*Sarah's morale sank again. She looked at the clothes that she had put out to wear before that abrupt phone call.*

*'I'd better do something before I commit suicide,' she thought.*

*It was then that she remembered that O'Rourke had given her a further day's pay in lieu of notice. Not that he had to, she thought, to be fair. But it meant that she could go shopping in town. Because she had some money, and because now she wouldn't be working tomorrow.*

*'I'll ring Julie,' she decided. 'Perhaps I can go round there and talk things over with her. That's what I need to do – talk to someone – get it all in proportion. And Julie might want to come to town tomorrow as well. New clothes and a day out . . . and who knows who we might meet,' thought Sarah.*

### ABOUT SARAH'S STORY

This tells us something about what communication does for us. There has to be a reason why we decide to communicate in the first place. If we consider what Sarah did, and what she was going to do, then it is clear that her thinking was a piece of 'intrapersonal communication', and that when she rang Julie she would be within the category of 'interpersonal communication'. And when Sarah talked over her situations and her feelings with herself, she was impelled to communicate by something within herself. The same could be said of her conversation with Julie – when it took place. Sarah wanted to feel better about herself, she wanted someone to talk to. We all want something to happen through communicating. In other words, we have needs, which communicating can help to satisfy. Having recognized a need to express ourselves, we identify aims or purposes to fulfil those needs through communicating with other people.

## 2.1 Needs and purposes for communication

Needs and purposes can therefore be seen as mirror images: a need is felt from within, a purpose recognizes the outcome we want.

People must have a reason for communicating. It is worth remembering that when people communicate, they may be fulfilling more than one purpose at the same time. For example, someone may tell you something that you want to know: their purpose may be to inform you, but at the same time, perhaps, to impress you with their knowledge.

The concept of purpose helps explain what people intend to achieve when they communicate. In our working lives at least, it helps to be clear about our own purposes when we communicate.

**Purposes relate to needs in that our purpose is what we intend to get done through communicating in order to satisfy our needs.**

We may not always be conscious of our purposes. In the example given above, the person might not be aware that they were 'showing off'. But by examining how they use words, gestures and tone of voice, we might be able to understand that this was indeed what they were doing. When we communicate face to face, it is the non-verbal forms of communication which often reveal our unconscious purposes or needs.

Similarly communication outcomes may be intentional or unintentional. If we hurt or upset people through what we say or do, we may not have intended to do this. An owl hooting outside a window does not intend to tell me that it is there and that it is night-time. That is not its purpose. For communication to have purpose, it must (even unconsciously) be directed from one person to another, or indeed from one animal to another. The people who manufacture a newspaper intend to communicate with their readers. The company which issues a report on its trading over the previous year intends to communicate with its shareholders.

There are several common purposes and needs of communication which are described below.

## Survival

**We communicate to survive.**

In wealthy northern countries it seems strange to talk about survival, especially in its basic senses of warmth, food and shelter. Yet some of our communicating is still about these physical needs. For example we would communicate in order to rent a flat (shelter). The flat might be rather different from a village hut, but it still does the same job. If we felt ourselves in physical danger, we would also communicate with others to try to get help.

## Co-operation

**We communicate in order to work with others.**

It could be argued that co-operation between people is the single great-est need and purpose in communication. It is obvious that our need to form social groups actually comes from our need to co-operate with each other in order to survive. Organized groups of people in any society work together to provide basic needs and also less basic needs. We use communication to get along with other people and to work with other people.

Chapters 3 and 4 provide further information on this.

## Personal needs

**We communicate to satisfy personal needs.**

This reminds us that, just as survival was about more than physical things, so also our needs are not merely physical.

We have a personal need to feel secure within ourselves. This leads to other needs – to have a good opinion of ourselves, to feel that we are wanted and valued by other people.

In the story above, Sarah had begun to feel badly about herself, to feel that there might be something wrong with her. She wanted to be wanted and valued, and so was turning to a friend for comfort. Communication with and from others helps to satisfy these security needs. All of this underlines the important fact that communicating isn't just about practical things like buying six kilos of potatoes. It is also about non-physical things such as emotions, feelings and ideas.

These personal needs are behind acts of communication such as dressing in the right way for an occasion; having a cry on somebody's shoulder; or giving people presents.

## Relationships

**We communicate to be involved with other people, to form and maintain relationships.**

This follows naturally from the last two points. We need to have friends, because friends support each other. We need to get along with our work-mates, because working with people is about more than job tasks, it relates to needs for co-operation.

When one talks about being involved with others, this could be in terms of number (pairs or groups); in terms of what binds those involved (friendship or love); and in terms of what description we may give the involvement (family or social club).

## Persuasion

**We communicate to persuade other people to think in the way that we do or to act in the way that we do.**

The most obvious example of this is advertising. The advertiser intends to persuade a certain category of people – car owners or old age pensioners, for instance – to buy a given product or service. Communication makes the connection with these people persuasively. It usually seeks to change the opinions or attitudes of those people regarding the advertised product or service.

However, persuasive communication is more common than we may realize and is not confined to flamboyant examples of advertising. We may want to persuade someone to loan us some money, or to join our drama group, or to help us with repairing our car. It is true that the word 'persuasion' has a certain sense of manipulation – to get what we want. But in this sense we are all manipulators, every day.

## Power

**We communicate to gain or exert power over other people.**

To a certain extent this may seem to be like persuasion – our purpose is to get someone else to do something we want. But the word 'power' introduces something new into the situation. It suggests that the communicator intends to put the other person in a submissive or helpless position. It can suggest that the communicator has special privileges in terms of what they know or the means of communication they can use.

For example, a blackmailer has power. This person may possess such significant information about another that we call this other person a victim. If the blackmailer threatens to reveal this information to others, then their purpose in communicating is to exert their power, usually to get money.

**Propaganda is communication used to control or manipulate others, usually large groups of people.** It involves the control of sources of information and of the means of communication. This control represents power. The Union of Soviet Socialist Republics used propaganda to reinforce their economic and military power for several decades this century.

Mass communications are particularly well suited to this exertion of power because they can broadcast or distribute information and opinions to great numbers of people from a central source. Those who have power control that central source. That is why there is always concern about who controls the media in any country. The media can exert power over their audiences. It is argued that the most important way in which they do this is in shaping people's attitudes and beliefs.

Even in democratic societies, information about the state and about defence issues is often closely guarded. In the United Kingdom in the past few years there has been a campaign for a freedom of information act which would provide more access to information about national and local government.

## Social needs

**We communicate to hold our society and our organizations together.**

The bigger the society or the organization, the more communication is needed. It is the practical problems of running large businesses, for example, that have led to the development of new forms and media of communication. Data processing with computers seeks to solve the problems of handling huge amounts of information quickly by using new means of electronic communication.

These more practical social needs are to do with what goes on outside ourselves. They are to do with making the whole system work for us. Hospitals, schools, manufacturing organizations and government organizations all rely on effective means of communication in order to function.

## Information

**We communicate to give and receive information.**

We are exchanging information with other people almost constantly. We may need to find out the time when a bus leaves. We may be keen viewers and readers of the news because we want to know about other people, events and places in the world. On a smaller scale, we are great gossips and conversationalists because we want to find out what is going on around us.

## Making sense of the world

**We use communication to make sense of the world and our experience of it.**

We suggest that making sense of the world is about four important things:

What we believe in
What we think of ourselves
What we think our relationships are with other people
What we think is real

These ideas map out the physical world, our social world and the world inside our heads.

When a child asks questions in order to find out, for example, how granny is also mummy's mummy, he or she is making sense of the world of family relationships. When we watch a television documentary on the forests of South America, then we are making sense of another piece of the physical world. If we become involved in a discussion about the rights and wrongs of the way we treat animals (as when we use experiments on animals) then we are making sense of the world of our values and beliefs.

## Self-expression

**We communicate to express our imagination and ourselves to others. We like to be creative with our communication in words, pictures, sounds and other forms.**

This is an important kind of need because it covers the creative aspects of communication. This creative expression of the imagination includes the kind of reasoning seen in a book on the possibilities of life existing on other planets, as well as that seen in a television play.

We use our imaginations to cover an infinite range of possibilities. One could argue that drawings representing the design concept for a new car show communication being used in the cause of self-expression. If stories are made up through the powers of our imagination then so is our view of ourselves.

Under this heading of self-expression comes the whole range of urges that all people have to express themselves through dress and body adornment. These may be regulated through social conventions. On certain occasions certain sorts of dress are considered appropriate: for example, if we attend a funeral then we wear dark clothes. These serve to express our feelings in socially accepted ways. However, we may seek to dress and adorn ourselves in ways that we think challenge social conventions.

It seems that humans have an innate urge to use their imagination and to be creative. Clearly, there is more to life than merely surviving or doing business. We use communication for more than carrying out transactions with other people. Our use of forms of communication, especially those using words and pictures, enables us to make up things that might happen, or create situations that will never happen. In particular we love stories and dramatic creations – fictions which give us amusement and pleasure and explore possibilities. Through a story we can be in places which we may never visit or meet people whom we would fear to meet. We can be involved with a relationship which reminds us of one which we once had, or one which we would like to have.

Each of us, then, communicates for a whole variety of needs and purposes. We could list other reasons in addition to those mentioned above. But all of them could perhaps be organized under four main headings: **personal needs, social purposes, economic necessities and artistic expression**.

Having seen why we communicate, in the next section we want to see what happens when we communicate.

## 2.2 Maslow's hierarchy

One much-used version of needs is that of Abraham Maslow, in which he describes people as being driven by sets of needs in a hierarchy, from the most basic at the bottom, to the most refined at the peak of a triangle (see figure 1).

Basic needs are about wanting food, shelter, sex. Just above that come the needs for safety – having a roof over one's head and knowing that one belongs to some group like family. Then there are the social needs for things

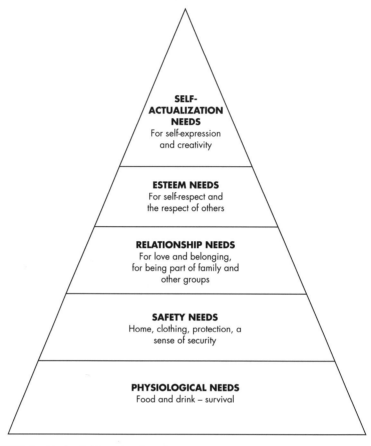

**FIGURE 1** Maslow's hierarchy of needs

like love and friendship, which urge us into relationships. These are followed by ego and esteem needs, which are about us as individuals wanting self-respect, recognition, even power. Finally, at the top of the triangle comes the most sophisticated need – for self-actualization. This is about self-fulfilment, about finding and being oneself. Certainly these needs get more complicated and personal as one goes up the hierarchy. This sense of development also loosely relates to us growing up and becoming more complex human beings. But in terms of our lives and actions one cannot really say that we simply move away from 'baser' needs. They are always there somewhere. Why we are driven by different needs at different times very much depends on circumstances, on how we are feeling at a given time, on personality. In one case a boxer is driven by needs which cause him to bite through his opponent's ear. In another case a sailor is driven by needs which urge him to rescue a fellow sailor a thousand miles from land and with the near loss of his own life. You can discuss what drives such different people in different ways.

## 2.3 Nature or nurture?

**Does the ability to communicate come from learning or from our genes?**

You should relate what follows to section 1.4. As a species we are biologically privileged by our relatively huge brains. It seems likely that to some extent this development is a survival/selection characteristic in which the ability to use speech and to visualize space and movement has helped us a great deal. But what we have done with this talk and this visualization, in respect of socialization or of creativity, is another matter. It is not apparent that anyone is born with special creative skills. We are not born talking.

Some linguists, particularly Noam Chomsky, have theorized that we are born with 'deep structures' in our brains. These are supposed to enable us to make sense of the conventions of speech, to learn to speak as babies. This was a theory which tried to explain how we learn to talk. However, there is no biological or physical evidence for these structures. But there is plenty of evidence that people learn communication skills by imitating others and by practising. Where writers or artists seem to run in families, this is not because of some inherited gene: it is because the children grow up in an environment which encourages one form of communication. It may also be because those children feel challenged by their parents' skills, and need to match these in order to satisfy their personal needs.

Education is a great nurturer of communication skills. Plainly, those who don't have certain kinds of education are not able to write, or cannot draw, and so on. This is why we believe that communication skills can be learned and developed. Our society has education because it believes that, apart from other knowledge and skills, it is useful and desirable to be able to communicate effectively in various forms. Communication is nurtured in children by family and the school. It (particularly speech) is the means by which we satisfy our needs, through which we function socially and economically.

---

**Why is it that we don't communicate at times?**

Hint: think of the times when one should speak up and when one should keep quiet.

---

## 3 What happens when we communicate?

### LUCY'S STORY

*It had been a tough day for Lucy. She had had a row with Janet Capstick, her supervisor at work, and now she was worrying about whether she would get the sack. Like many arguments, it had started with something apparently trivial and then got out of hand. The trouble was that Mrs Capstick, it seemed to Lucy, was a bossy woman. She wasn't that much older than Lucy herself, but seemed to think a lot of her position. And she was a great one for the rules. Lucy was on contract work, with thirty others, operating a telephone answering service for this insurance company. The rules were tight. If you were even a minute late in logging on, it counted against your pay. Today had been too much for Lucy. She had started on at Lucy in the first tea break.*

*'Could I have a word with you, Miss Johnson?' she had said, with that insincere smile on her face.*

*Lucy felt herself go all brittle. She followed her supervisor out of the tea room into the corridor. She really couldn't think what the problem was. But she felt resentful already. It wasn't the first time that they had had words.*

*'I wish to point out to you that you are improperly dressed,' Janet Capstick almost hissed into Lucy's ear. Lucy thought that she would laugh, but then realized that she would have to take it seriously. This person had no sense of humour.*

*'But I thought we sorted this out the other day,' she said. 'I'm wearing tights, I'm wearing an ordinary skirt. What's the problem?'*

*Capstick went a little pink. 'Your blouse. Too see-through. Too low. Not enough buttons.'*

*'Too much for who?!'*

*'It's the company's rules. They are quite clear. And indeed this is the third time that I have spoken to you about your dress.'*

*'Mrs Capstick, I'm working in a room full of women. I don't deal with the public. And as it happens, I was going to wear an ordinary top, only it's in the wash. I'll have it tomorrow.' I'm not going to strangle her, thought Lucy. I'll be polite. I need the money.*

*'Well, I'm afraid that is not good enough.' Janet Capstick stared at Lucy steadily and unnervingly. Lucy wondered if she would try it on if Lucy was as tall as her. 'I would like you to go home and change now, and be back in half an hour.'*

*Lucy couldn't believe her ears. 'You aren't serious, are you?!'*

*'I will be making a note of this incident on your file. I'd advise you to do what I ask – now.'*

*Lucy felt her eyeballs beginning to bulge. 'This is ridiculous. You really are a power freak.' She turned on her heel, and tried to walk away with dignity.*

ABOUT LUCY'S STORY

You may have noticed that this story suggests that people do think about communicating, not only after the event, but also while it is going on. Things that matter to the exchange are clothes, words, surroundings – the physical context. Phrases like this are the communication terms which we use to describe what communication is and how it happens.

You may also have noticed how the story of this communication is about a developing, changing situation, with various factors coming in. The relationship between Lucy and Mrs Capstick develops. It still isn't over: we don't know what will happen next.

We have already talked about communication being dynamic. Whether we are making the communication or we are taking it in, something is happening continuously. Communication, even reading a magazine, is an activity; it is a doing experience, it is a process.

## 3.1 Communication as a process

**When we are in a conversation, there is a continuous exchange going on.**

Ideas or facts or opinions are being turned into words and shifted from one person to the other through speech. In chapter 2 we will look at how, in another part of the process, non-verbal communication is also conveying messages.

**So when we talk about the communication process, we are talking about this active flow.**

And what we want to do is to explain what's happening, why and how. We want to know what is going on in the process, so that maybe we can improve our handling of it. Through knowledge comes understanding and the possibility of change. We look at the communication process from various angles in this book in order to become better communicators.

We use communication terms to describe various aspects of the process, breaking it down into stages and parts. We use terms to identify factors which may affect how communication is carried on. We interpret the evidence thus produced and try to make sense of it. Interpretation is not only about making deductions, but also saying why these deductions are significant.

For example, if we see context as a factor in the process, then what is important is to say why it matters in the examples that we are looking at. Theory needs to be applied.

One of the earliest and still the most useful attempts to describe the communication process in separate parts was made by Harold Lasswell in 1948. He said the process of communication could be described in these terms:

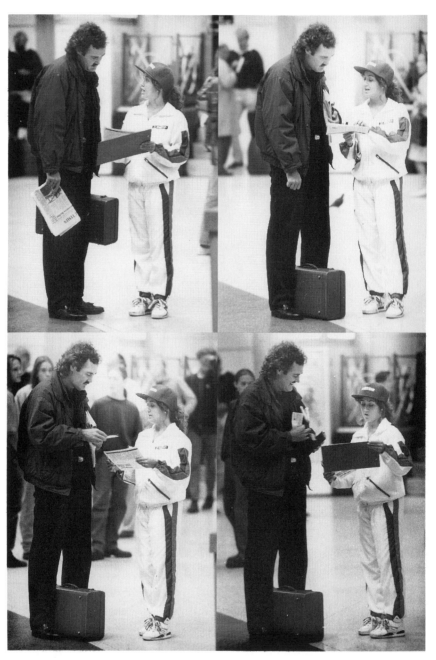

Communication processes

*Who*
*says What*
*in which Channel*
*to Whom*
*and with what Effect*

This is the same as saying that every example of a communication process can be broken down into the following terms:

*A Sender*
*directs a Message*
*through some Form/Medium*
*to a Receiver*
*with some Effect*

One may add other points to this list. These points are all examples of communication terms, or concepts, which identify different aspects of the process.

**Context** refers to the idea that every act of communication must happen in some sort of surroundings. Only what we mean by this is actually quite complicated. Most obviously there is the *physical context* – whether we are talking to someone in our living room or on the terraces at a football match. But then there is the *social context*, which is to do with the occasion involved and the people in it. This might be a group of friends in a club or a family meal or a group of mourners at a funeral. And then there is the *cultural context*, which refers to an even broader set of circumstances and beliefs, which still may affect how we talk. For example, it would matter if the funeral was in a Hindu or an Anglican context. It is particularly important to see that **the media are part of the cultural context in which we operate**. How we talk, what we talk about, what music we listen to, has a lot to do with the influence of the cultural context of the media.

**Purpose and need** are also factors in the process. They refer to the basic question of why any act of communication takes place. Everyone has a need that causes them to communicate, and everyone has a purpose in communicating.

**Audience** refers to the receiver mentioned above. This idea focuses on where messages go to, on the person or people to whom the communication is addressed. **The nature of the audience always affects the treatment of the message.** You don't talk to teachers in the same way that you talk to friends. You don't talk to one person in the same way that you talk to a group. You don't write a letter to a relative in the same way that you would write to your local councillor.

Of course there are other factors at work, such as the important question of what you are trying to say anyway. You need to look at all these factors, including audience, as you try to describe process and the nature of communication.

**So, communication is a process, and this process can be broken down into parts which help explain what is happening, how and why.**

When we use certain terms to explain parts of the communication process, we will try to suggest what they mean and give examples. But also remember that there is a glossary near the back of this book which you can use to check out special words.

## 3.2 Exchange of messages

One dominant idea is that **when we communicate, we exchange messages**.

We give messages and we receive them. These messages are taken into our minds, interpreted, stored or acted upon.

The messages can be about all sorts of things. They could be about something that is happening – a fire in the house next door; or about someone's feelings – they are very unhappy because a relative has just died; or about opinions – we tell someone that we think a certain film is well worth seeing.

In this sense we can also list certain functions of messages (and of the act of communication which puts them across). These functions could be:

to warn,
to advise,
to inform,
to persuade,
to express opinions,
to amuse.

You will recognize some of these words from elsewhere in this chapter. So, rather than our giving you examples this time, see if you can devise word messages which do the sort of jobs we have just listed.

The idea of message, in its broadest sense, is held to cover a wide range of communication forms and media. Maps give us messages about the area of land they depict. Graphs can give us messages about things like the increase in the number of goods which we import into our country. Photographs can give us messages about what people look like in countries that we have never been to. It is even argued that a piece of music is a kind of message from its composer – perhaps about an experience, a mood or feelings.

When we receive such messages we are involved in an exchange process with their makers, just as we are when we make messages ourselves.

## Sharing

**When we communicate we are also part of a process of sharing.**

Communication forms and media carry messages that allow us to share thoughts, feelings, opinions, information and experiences with others. This makes the point that communication, especially in our everyday dealings with others, isn't just about facts. It is about emotions, attitudes and beliefs. These are important to us. They are bound up with the personal and social needs which we have already described.

Such sharing, especially on a personal basis, affects many aspects of our lives, including the time we spend at work. It is all too easy to see work as a business of handling messages of a factual nature. But if our jobs involve dealing with people, then this cannot be the whole truth.

At work, for example, we are frequently concerned about what people think of us, and we of them. We spend time, however briefly, exchanging messages about personal background and experience. Indeed, there is evidence to suggest that how well we deal with 'job messages' depends on how well we are exchanging 'personal messages'.

So sharing is an important aspect of the exchange of messages.

## Neutrality of messages

**Messages are rarely neutral.**

It is possible to argue that simple messages of fact are neutral. For example, a message expressed in word form, such as 'There are two wheels on my motorcycle', seems quite objective.

But then such messages rarely come on their own. In the example just given, there would probably be other verbal and non-verbal messages around that sentence. It would be said in a particular situation and could be said in a particular way. In this case, the speaker could be addressing a friend whose motorcycle is laid up with a smashed front wheel. In that case, the message is not just a statement of fact. It is also saying something like, 'My bike's OK but yours isn't. Hard luck!'

And of course messages in advertisements are never neutral. Even a factual list of functions in a car advertisement is not just a neutral list. It is a selected set of messages about the good points of the car. We don't hear about any possible bad points. We shouldn't be surprised about this lack of neutrality. Any student of communication who examines the purpose behind the message in the communication can see very well why the messages are not neutral.

This isn't to make a moral judgement on the purposes of messages. People may say things with the best of intentions. But we should understand that they do have intentions and are dishonest or unconscious of what they are doing if they say that they don't. This leads on to the idea that messages we exchange may be overt or covert.

## Overt or covert messages

**Some messages are clear and obvious; some are hidden and not so obvious.**

This is another argument for the study of communication. It means that we should look carefully at what is actually being expressed in any example of the communication process.

**Sometimes a piece of communication actually intends to hide some of its messages.** How good it is at doing this depends on how sharp the receiver is at decoding the communication. For example, an advertisement could be saying overtly, this is a good fabric conditioner which makes your clothes feel soft. But it may also be saying covertly, you aren't a very good mum to your family unless you buy this fabric conditioner. Incidentally, it also conveys opinions about what the advertiser suggests good mums should do!

**Sometimes there are hidden messages in a piece of communication which are not intended by the sender.** For example, a friend might tell you overtly that she has not been out for the past two weeks and hasn't seen many other friends. What she could be saying covertly is that she is lonely and wants some company.

## Multiple messages

**Communication usually involves the exchange of more than one message at a time.**

This is implied by what we have just said. If there are overt and covert messages in a piece of communication, then clearly when we communicate we don't just pass back and forth single, simple messages. Indeed, there is another proposition that goes with this. Communication usually takes place through multiple channels. In the examples given above, we can see that the advertisement probably communicates through pictures and words and the people communicate through speech and non-verbal communication. Indeed, where people are concerned, it is often the non-verbal channel which carries the covert message.

## The nature of messages

We shall discuss messages under the heading of linear models later. But it is worth emphasizing the fact that **messages are not just about what is said. They are about how things are said, and about what channel (or code/codes) is used.**

The American writer D.K. Berlo refers to this when he describes the message in three parts: the *code*; the *content*; and the *treatment*.

He also points out that everything we know or experience (including communication from other people) can only enter our consciousness via one or more of the five senses – sight, hearing, touch, taste and smell.

Berlo also refers to the fact that our knowledge, attitudes, communication skills and cultural background affect how we communicate with others. In other words, our effectiveness as communicators depends on what we know', our attitudes, how good we are at communicating and how we have been brought up to communicate.

Whatever happens when we communicate is something that we have learnt to do, in certain ways, for certain reasons.

However, there are other ways of explaining what happens when we communicate.

## Communication and meaning

Although we are going to talk about meaning in the next section, with reference to signs, the idea of meaning is important enough to comment on now.

Messages are really about meanings. We use the word 'message' as a convenience. It makes some kind of sense when for example one is talking about passing memos around an organization. But in fact communication is not really about passing around little 'packages' from one person to another through talk or pictures or whatever. It is rather more complicated than that.

Every piece of communication, whether it is a conversation or a photograph, means something to those involved in creating it or receiving it. What those involved think the communication means is, however, not cut and dried. Most pieces of communication mean more than one thing to most people (see 'Multiple messages', page 24). What is more, they may not mean the same thing to everyone. Even an invitation to a party 'starting at 8.00' won't mean the same thing to everyone (see figure 2). People will arrive at different times.

Some forms of communication tend to be more ambiguous in their meanings than others. So one is more likely to argue about the meanings in a photograph, than what is meant by the write-up of a physics experiment.

When we 'take in' some example of communication, when we decode it, what we are really doing is to deconstruct it and reconstruct meanings in our mind (see figure 3). A lot of this book is really about the factors which affect how we construct those meanings. If someone yells at us 'Look out!', what do we do? We work out that we are being warned about something. We work out that we should use our eyes. But do we look behind us? Or

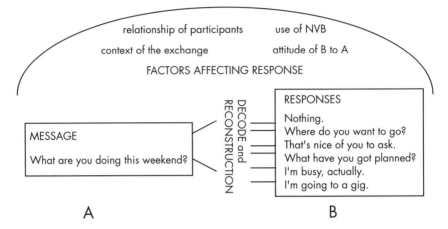

**FIGURE 2**   The response that we give to a message depends on what it means to us. There may be many possible responses affected by a variety of factors.

look up? Do we duck? Do we yell back? What do we assume the warning is about? There may be factors in the situation which help narrow down the meaning of the message. But having deconstructed the shouted words, still there are different meanings that we may reconstruct in our heads. And that is important to remember: that the meanings are in our heads. Communication may involve physical objects or physical activity. But ultimately it is all in the mind. As James Watson says, 'Can we ever be sure that we have understood a message or conveyed a message as we intended?' (Watson 1985).

## 3.3 Communication as signs

**Communication is all about the giving and receiving of signs which have meanings attached to them.**

This is one of the most convincing views of what happens when communication takes place, because it seems to apply to all examples in all situations.

So the idea is that when you speak to someone, you are making signs at them. As long as they know what these signs mean, then they can decode them and the message will have been put across.

The same could be said of any form of communication. A non-verbal sign might be a wink, meaning 'Keep quiet, it's a secret between us.'

A picture sign might be a low camera angle, meaning this person is important and dominating. A musical sign might be a black mark (called a crotchet) which means play this note for a specific length of time. And this page is covered with signs, called letters and words. We hope that they mean something to you.

## Signs and meanings

**But a sign can only be a sign for us if we assign meaning to it.** And there are four problems here:

(a) To say that something is a sign doesn't tell you what its meaning is.
(b) The same sign can have different meanings in different places or at different times.
(c) One sign can have more than one meaning.
(d) The same sign can mean different things to different people.

The answer to the first problem is that **we learn to connect a sign with a meaning**. Mainly, we learn to do this through parents and friends, as part of growing up. We are also taught formally in school. And we should go on learning something about signs and their meanings for the rest of our lives.

If we want to learn the word signs of the spoken French language, then we go on a course where we are taught to make the signs, and are taught to attach meanings to the signs. This second point is important because, of course, being able to say a French word correctly doesn't tell one what it means. Signs are useless unless one knows the meaning. Which is why archaeologists have spent years trying to decipher (decode) some ancient scripts.

The second problem must also be solved by **learning the 'rules' for the right place and the right time**.

Don't tell an American that you want to wash up if you mean that you want to help with the dishes. An American will think that you want to wash yourself. And beware especially of non-verbal signs. You might, as an English person, raise your hand casually, palm outwards, in greeting to someone

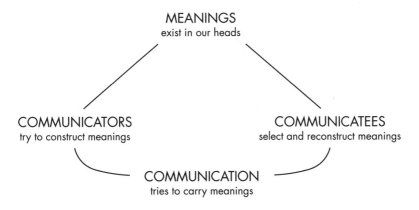

**FIGURE 3** Communication and meaning: it's all in the mind

whom you pass by at work. But for a Greek, the same sign looks suspiciously like an insult! Even within our own culture, we know that putting an arm around someone's shoulders signals different things according to the situation that we are in (and who is involved).

The third problem is obviously connected with the last one. Indeed the last example could also apply here. But place, time or person doesn't have to be involved in this case.

Take a written word sign such as 'bow'. As a sign on its own it could refer to the action of bending the body, and an object which projects arrows, and an object which is drawn across the strings of musical instruments. Knowing all the possible meanings of the sign doesn't help, even though it is a lot better than having no idea at all of what the word means.

From this example we learn that **we often understand the meaning of a sign from other signs around it**. A sentence (string of signs) such as 'She raised the bow and loosed off an arrow at the target' helps pin down the meaning of the word.

Or, to take the example of a party game such as charades, we know that the more dress and gesture signs the player gives us, the more likely we are to guess the character being portrayed.

So, if communication is about exchanging signs, or giving and receiving meanings, then the ability to use a wide range and number of signs is likely to aid communication.

It may also appear that in some cases we have more than one sign for the same meaning. The sets of words 'naked, nude, starkers' and 'slim, thin, slender' are examples. But in fact, because in the first case the words mean rather more than 'without clothes', one can say that they are not just different signs for the same thing. You work out exactly what they do mean.

The fourth problem may also seem to overlap with the second. But the point is that **even when people are speaking the same language in the same place at the same time, signs can still mean different things**. Take the word 'disgusting'. A dictionary might have us believe that it means something like loathsome or nauseating. But, for example, do parents really mean this when they express their disapproval of the state of their child's room by saying it is disgusting? They probably don't mean that the room actually repulses them. More likely they mean that they disapprove of its untidiness. And if we use a sentence such as – 'It's a disgusting state of affairs when you can't rely on the buses to run on time' – we aren't really talking about physical loathing. We mean that the situation is very annoying and unsatisfactory, so far as we are concerned.

So we really do have to learn a wide variety of possible meanings for signs, and be careful about choosing the meaning which seems to best fit the communicator's intentions. The reverse is also true of course – we must be careful about picking the signs we use, in order to be able to express what we really intend. It is not easy to say what we mean.

## Codes

**When we communicate through signs we use codes.**

**A code is a system for using signs. This system is based on rules and conventions shared by those who use the code.**

Morse code identifies itself literally. It is a code of long and short electrical signals (dots and dashes) which stand in place of other codes and signs – such as the alphabet and writing, or numbers.

Speech is a series of sound signs which forms a code that we know as spoken words. A photograph of a person represents two forms of communication and two codes. One is the non-verbal code composed of the various dress and body language signs which we see represented in the picture. The other is the pictorial code composed of signs such as de-focused background or closeup on head and shoulders.

**The forms and codes of communication are bound by certain 'rules' as to how they are used. These 'rules' are called conventions.**

In some instances the conventions are quite strong. One has an organized system of signs. Here the best example is that of spoken or written language. We have all been taught the rules of spelling and grammar; and if we haven't, then we must have learnt them from others. The act of speaking involves knowing which sign goes where. And just as we share knowledge of signs, and more or less agree what they mean, so also we more or less agree on these conventions. Without the organizing power of these conventions, we wouldn't be able to communicate at all. Anyone who mispronounces or mis-spells a word badly, fails to communicate that word and so fails to communicate what they mean. And when someone mis-spells a word only slightly and is still understood then it is still the organizing power of those conventions that has saved the day for them and got the meaning across. Because we know how words should be spelt we can work out what a mis-spelt word is probably intended to represent.

**Codes are sets of signs. Conventions are rules for using these signs** (see figure 4).

It is possible to divide a code into *primary and secondary codes*. A secondary code is a particular form of the primary main code. The primary codes represent the main set of signs for a given form: verbal, non-verbal, pictorial, and so on.

Secondary codes are composed of special sets of signs that work within the primary code. Secondary codes are often related to work (computer talk), or social/sub-cultural groups (bikers). These secondary codes may also have

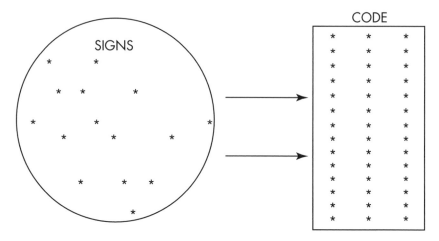

**FIGURE 4**    Signs form a code when organized by conventions

conventions governing their use. We slip into them on many occasions because we think they are appropriate (people baby-talking to young children). Our use of codes is not always appropriate to the occasion or to those present. You might consider the arguments for and against using baby-talk with children as an example.

## 3.4 Communication as behaviour

**This view suggests that the act of communication is a kind of behaviour. It also suggests that we communicate with others in order to modify their behaviour.**

The first proposition suggests that communication is as much a kind of behaviour as eating, or banging a nail in a piece of wood. Again, this raises the question of what we know how to do when we are born and what we learn to do afterwards. There are those who think that we learn to do everything after we are born. Others would say that, in the case of speech for example, we are born with a certain *competence* to make speech. Then they would say we develop *performance*, or the skills of speaking.

Either way, there certainly is a lot of learning involved. And it is true that just as we may learn to use a knife and fork or chopsticks to eat with, so we learn to use words in certain ways to put over what we mean, whichever language we may be talking about. And it may be said, just as we learn to behave in different ways according to our upbringing, so **we learn to communicate in different ways according to our upbringing**. So the idea that communication is a kind of behaviour helps us look at why we communicate as we do. If we aren't much good at drawing it could be said that this is because we haven't been taught this particular form of behaviour. Or even if we aren't much good at apologizing to people this is because we haven't learnt much about how to do this.

The second proposition – about modifying the behaviour of others – is easy to understand if, once more, one looks at the example of advertising. Generally speaking, an advertisement wants to change our attitudes so that we then change our behaviour. For example, it might want us to feel favourably disposed towards a certain company's life insurance policy, so that we then go and take out a policy with that company. However, the proposition can be applied to a wider range of examples. For instance, it could be said that a baby cries in a certain way because it has found out that this will cause its mother to give it food. It has changed the mother's behaviour.

The idea that communication changes behaviour doesn't have to be confined to simple examples, where something is seen to happen immediately. It could be said that everything we learn, every piece of information that we acquire, changes our behaviour to some extent in the end. Every piece of communication which we experience may affect our attitudes and beliefs in some small way.

**We cannot help but change others and be changed by others when we communicate.** So, for example, a person might choose a career in social work because he or she had read a publicity booklet which intended to persuade readers that this is a good and worthwhile occupation. On the other hand, someone might choose this career simply because of the many things heard, read or watched about it on television. No one was intending to change this person's attitudes and behaviour. But it happened because of an accumulation of messages.

This idea of communication as something which acts as a stimulus and which evokes a response relates to behaviourist psychology. This may be briefly described as **S–R theory**.

People like B.F. Skinner were convinced that all creatures' lives were defined by the responses that they gave to various kinds of stimulus, and that these responses could be modified by changing the stimulus. At its most simplistic, the approach proposed that anyone could be made to do anything provided you could find the right stimulus. Primary stimuli would be forms of pain or pleasure.

Propagandists might like to believe this! If one can only find the right kind of communication, then people can be persuaded to do and to believe anything. Fortunately, it is not that simple. People make sense of stimuli (such as words or pictures) in different ways for different reasons (see figure 5). Communicating is not like pressing buttons.

Nevertheless, when one is looking at communication between people it can be quite illuminating to hang on to some idea of response, to look at why people make the responses that they do. For example, in social

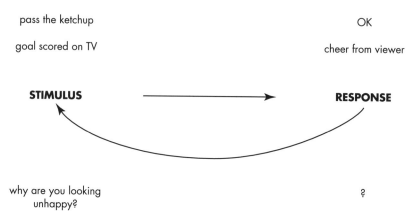

FIGURE 5    A stimulus–response model for communication. But is it that simple?

interaction, we now know that there is a lot of cueing of responses – in taking turns to talk, or in getting to like someone. So one should not ignore S–R theory either.

## 3.5  Models of communication

**Another way of describing the communication process is to use a model.**

A model is a simplified description of a communication process, usually set out in graphic form as a diagram. It can show the elements of a communication process and the relationships between those elements.

A model is a medium which is mainly graphic. The parts of the process are laid out, for example to describe what comes first, second, and so on. And the parts are labelled using communication terms. Models are useful because they lay out the process, or a view of what the process is like, in a simple, visual way.

**Because there are different terms and different views of what makes up the communication process, so there are different models.**

And one can change the terms of a communication model without changing the layout. For example, we can talk in general terms about the receiver of a message, whatever the situation. But in fact, if we were referring to receivers of music at a concert or receivers of a radio programme, then it is more appropriate to use the term 'audience'. And this is what models for mass communication tend to do. They do this because the term 'audience' draws attention to the fact that there is often more than one receiver for a piece of mass communication, and to the fact that such receivers are not engaged in the communication process in the same way as people talking face to face.

Models and the terms used in models may be changed to emphasize particular points about a situation – e.g. the difference between making a speech and reading a book.

There are a variety of models used in this and other books. You will find some models worked out by other people useful. But remember that communication studies is about doing. Be prepared to make up your own models. Models can be more or less complicated, according to the number of terms used, and the ingenuity of the layout.

We will start with the most simple style of model.

## Linear models

**These lay out parts of the process in a line, as if communication is all about sending messages from A to B.** In fact, communication is rarely that simple, but it is a good enough way to begin. This model, shown in figure 6, with a simple situation indicated below it, suggests a few terms and ideas.

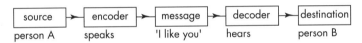

**FIGURE 6** Basic linear model of communication

*Source* and *destination* make the point that communication always comes from someone and goes to someone. But it matters as to who exactly the source and destination are. For example, one would want to take into account whether person B is male or female.

The idea of *codes* has been described on pages 29–30. Communication has to be expressed through some form or medium and these all have their own codes. For example, the message in figure 6 could have been encoded through a non-verbal sign, such as touching. This is a different code from that of speech. In any case thoughts or feelings have to be expressed in some form to be 'decoded' and understood by someone else.

And then there is the term *message* – what is said, or expressed one way or another. As we have said, D.K. Berlo has broken this term down into three parts: content, code and treatment. In the example given above, the content is 'I like you', the code is that of speech and the treatment depends on how it is said – warmly, lovingly, factually, and so on.

## Exchange models

**These indicate that communication is at least a two-way process.**

In the case of a group of people, it may seem to be more than two-way. In the case of someone watching television it may be difficult to see how there is a response to the messages coming from the television set. This will be discussed in the last chapter of the book. But for situations discussed in chapter 2, this kind of model, shown in figure 7, is very useful. This model makes the point that messages go both ways in a conversation. It also says that everyone is a decoder and an encoder. That is to say, we have to find some way of putting together and expressing what we have to say, as well as some way of taking in what the other person says.

But then, we also have to make sense of what is said. This is where the term 'interpreter' comes in. We are all interpreters of messages, all day and every day. How we interpret messages is another matter. This will be discussed later. But we will find that there are reasons why people may interpret the same message in different ways. Here is a fundamental reason for studying communication. If we all got our messages across exactly as we intended, there would be fewer problems between people. But this doesn't happen. When we examine the idea of perception, we will see that because we all have different kinds of experience, and make different kinds of assumption, so we interpret messages in different ways.

Sometimes the difference isn't great. Sometimes it is, and it matters.

For example, looking back to the situation of the first model, if the person who is the source of the message (person A) is female and the person who is the destination (person B) is male, and if person B interprets the message as loving when it was meant to be just friendly, then the two people

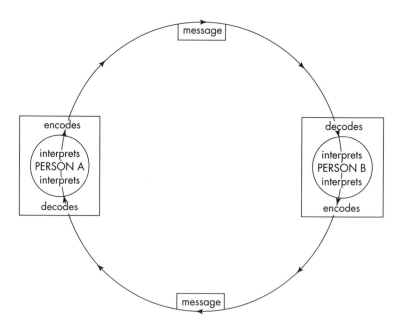

**FIGURE 7**   An exchange model of communication

concerned have got problems. We will return to examples of problems throughout this book.

## Contextualized models

**These models add the dimension of situation or surroundings.**

This matters more or less to how communication takes place according to the particular example. But **context always affects the act of communication**.

For example, we would communicate differently in the situation of a formal dinner party with our boss, as compared with eating fish and chips in the kitchen with friends. This example shows that context has both physical and social aspects.

Figure 8 is a model which includes context. One other term is important.

This new term is *feedback*. It reminds us that communication is often two-way: that there are responses to messages sent. And that we adjust the way that we carry on a conversation, for example, according to the feedback that we get from the other person. The channel which conveys feedback does not have to be speech but may be non-verbal – for example a bored expression or a movement of the feet in readiness to leave.

You will also notice that we have changed the words 'source' and 'destination' in figure 6 to 'sender' and 'receiver'. You may come across these terms in other books. Try to decide for yourself which words are most useful.

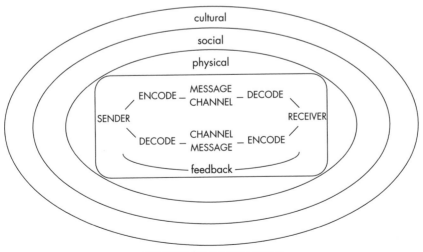

CONTEXT OR ENVIRONMENT

**FIGURE 8** Contextualized model

## Conclusion

We have argued that **the act of communication is one in which meanings are exchanged through signs.** We have made a number of suggestions about what happens when we communicate. And explaining what happens when we communicate helps explain what communication is.

Generally, in this chapter we have given ways of:

explaining why we communicate,
describing how we communicate.

Now you can check what we have said by looking at the summary which follows. After that, we suggest some activities which will bring out some of the points we have made, and which will encourage you to check our ideas and explanations as to what communication is.

---

**Do we know what we are doing when we communicate?**

Hint: when are you conscious or unconscious of the effect of what you are saying?

---

## Review

This is to help you check on the main points of this first chapter, 'What is communication?'

First we said that communication is something that we experience in various ways. So then we asked ourselves:

### 1 HOW DO WE EXPERIENCE COMMUNICATION?

1.1   Through various means of communication which you should be able to define and give examples of, from the list that follows:
forms,
medium,
the media,
other kinds.

1.2   As a connection between people, joining friend with friend, or newspaper reporter with newspaper reader.

1.3   As an activity, because it is something that we do. We make communication in order to make things happen in our lives.

1.4   As something which we have learnt to do, like other skills and abilities which we have.

1.5 Within four main categories of communication activity. Again, you should be able to define and give examples of these from the list that follows:

> intrapersonal communication,
> interpersonal communication,
> group communication,
> mass communication.

1.6 As something we use, e.g. to inform, persuade and entertain.

1.7 As a means of expressing our culture and our beliefs.

Second, we said that there has to be a reason for communicating to take place. So then we asked the question:

## 2 WHY DO WE COMMUNICATE?

2.1 To satisfy needs that we have within us,
to survive, physically and as social beings,
to feel secure and valued by others,
to be involved with others, in relationships,
to conduct the everyday business of our lives,
to give and receive information,
to play with ideas and stories,
to express ourselves,
to make sense of the world.

2.2 Maslow sees needs ranging from the simple to the complex.

2.3 We may ask ourselves whether communication comes from learning (nurture) or from genetic inheritance (nature).

## 3 WHAT HAPPENS WHEN WE COMMUNICATE?

3.1 We are involved in a process in which many things are happening at the same time. The process can be broken down into various parts, according to a given situation, which can be described through special terms. This process is all about making sense of the world, making meanings in our heads.

3.2 We exchange messages, which may be about facts, opinions or beliefs. This means that we share information, feelings and ideas with others. But we have to take account of the fact that messages are rarely neutral, that messages may be overt or covert and that messages are usually multiple (more than one is exchanged at a time). The term 'message' can be divided into three parts: content, code and treatment.

3.3 We are giving and receiving signs and their meanings but signs can have more than one meaning: they mean different things to different people; they change their meaning according to time and place; and meanings only belong to a sign because we agree that they do.

Together the signs in a form of communication make up codes. These codes depend on conventions which govern how they are used, which we learn and which help the communication to make sense.

3.4    We are involved in a kind of behaviour which may well be a way of trying to change the behaviour of others. Some people see behaviour as a process of stimulus leading to response, and so on.

3.5    We can see this process very clearly through the use of models. These fall into various types. You should be able to define and give examples of the following types:

> linear,
>
> exchange,
>
> contextualized.

## Debates

### How do we draw a line between communication which is intentional and that which is not?

- One problem is knowing or finding out what was in the mind of the sender (purpose).
- Another problem is that communication may take place even without the intention or knowledge of the sender (non-verbal leakage).
- Another problem is that the effect of the communication may not match its intention (perception).
- Another problem is that communication will have some effect, whatever it was or was not intended to do by the sender (one cannot help communicating).

WHAT DO YOU THINK?

### Is it true that most communication is designed to change the behaviour of others in some way?

- Points about intentionality also apply here.
- One issue is about whether those communicating need to be in the same place at the same time in order to affect the behaviour of others (context).
- Another issue is about one's general approach to communication: a behaviourist psychologist would probably agree with the point of the question (S–R theory).
- Another issue has to do with what you would define as behaviour (forms of communication).

WHAT DO YOU THINK?

**How far is communication defined by one's culture or sub-culture?**

- One point of view suggested by the question is that the way we talk depends on the way we are brought up.
- Another view would be that the way we talk (communicate) actually defines the culture we belong to.
- Another view would be that the real point is not about how we communicate but about how we think.

WHAT DO YOU THINK?

**Do we learn to communicate or are we born with some ability to do this anyway?**

- This question is all about what is known as the nature–nurture debate – what are we born with (genetic inheritance) and what are we nurtured into (socialization)?
- One problem is that babies can't talk, so it is hard to work out what they 'know' or don't know.
- Another problem is in deciding when communication is intentional or not.
- Another problem is in trying to separate out environmental influences from what we may be able to do naturally.

WHAT DO YOU THINK?

## Assignments

### Assignment One

Draw a diagram using any of the communication models in this chapter – or adapt one for yourself – to describe the process of communication through contrasting examples such as: a photograph from a family album, a radio programme, a telephone conversation, a job application form.

You should cover factors such as source, audience, purpose, context, feedback.

### Assignment Two

Write an explanation of how the ideas of sign, meaning and conventions relate to the fact that the words 'great' and 'grate' sound the same; and the fact that the word 'spirit' can refer to different things.

Using magazines, make a collage of photographs to bend or break the conventions for showing women in perfume advertisements, and for showing politicians in news articles.

## Assignment Three: Case Study

Refer to the advertisement for Clearasil at the beginning of this chapter, as source material.

You are on work experience with an advertising consultancy. As part of this experience your supervisor at the company asks you to carry out some tasks to test your awareness of how adverts communicate with their audience.

Complete the following tasks.

(a)    In which three magazines would you prefer to place this advertisement, and why?

(b)    Suggest two other kinds of background against which you would place the female models, and say why.

(c)    Describe the audience most likely to respond to this advertisement.

(d)    Write a brief assessment of the audience's needs, which you think are suggested by this advert.

(e)    Draft a questionnaire designed to find out how the intended audience responds to the advert.

(f)    Design an alternative version of the advert intended to appeal to males.

## Suggested reading

Ellis, R., and McClintock, A., *If You Take My Meaning*, 2nd edition.

Fiske, J., *Introduction to Communication Studies*, introduction and chapters 1–4 (but be warned that some of this book is written for an advanced level).

Myers, T.M., and Myers, E.G., *The Dynamics of Human Communication*, chapters 1, 2 and 5.

See also the resources list at the end of this book for further details of these and other books.

# Chapter 2

# Interpersonal communication

Language is a subtle medium and it can transmit information of both a semantic and social nature often simultaneously. It is, of course, aided by the multifarious nonverbal channels – the tone, the paralanguage, the posture, the gesture, the eye-gaze. That is what makes conversation so fascinating and so complex.

Andrew Ellis and Geoffrey Beattie,
*The Psychology of Language and Communication*, 1986

This chapter provides information about communication between individual people. It includes accounts of how speech and non-verbal communication enable us to relate to one another. There is also comment on how we present ourselves to others, how we perceive other people, and on barriers to communication.

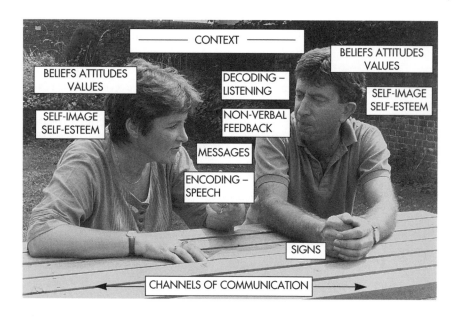

# 1 Means of contact

## HAZEL'S STORY

*The Spanish beach was crowded and as hot as a warm bath. Hazel tipped her straw hat back a little. The cries of children sounded like complaining seagulls. Only there weren't any seagulls around this beach. Hazel shifted position on her beach towel and opened one eye. There wasn't even the noise of the cicadas which could usually be heard scraping away. It was too hot and too near the town for them. Hazel opened the other eye, wide. The children were gone.*

*She sat up abruptly. Ten minutes ago Laura and Tim had been playing at the water's edge, in a straight line with her big toe. Hazel scanned along the water line anxiously. Surely they must be all right. After all, Laura was 6 years old and Tim was 8. And two kids can't go far in ten minutes or less. She looked around the encampments filling the beach. A dark-haired, handsome youth grinned at her, encouragingly. Hazel scowled at him. Another time, Don Juan, she thought.*

*Panic began to set in when she stood up and still saw no familiar blond heads. Pauline and Roger will go mad, she thought. I'll murder those kids. Aunty Hazel is not going to be popular.*

*Within twenty-five minutes she was at the local police station and wishing that she had learnt some Spanish before they came on this holiday. Luckily, someone had helped her on the way, when she was trying to find the word for 'police'. That, and some determined gestures, had got her to the right place. But the kids were still missing. And she felt silly, clutching a striped beach bag and with only a beach robe over her bikini.*

*The Spanish policeman who was trying to help her was courteous and charming. But he didn't speak any English. Hazel tried a few simple words and then gave up, as they smiled at one another uncomprehendingly. There was plenty of good will on both sides, but that was all at the moment. Hazel wished that her brother-in-law was there. He spoke a little Spanish. Even the word for 'child' would be a help. Something had to be done. She beginning to believe that something terrible could have happened to the children. Perhaps she should just go back to the beach and wait.*

*Hazel looked the policeman in the eye and took a deep breath. She made a flat-handed gesture, with her palm, about the height of Laura's head from the floor. Then she shrugged her shoulders and tried to look anxious. The policeman looked on with interest and then pointed suddenly to a picture on the wall. It was a photograph of a child.*

## ABOUT HAZEL'S STORY

This tells us about the different ways of making contact with other people. We tend to take things like words and gestures for granted – until they don't work the way we want them to. These verbal and non-verbal forms of communication are in fact the channels through which we pass messages to others. Most of us have forgotten the experience of early years, when we were learning the signs which belong to these forms, and what they mean. It is only when we are stuck in a situation like Hazel's that we may rediscover what it was like to be a young child, cut off from others, without means of contact. But even a young child who cannot speak still has some ways of getting through to others. Hazel got through to the policeman when she smiled at him, and when she used her body and her hands to express what she meant. For interpersonal communication to happen, there must be some means of contact with the other person. There are two principal means of contact: non-verbal communication and speech.

## 1.1 Non-verbal communication (NVC)

**We make and receive non-verbal signs whenever we are with others.**
These signs are not words, but they are often used with words. They affect the meaning of what we say. They are produced by various uses of our bodies, by the way we dress ourselves and by the ways in which we can utter the words which make up speech. They say a lot about our feelings and our attitudes towards others. And they can be used apart from words. We become well aware of this when a policeman raises his hand to stop our car at a junction, or if an angry driver waves his fist at us.

**These non-verbal signs can be placed under three main headings: (a) body language; (b) paralanguage; (c) dress.**

### (a) Body language

**This tells us a lot about people's feelings, attitudes and intentions.**
Actors understand this very well when they put on non-verbal signs in order to convince the audience of the part that they are playing. Some books try to convince their readers that the key to success with the opposite sex lies in the use of non-verbal signs. This is only partially true. People may like us if we are pleasant and friendly towards them; and a lot of this friendliness is shown through body language. But it is not the only thing that matters. There are a great many signs that we give off when we are talking to someone. It is the meaning of all of these together which counts. And meaning varies according to the situation and who is involved. Having said this, it is also true that we are capable of paying more attention than we do to what other people are saying to us through their body language. And we are capable of controlling our body signs more carefully than we do, so that, for example, we get on with people better. In other words, our communication skills are learnt, and we can learn more. In which case it is useful to have some idea of what we are doing.

Body language includes five main elements, as follows:

**Gesture**: the way we use our arms and hands.

It is common to see people wave across a crowded room to attract attention, and then beckon someone to them. We use gesture to express things like height and width of objects we are describing. But there are more subtle signs, such as the steepling of fingers to express confidence. And for some people, gestures are part of their job – the tick-tack men at a racecourse, signalling bets and results. There are some complete languages of gesture – codes: so-called 'deaf and dumb' language, for example.

**Expression**: the way that we signal with our faces.

This usually says a lot about mood and emotion. The eyes and the mouth dominate expression signs. These are the signs which people look for first when they are trying to weigh up someone. We are capable of distinguishing subtle variations in smile or look. If someone gazes at you a lot, then it means they are interested in you. If two people gaze at one another a lot then it means that they have a positive and trusting relationship. Or again, we are able to distinguish between the raised eyebrow of surprise, of fear or of acknowledgement when we meet a friend. In short, we do a lot of looking during the process of encoding and decoding body signs.

**Body posture**: the way that we hold our bodies.

A relaxed posture expresses confidence in the person whom we are talking to. On the other hand, at an interview you would be well advised to sit up straight and look interested! To take another example, when one talks about a confrontation, it means just that: bodies positioned front to front. Together with closeness and direct gaze, this signals mutual aggression. So it isn't surprising to find that, in the West at least, people normally stand with their bodies slightly averted from one another, when having a conversation. This is considered polite. It signals that your intentions are friendly or neutral.

**Body space and body proximity**: how near to others we stand or sit.

First, everyone needs a certain space around them, to feel comfortable. Factors such as the age or the sex of people involved in an exchange can make a difference to this. But generally, adults won't let another person get within arm's reach unless they know them pretty well. Indeed, one can guess the degree of people's friendship from the way that they treat each other's body space. It may be possible to get on good and friendly terms with someone by 'dipping' into their body space. But it is advisable to think hard about the person and the situation because this may also upset them. This is when one starts talking about body proximity. People often rate their status according to proximity. So, while it may be all right to get close to friends and loved ones, the boss may take a dim view of what could be seen as 'familiarity'. The meaning of body proximity, like that of other non-verbal signs, varies from culture to culture.

**Touch**: is about who we touch, when, where and how.

It tells us a lot about relationships, status and degrees of friendliness. Women tend to do more touching with women, just as young children do more touching than adults. But obviously there are all kinds of special situations with special rules, such as those concerning lovers. It is also notorious that the British are one of the least 'touching' nations in the world, which can provide serious problems in our relationships with those from other cultures. There is some evidence that more touching – within the broad social rules – would help us get on better with others, including those from our own culture. Usually, when we are touched (however briefly) by the other person, during an interaction, then we feel more friendly towards them. Salespeople have been known to exploit this reaction.

## (b) Paralanguage

**This tells us a lot about how to interpret the meanings of words during a conversation.** It describes the non-verbal signs which accompany speech.

There are those signs which are separate from the words themselves. They are often about immediate reactions and emotions. We may whistle or gasp in surprise. People making public speeches are fond of 'er' and 'um', which is really a sign for 'Hold on, I'm thinking up the next bit.' We may scream with fright or groan with pain.

There are those signs which are represented through ways in which the words themselves are pronounced. They are signs such as pitch, stress and volume. We don't speak like robots in a flat and even way. So when the voice rises at the end of a sentence, for example, it may tell us that this is a question. Try delivering this set of words as a statement and as a question and you will see what we mean – 'You'll meet me at eight o'clock tonight.' Another example of this kind of paralanguage is to be seen in the fact that we often know that a person is angry when they begin speaking loudly. And again, it would be impossible for people to be sarcastic or speak ironically without the aid of these special signs.

Paralanguage can suggest things about a person's state of mind or their emotions. When we say that a person is calm or excitable or nervous, then it is the way that they deliver their words which can tell us this. So if we want to present ourselves well at an interview, then we could try to use the calm and even tones of someone who is confident and who is thinking about what they are saying. At the same time, we would try not to speak in a flat, monotonous manner, because that would suggest that we are boring or bored.

## (c) Dress

**The third kind of non-verbal communication that we use is to do with dress, hair, jewellery and make-up.**

This one says a lot about personality, role, job and status. For example, characters in television comedy and advertisements are given certain kinds of dress to make them easily identified. An extrovert type may be given wild and colourful hair, with bright clothes. Housewives are put in aprons. Stockbrokers wear dark jackets and pin-stripe trousers. And important people are seen in a Rolls-Royce, wearing expensive clothes.

You could try making your own analysis of the dress of a policewoman, a priest, a nurse and a teacher.

Dress also signals people's identity. When we group people by class or job (soldier) or sub-culture (punks), often it is clothes which first identify them with the group.

As well as dress and personal adornment of various kinds, we use objects and possessions to reflect or express ourselves. Obviously your desire to create a particular personal statement through the clothes you wear, or the bike or the car you own, or the furniture with which you surround yourself, may be limited by the amount of money you possess. But other people are likely to interpret all of these as reflections of you. All of us have a tendency to read meanings into objects.

## Comment

**NVC has a number of characteristics and functions.** Some functions occur when it is used with language. For example, it may reinforce something that is being said, as when a speaker chops one hand down upon the other in an emphatic gesture. Or it may elaborate on what is said when, for example, a speaker uses a level hand palm down to add to a description of the height of a child. Sometimes a non-verbal sign can have the function of modifying what is said. For example, it is possible to smile at someone at the same time as 'telling them off'. The smile takes the edge off the spoken disapproval.

**NVC is a primary code of communication**, as much as written language. It also has its share of secondary codes. For example, the floor manager of a television production has a special set of signs by which he communicates with programme presenters.

**NVC is also controlled by conventions** (rules) in the way it is used. These conventions are not as exact as the rules of grammar, which control our use of language. But they do make it probable that, for example, we will look at someone just before we smile, just before we shake hands with them.

**Ritual kinds of non-verbal behaviour are also common.** Chanting and flag-waving fans at the football match every Saturday show this. Some rituals are well known and public, such as those in a church service. But others may be less obvious, if no less a matter of habit. See if you can think of any examples of ritual NVC which you know of, at home, at school, at work.

**Non-verbal cues may be involuntary or intentional.** Signs such as blushing are considered to be reflexes which we can't control. It is in fact quite difficult to control many non-verbal signs. But it can be done to an extent – politicians practise such control for their public appearances. It is an interesting question as to whether NVC is intentional or not. We learn to use the signs subconsciously in most cases, yet they are not produced by accident, and so it would seem that there is some intention there to communicate. Perhaps we should all try to be more conscious of what our intentions are.

**NVC is specific to nations or cultures.** A culture or sub-culture is a collection of people who have strong beliefs and values in common. They may have a certain religion, recognizable arts of their own, what we would call a way of life of their own. Cultures can often cut across national boundaries, as is the case with Jewish people. Cultures can exist within nations, as is the case with West Indian communities in Britain.

Television and travel have helped carry non-verbal signs (and words) across national boundaries in the world today, so that people are tempted to think that gestures and expressions mean the same everywhere. This is not so. One may see the same signs in other places, but they don't necessarily mean the same thing as they do in Britain.

Even though a very few signs are used quite widely, such as the lifted eyebrow flash to express surprise, many other signs do not travel well. Men from Middle Eastern cultures like to stand close and face the person whom they are talking to. Men from western cultures don't like this directness and closeness so they are inclined to dance away from an Arabic speaker, who of course quicksteps after them in order to show what he considers to be polite signs of conversation.

Precisely because this is an age of international travel, we should think about our NVC as much as our words when on holiday or business abroad.

So NVC is a complex combination of signs through which we can communicate even when we aren't talking. They give rise to the proposition that we cannot help communicating, whether we like it or not. So, whatever clothes you put on, other people will be noting these, and to some extent, trying to read something into them.

**NVC relates to our perception of others** (section 3 of this chapter). A significant part of what we perceive in others is in their non-verbal signs.

**NVC helps build and maintain relationships.** Because non-verbal signs say a lot about our attitudes towards one another, so they influence the nature of our relationships. Positive relationships depend on positive attitudes. These attitudes can only be understood through appropriate uses of NVC.

**NVC relates to the idea of feedback** (section 2.7 of this chapter). We give off and make sense of these signs very rapidly indeed, even at the same time as we are talking or listening. So it is hard to 'notice' everything that is going on. This is where it is useful to look at videotape recordings of people in conversation and slow them down so that one can see just how the people involved are signalling to one another.

For example, in an interview one could look at several units of inter-action. In the first place there is the 'handshake' procedure, when the two people greet one another. Then there is the period of initial assessment where usually insignificant questions are asked, but the two people are weighing each other up in terms of personality and attitude. And then there is a period of evaluation, where as well as handling a question-and-answer session on a verbal level, the two people are checking and confirming (or not) their first impressions of each other, on a non-verbal level. And there is plenty of evidence that non-verbal impressions can strongly influence the outcome of an interview.

We have used the term 'non-verbal communication' in this context, which suggests an intention, conscious or not, to convey some message to other people through non-verbal signs. **It is useful to separate non-verbal communication from non-verbal behaviour – the latter phrase notes that we may act in various ways without any intention of communicating to other people.** However, all human behaviour is likely to have meanings assigned to it by other people. As many writers on communication comment, 'One cannot not communicate.' Whatever one does or does not do may be interpreted by other people as meaningful actions.

## 1.2 Speech

We have already seen that there is more to conversation than the acts of delivering and hearing words.

The exact meaning of what we say depends on our use of paralanguage in particular. And of course other non-verbal signs accompany the words. A fist in the palm of the hand may help emphasize the importance of what we are saying. On the other hand, a mocking smile may accompany an apparently pleasant remark: it could contradict what we said, and point to an opposite, true meaning.

**Spoken words are sound signs.** We have a tendency to regard words as somehow natural and true, as if they are an absolute fact of life. In our last story, Hazel found out that this certainly isn't true, when she realized that she couldn't make the right sounds to communicate with the policeman. Actually words themselves are made up of small units of sound called phonemes. We combine these to make a spoken word, and that word is only a sign. The fact that the signs mean something to us is the result of a long process of learning. The word 'dog' could just as well be the word 'bart'. If everyone thought of the same animal when the sound 'bart' was uttered, then it would do just as well as 'dog'.

And, as with other cases that we have looked at, we often need more than one of these sound signs to work out what they actually mean. For example, for most people, the spoken words 'there' and 'their' and 'they're' all sound pretty much the same. Try saying them. It is only when they are uttered *in the context* of a sentence that we can be sure of which one is meant.

**Speech is a code of signs, ruled by conventions.** This follows what we have previously said. Many other forms of communication, such as NVC and pictorial images (film and photographs), consist of codes. The rules by which these codes are used are called conventions.

We expect words to appear in a certain order (called syntax) and to be combined in a certain way to produce 'proper' English (called grammar). What we call the English language is a primary code of communication. We learn its signs and conventions at an early age because it satisfies a lot of our basic human needs to be able to speak. We will also learn some of its secondary codes and their conventions because they also have special uses. For example, air traffic controllers and airline pilots have their own code within the main code of English, which uses special words in special ways. People who haven't learnt their code can't understand them.

**Utterance** is the formal term used to describe a collection of words which express an idea. This could be a phrase rather than a sentence. But it will put across meaning because it does use conventions. So, 'terrible weather yesterday' is an utterance, even though it is not a sentence with a verb. It also illustrates how the way that we talk, the way that we assume others understand us, does depend on a variety of factors such as shared experience.

**Dialect** is also an example of a code. It represents regional differences from 'standard' English. These differences are to do with vocabulary, or the collection of words that one uses, as well as to do with the ways in which those words are used. A common example is the shifting of pronouns, where a dialect speaker might say 'I' instead of 'me'. There are many examples of dialect words in use. In the west of England, where we are writing this book, people often talk about 'daps', where others might talk about gym-shoes, or even plimsolls. Dialect is not improper English. It is another version of English. In a given region it may be the main spoken language code in use. Many people use more than one code anyway: standard and dialect. The reason that it is useful to be able to use 'standard' English is that it does provide a good chance that one will be clearly understood by English speakers wherever one may be.

**Accent** should not be confused with dialect. Certain accents may go with certain regional codes, but accent is part of the sign system of para-language. Everyone has an accent. It says a lot about our beliefs and values, especially with relation to class, that many people are brought up to think that there is a middle class which has no accent and that this is 'normal' and 'proper'. This is purely a matter of opinion. English people who have not been brought up to distinguish the relevant signs have no idea what a proper Scottish accent should be. The idea of 'proper' is just a meaning which we have chosen to associate with certain signs.

**Received pronunciation (RP)** is a phrase used to describe one accent which is associated with the 'correct' pronunciation of words. From one point of view it is not a bad thing if there is some notion of standard, if it means that people can speak English in such a way that they can understand one another easily. On the other hand, the phrase has strong cultural meanings which not so desirable. RP is too often assumed to be good and right, and any deviation from this is wrong – which is nonsense. RP is associated with status, acceptance and even power within our culture. It becomes a sign for these attributes. This situation is undesirable, but has its equivalent in many languages and cultures (compare, for example, Parisians' attitudes towards southern French accents).

**Register.** This follows on from our last point. We have the ability to choose our speech from two kinds of broad code, labelled upper and lower register. The distinction is usually thought of in terms of the difference between ordinary English and 'posh' English. In fact, once more this is a rather snobbish way of looking at it. Upper register is simply a rather more careful kind of English with a wide vocabulary and formal syntax, which we would use when we want to be careful about what we say – for example, if we were giving evidence in court. Self-conscious use of upper register sounds strained and silly: for example, the policeman in the same court who is 'proceeding in a northerly direction', instead of walking down the road to where it meets the High Street. The point is that we need this careful upper register when we have to explain things accurately or argue things through logically. That is all. It is no good saying 'Put a bit of the yellow liquid in the brown stuff' when trying to explain something to a trainee in the laboratories of a chemical company. The result could be a bang!

**Speech uses idiom and colloquialisms.** It isn't necessary to have an English language lesson to be able to analyse and use spoken communication more effectively. But it is useful to have labels for some of the more common ways of handling language. Colloquialisms are the characteristics of everyday, casual speech. They appear in lower-register use. Simple examples are 'won't' and 'can't' for 'will not' and 'cannot'.

'Idiom' refers to some of the slangy and non-literal ways in which we use everyday speech: the sort of things that make it hard for people from other countries to learn English. We know what we mean when we tell someone to 'Belt up!', but it is an odd thing to say if you think about it from the point of view of, say, a German.

**Speech is part of culture.** That is to say, we develop the kind of spoken language which expresses the things our culture believes in, its ideas, even just the objects with which it is familiar. This is why translating from one language to another is so hard. The French, for example, don't have exactly the same set of ideas and objects as we do, with merely a different code of sound signs. They talk about *ennui*: we translate it as 'boredom'. But this isn't exactly what it means to them. It also says something about tiredness of the spirit. More obviously, it is hardly surprising to find that Eskimos have many different words for different kinds of snow. They need them in a land where their lifestyle and their very survival depend on different kinds of snow.

If the study of communication is a study of how we produce meanings from signs, then we should be aware that culture affects this process, and that spoken language helps define the culture. What people mean when they say something depends partly on their background, and their culture is very much part of this background. Because there are cultural variations within what we broadly call English culture, we can come up against problems even in one country. For a start, there is the question of our so-called ethnic minorities. Someone whose background is Pakistani and who is being interviewed for a job may feel it necessary to say a lot about their qualifications. Their use of English might be 'good', but their intention and meaning would be subtly different from that of the average English person. In their subculture, it is a matter of status and sound argument at an interview to stress good qualifications. The interviewer may see this as slightly irrelevant and a little boastful. In this example, the cultural factor does matter. Also, different people from different backgrounds in different parts of one country may represent cultural variations. They may use language slightly differently, or mean different things by it. People often talk about the differences between the north and south of England. What are these differences? Are they to be seen in the use of spoken language?

Spoken language is very good at dealing with ideas, opinions and arguments – what we call abstracts; things to do with the world of the mind, as opposed to a physical and material world. Speech is quick, immediate, flexible, a form of communication that everyone has some ability to use and which doesn't require assistance from technology – not even a pen! Our relationships depend on speech because we have made it a tool for describing and discussing feelings. Our sciences depend on speech because we have made it a tool for explanation and reasoning. Words allow us to suggest things that might happen, but haven't, and to discuss things that have happened, but aren't happening any more. All aspects of our working and social lives depend on being able to use words. But best of all they allow us to reason and to deal with feelings.

**Speech contributes to our social identities.** How we talk gives us and others a sense of who we are. This is most obvious when we speak in some kind of role. So the captain of a team would be expected to be loud, firm and directive if they said anything while a game is in progress. In this way speech is an expression of how we see ourselves at a given time. This ties in with what we say about self-presentation. So, apart from particular roles and specific situations, we may also see ourselves, for example, as a caring person. In which case, our paralanguage will support this self-image, and what we talk to people about will also express this sense of caring.

**Speech gives social recognition.** By this we mean that we use words and talk to acknowledge who it is we are talking to. Sometimes this is obvious in forms of address, such as calling someone 'sir' or 'Lady Brown'. But it is also common though less obvious in other ways. For example, one form of greeting may be 'How's it going?' You may or may not really want an answer to this. But uttering the phrase gives recognition to the other person. Similarly, it is important to talk 'properly' to children, perhaps about something they are doing, because this talk recognizes them as human beings with valid interests. Such recognition usually brings an equivalent response. Being recognized helps them to grow up.

**Speech creates social meanings.** The way we conduct a conversation in respect of words chosen, as well as non-verbal factors, says a lot about our understanding of the social circumstances of the conversation. Compliments from a male to a female at a party about her appearance will not just be about how she looks. Both people also know that what he says carries other implicit meanings such as – this is the kind of situation where I expect to be able to say things like that – I'm drawing attention to the fact that you are female – I'm starting to 'chat you up' – and so on (now see figure 9).

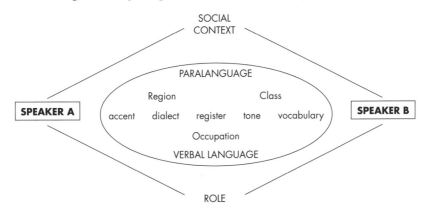

**FIGURE 9**   When speaking with others we have complex choices to make about our expression and what is appropriate

---

**Do we mean what we say?**

Hint: when have you unintentionally given someone the wrong message?

---

## 2 Dealing with others

### 2.1 Strategies

**A strategy is a short piece of communication behaviour or interaction. It involves the deliberate use of verbal and non-verbal signs to achieve a communicative purpose.**

We use these strategies the whole time, though we may not be aware of it. One of the earliest and most simple strategies that a baby uses, for example, is the hunger cry. What starts off as a reflex becomes a deliberate yell for food, and then perhaps for attention. The child learns to generate communication signs deliberately.

Salespersons are actually taught strategies for dealing with people so that they stand a better chance of making a sale. In effect this involves learning a set of verbal and non-verbal signs which, it is hoped, will have the desired effect. So, among other things they may be taught to do a lot of smiling, to find excuses (such as the use of brochures) for getting inside the client's body space, to refer to details of the client's lifestyle or home approvingly, to agree (or to appear to agree) with everything the client says, to relate their product or service to the client's known or supposed needs. All this proves that communication can be controlled, can be used for an effect – whether or not we approve of what the effect is. And it comes about as a result of using one or more strategies.

Of course, not all strategies are persuasive. You might consider what you think people do when they use strategies for encouraging a child in its reading or for comforting a woman whose husband has been injured in a traffic accident.

We use the most common strategy every day in its various forms. This is the 'greetings strategy'. A strategy doesn't have to be a lengthy piece of interaction. Greetings can be quite short. But still, what happens is that various non-verbal signs and words are used to show that the people involved recognize one another, feel friendly towards one another, and confirm the nature of their relationship.

Some strategies, like the greetings ones, can become a matter of habit. If the same pattern of communication is used again and again then it becomes a ritual. Some strategies are used more consciously than others.

Obviously, if we are not familiar with a given situation then we have to think more consciously about what strategy is most useful. But once a general type of strategy has been tried once, then it is easier to think up variations on it. For example, pupils have quite a stock of useful excuses for being late for school, from 'The bus came early' to 'The cat was sick on my school bag'. But the basic strategy remains the same – it always includes elements such as the breathless arrival, the sincere, direct gaze and the verbal apology.

There are a great number of strategies that we use, so many that it is hard to categorize them. One way of doing so is to look at communication needs as mentioned in chapter 1, and place all strategies under one of these headings. Other ways of describing strategies have already been mentioned, in effect, through examples in this section. So, we have strategies for persuading, for approving or disapproving, for making excuses and for avoiding people and problems.

Finally, one very common set of strategies that we have is to do with conversation. One could say this is the basic stuff of everyday interpersonal communication, but again, conversations don't just happen and develop by chance. We communicate because we want to. We use strategies to shape conversation. The most common ones are these: starting and finishing a conversation; interrupting people; keeping the conversation going; changing the direction of the conversation.

All these strategies may happen quite quickly, but still, the signs achieve the purpose. For example, in the case of interrupting we may use a sign such as a small cough to distract the speaker, we will use eye contact and perhaps a small finger movement to say that we are ready to speak, and we may nod our head vigorously to signal that we have taken in what the previous speaker has to say, and that he or she can now shut up!

## 2.2 Games

**A game is an interpersonal strategy used to put someone down.** The usage was coined by Eric Berne to describe one aspect of his theories of transactional analysis. His book *Games People Play* is all about the way that people misuse communication skills. He concentrates a lot on words, but games are also played through NVB. Games are often seen in relationships – friends, marriages, boss–worker relationship. They are about the one person exerting power over the other, and trying to make the other person feel bad. Berne calls that other person the Victim. He describes different sorts of games and gives them titles.

The most basic game is called 'Yes, But'. This could be played by your friend on you, where you are trying to help them get through an assignment. Every time you make a helpful suggestion they have another reason why it won't work – 'Yes but I have to go and see my Gran that night.' Finally you get really cross with them blocking you, and then they say something like, 'Great friend you are!' Or, 'I told you it was impossible.' Then you feel guilty. That's what they want. Don't rise to it. Do your friend a favour, tell them to stop making excuses.

A more sophisticated version of this game is called 'Wooden Leg'. This is where someone has a genuine problem, perhaps a disability, but they exploit it. You have to be tough to break this game. We know a true story about a girl in a wheelchair at a school, who was forever using her condition to get what she wanted and to make others feel bad if they didn't give it to her. For instance, she would force her way to the computers in the IT room, though there weren't enough for the class, complaining that people were not thinking about her disability. Other pupils gave way, feeling guilty. What they should have done is to say, no, the fact that you are in a wheelchair has nothing to do with you taking your turn to get some machine time, so wait.

There are particular ways that the game player can lead on the other in a game, and can wind them up. You will need to follow this up with further reading if you are really interested.

## 2.3 Presentation of self

**We present different personalities to other people according to the situation we are in.**

The idea that we present ourselves to others in different ways at different times comes from a book by Erving Goffman. It provides a useful and entertaining account of how we play parts when communicating with others, whether in public or in private situations. He uses a number of terms to explain his ideas. The most useful of these can probably be included in one sentence. *We stage a performance through a persona.*

**The idea of staging is that we do put on a show**, especially in public situations. If a woman is paying for petrol at a filling station and then discovers that she has no money with her, she may well put on a performance to cover her embarrassment and to explain why she can't pay. In which case, the place and situation becomes the stage. And the stage does make a difference to the performance. For example, imagine a situation in which you are a motorist and your car won't start. If this happened at the air line in a filling station, you might mutter, but then you would look for a reason for the problem, and go back and ask for help. But if this took place in a driveway at home, then you might feel free to put on another performance involving strong language and banging of car doors to express feelings.

And again, staging can involve using the props on the stage. In the case of an interview, the interviewer can arrange props to assist in staging: an easy chair to relax the interviewee; folders in front of them to appear well informed; glasses to suggest intelligence and authority. Or, to take another example, a young man inviting a new girlfriend to his flat for a meal will tidy the place, perhaps put flowers on the table, choose some music. In fact, he will dress the stage for his performance, having regard for the needs and purposes of his communication.

**The persona is the character that we adopt to play the part.** Different parts in different situations require a different persona. A receptionist in a hotel would put on one kind of persona to do his job and another kind to talk to a girlfriend who takes him out for a meal.

Each persona in this case is defined by its characteristics, as one would define personality. The first one might be described as pleasant whereas the second one might be friendly. The persona is part of our way of dealing with people. It is the character out of which we communicate. In this sense it defines how we communicate. To decide (subconsciously) on using a particular persona is also to make a decision about communication style – how we talk to and use non-verbal cues with the other person.

The ability to shift from one persona to another, to choose one, is an important part of being an effective communicator. Some people believe that we have a fixed personality, or even that there is somehow something dishonest about adapting our behaviour to different situations. This is not so. We need to change. It would be absurd and insensitive for someone to present the same persona for dealing with a working colleague in a production meeting and when visiting the same person in hospital after an accident.

The use of persona tends to be most obvious when one is talking about public situations, whether they involve work or leisure. If there is such a thing as a basic personality, then we would probably agree that this is the self that we present to friends and family. But still one should note that persona and performance can describe how we make contact with others in some fairly private situations. A doctor examining a patient is, in one sense, having close and personal contact with that patient. But he communicates as a particular persona in a particular way so that they both understand the 'rules' of that situation.

Or there might be the case of a visit to relatives. They may be family and it may be a private situation, but still it is possible that we would adopt a persona for dealing with, say, an aunt or uncle.

The idea of a persona is very close to the idea of role, which we will be looking at again in chapter 3. Roles exist in groups. They are about personality, behaviour and position within the group. People have roles as a member of a group – family, or friends or work group. Sometimes these roles are recognized by labels such as daughter or supervisor. A persona goes with the role. A supervisor of a group of clerical assistants would communicate in a way that they saw as being appropriate to that role. But they would also adopt a persona which fitted the role. The way that they communicated would also be affected by this persona.

**A performance is the act of presenting the self**, it is the act of communicating. The term is meant to suggest an intentional use of speech and NVC. The performance makes contact with the other person. A performance will probably involve some of the strategies that we have already referred to. There are some obvious and professional examples of performances. For instance, try watching a quiz show presenter on television. Watch the way that they glad-hand the game players, especially if these are members of the public. Watch the way they introduce and conclude the show. Watch the way they whip up excitement or produce laughter. This is all part of their performance. But then consider the example of parents telling off a child. This is also a performance. Watch for the way that they grab the child's attention, then enforce silence and stillness. Watch the way they hold that attention through the telling off that follows. Watch the way that this involves a mixture of disapproval, explanation and threats. Of course, the fine detail of the performance is composed of signs. Verbally, there may be phrases such as 'Don't do that!' or 'I'm not bringing you here again.' But don't miss the non-verbal aspects of the performance – gaze from beneath the brows, stiff body posture, threatening hand gestures. This is the stuff of the performance. This is how contact is made.

## 2.4 Communication skills

**A communication skill is an ability to use a means of communication effectively, with regard for the needs of those involved.**

It should be emphasized that when one is talking about interpersonal communication being 'effective' this is not the same thing as getting one's own way. The idea of effectiveness includes consideration for, and understanding of, the other person. It follows that any communication skill involves more than mere mechanical ability to use the means of communication concerned. To be literate and to be able to write a letter requesting particulars of a job requires one level of skill. One also has to know and use the conventions of the given format (the letter). But to be able to write a letter of application for a job that is persuasive and attractive enough to get one an interview requires deeper skills. In this case effective communication involves a sense of style, among other things.

### Making contact with others

Communication skills that require us to deal directly with people are based on the use of spoken and non-verbal communication. Initiating, managing and ending contact with others is a basic human experience of everyday life. It is so basic that we may not realize that we do learn skills in managing these contacts, whereas everyone is aware that they are taught to read. If you think of the number of situations in which you deal with other people every day then it is also obvious that these skills of contact are tremendously important. How we manage them is not something 'natural'. Not everyone does it well. And we all have something to learn about getting on well with others. Peter Honey says of other people, 'their attitudes towards us and, more importantly, their behaviour towards us, are determined largely by our behaviour towards them' (Honey 1990).

We have already referred to strategies and self-presentation. Looked at another way, it is reasonable to say that:

**It is a skill to be able to use strategies effectively.**

**It is a skill to be able to present the self effectively.**

Before we write about feedback and perception, which are very much concerned with skills, it is useful to comment on relationships in particular.

## 2.5 Shaping relationships

**Interpersonal communication is most important in that it helps define our relationships with other people**. It can make them or break them. It can help maintain them. And our lives are a network of relationships. The communication skills that we have already described are most influential in terms of making the contact that is to do with these relationships .

Relationships are not only to do with family, friends and lovers. We have some kind of relationship with everyone around us, not least those we work with. These relationships may not all be good ones. But even then, communication provides us with the means for a remedy. If we want to like and be liked, then we have to do something about it. Our skills in using verbal and non-verbal communication will be most important in this case. Since we cannot avoid having some kind of relationship with so many people in our everyday lives, it seems at least sensible to make these friendly and positive. We can work towards this by, for example, developing skills in giving signs of recognition and approval. We hope that others would do the same for us. When we begin to talk to another person, we begin to establish a relationship with them. It is up to us what the nature of this relationship is. But we cannot avoid this fact: communication is never simply about passing factual information, where two people are concerned. Nor is it just about having mechanical skills of communication – the practical ability to use words. It is about what we use those words for, about why and how we use them.

This is why people, even on matters of pure business, who are seeking information, say, over the phone, will start off their conversation with some enquiry about the other person's health or family. We would do well to remember that communication between people is basically about people.

Communication does not just define a relationship, it is also defined by it. As Peter Hartley says, 'any communication between two people will be influenced by the relationship which exists between them' (Hartley 1993).

A relationship is about the roles of those concerned, it is about shared experience. It has been noted that people starting a love relationship talk more than those who are well established. Those who don't talk so much don't love each other any the less. But the nature of their relationship defines how much they feel the need to talk and what they feel they need to talk about. In a secure relationship – friends, family, lovers – people may well talk more freely about feelings. But equally people can be in a family relationship and feel insecure, and not talk freely. It doesn't matter that in principle they are, for example, sisters, and 'should' have a relationship. The way they talk will show what their relationship is really like.

Relationships also go through stages, in which those involved explore one another's knowledge, opinions, values. They can move from the experimental to a secure stage – or not. Again, the way talk is used will say something about the stage people are at.

Other aspects of interpersonal communication will also both help make a relationship and reflect on its nature at a given time. For example, self-disclosure – talking about your background and your beliefs – helps open up a relationship. It is a recognized skill in developing positive communication. If you can talk quite freely it will help people trust you. Hearing people talk freely may also tell listeners about the state of their relationship – good friends who trust one another.

## 2.6 Defining social situations

It is possible to categorize interpersonal communication and the situations in which it occurs in terms of oppositions. These labels are quite useful because they suggest contrast in the way that communication is used; also because they offer a quick way of looking for a range of situations through which to discuss how we make contact with others.

**Formal/informal**: suggests a difference between calculated and spontaneous use of communication. It suggests another contrast of public/private situations. It says something about how conscious we may or may not be of the effect of our communication on others. It would be the difference between a casual visit to the cinema with a friend and attending a première of a film where one had to talk to royalty and the famous.

**Public/private**: suggests a difference of context, where the communication takes place. This in turn suggests a difference of presentation and an awareness that others may be observing the communication. In public we tend to restrain our non-verbal cues, the messages about feelings. We do not say so much about ourselves. It would be the difference between discussing one's political views with the family and talking about them in a television interview.

**Distant/intimate**: suggests a difference of relationship between the people communicating. Also possibly a difference in the situation which they might be in. If there is distance between us and the person we are talking to, then we are inclined to be formal in the way that we use language. If the situation is intimate, then we would reveal more of our real selves, and therefore build a closer relationship with more trust. It would be the difference between discussing supply problems with the boss and discussing marriage plans with a partner.

**Ritual/open**: suggests a difference in the predictability of the communication used. Also possibly a difference in the familiarity with the situation of the people involved. Ritual situations often confirm relationships, attitudes and feelings of security. But they don't open up a genuine dialogue in which communication is used to explore feelings and ideas. It would be the difference between a market researcher asking someone to answer questions for a standard questionnaire and meeting someone on a blind date.

**Functional/expressive**: suggests a difference in the quality and purpose of the language used. The two kinds of situation make different demands on the participants. In the one case it suggests that there is a practical job to be done, in the other that the communication is needed in order to discuss and to speculate. It would be the difference between trying to buy a spare part for a car and trying to interpret the results of an experiment carried out in a laboratory.

## 2.7 Feedback

The idea of feedback was introduced in chapter 1 when we talked about contextualized models.

The idea of feedback has two main aspects. One is the idea that messages are sent through verbal or non-verbal channels in response to messages from another person. The other is that these response messages are acted upon: that an adjustment of the content and style of communication may take place as a result of feedback.

This is important because it can be argued that if we are poor at giving off, recognizing or acting upon feedback, then we are that much poorer at communicating with others.

**Feedback can, of course, be verbal as well as non-verbal.** If a person invites someone to come round and see them, and the other person says that they can't do that, then that person has given verbal feedback.

But it is non-verbal feedback which is, if anything, more important. This is because it isn't always recognized and yet research suggests that it is the most influential channel in terms of affecting our attitudes and emotions with regard to the other person. For example, simply smiling and nodding at the other person suggests that we like them and approve of what they are saying. This feedback will encourage them to talk.

In another instance, it could be that we give negative feedback to someone else. For example, we might unconsciously clench our fists while talking to this person. This suggests tension within us, and probably some feeling of aggression towards this other person. They will get the message and either respond with a degree of aggression themselves, or perhaps just keep quiet.

This reminds us of the point that non-verbal signs are usually used unconsciously. This means that they can often be taken for a true sign of someone's feelings.

This should also remind us of the idea of strategies.

These can also be used consciously or unconsciously. And again, it is often the non-verbal signs in the strategy which are the most useful in achieving whatever it is we want to get done. For example, if we sense from their feedback that someone is losing interest in what we are saying, then we can use a strategy to try and recover that interest. If we were talking about a television programme, then we would try and make it sound more exciting. In particular, we are likely to start using more large gestures to describe action, so that the eye of the other person is drawn. We would vary the pitch and tone of our voice, so that it won't sound too boring. We would look more at the other person, stand a little closer and perhaps touch them lightly.

Our strategy would be a response to their response. And this tells us that a conversation is a continuous process of feedback of messages and adjustment of each person's approach to communicating. Once more, the rule seems to be that effective communication is, in various ways, a matter

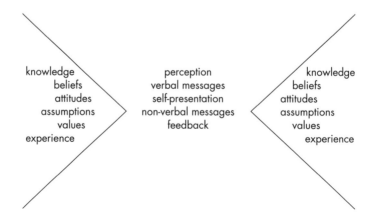

**FIGURE 10**  Interpersonal communication factors

of paying attention to the other person, of considering what they need. A good communicator is observant and sympathetic.

This can apply to many of life's situations and experiences. If a child is learning to tie his or her shoe-laces for the first time, then approving pats and saying 'Well done' will encourage the child to stick at it.

If a supervisor is trying to get her clerical team to put in an extra half-hour in order to clear a job before the weekend, then she is likely to get them to do this by saying complimentary things about their work, reinforced with smiles and nods, and other signs of interest in what they are doing.

**Feedback regulates our contact with others.** It helps decide how well a conversation will go. It is our reaction to other people's communication, and their reaction to ours.

## 2.8 Gender

**Interpersonal communication both defines and is defined by gender.** There are important debates going on now about the social roles of female and male. There are issues surrounding the treatment of women at work, and the equality of their opportunities. Understanding of how males and females see one another and talk to one another can help inform those debates and issues.

At the same time, questions of equality should not be confused with matters of difference. Gender differences and the social–biological interplay between these are represented through our uses of verbal and non-verbal communication. The ways in which a male talks to a female who is pregnant with their child may be a particular example of such gender difference.

In this area we are back to the important questions of meaning – what do we mean by what we say and how we talk to someone of another gender? Objections to some uses of language in particular by men towards women are in effect based on the belief that what is said means something objectionable. To use a cliché, the insertion by a male of the phrase 'my dear' into an utter-ance used towards a woman, is taken to mean something condescending. It is considered to be an expression of a male sense of superiority and of a subconscious attempt by the male to diminish the woman.

These meanings and implied attitudes help explain the rather difficult word **discourse**. This describes how we have particular ways of using languages (codes) to produce particular meanings about particular topics. You can have a discourse about all sorts of topic areas – the law, childhood, masculinity. The ways that boys and girls talk about one another reveals that two gender discourses do exist. You can look at girls' magazines to discover some words and indeed picture language that is used by girls about boys. Even more revealing are some of the words used by men to talk about women. You could easily collect these for yourself and work out what they

mean in terms of attitudes and values. This kind of communication is important because it is part of the process of socialization. Boys and girls grow up
having a certain understanding of what it means to be a male or a female
because of the words that are used about them. It is one thing to use words
which describe general gender differences – strength, for example. But it is
another thing to use words which create unequal ideas about difference –
about strength of mind or intelligence, for example.

Finally in this varied survey we return to gender in conversations. A
number of defining differences have been discovered here, especially those
which are about women deferring to men. For instance, many women like to
talk about feelings; many men do not. Many men like to talk about things,
such as cars; women are not as interested in such things. Men like to talk
about themselves, about their achievements; women listen to this when, as
they have admitted in surveys, they would rather not. 'Women talk about
family, friendships, feelings, clothes, health and food. Women engage in
more self disclosure, talk about more intimate topics, especially to other
women' (Argyle 1992). Of course these are general differences, and there will
be exceptions to this kind of communication.

## 2.9 Culture

**Interpersonal communication varies according to the culture in which
it happens.** We have just talked about gender (and discourses), but what
these mean to us does depend on our culture. This is one of the problems
about getting into issues of gender. Some spoken language and the language
of dress codes for women in, say, Iran or Afghanistan may raise 'feminist'
issues for at least some westerners. It does not for many of the people in
those countries. What they mean by what they say when they talk to one
another is not what we may think is meant. Wearing a veil is a sign of being
a proper and modest woman, not a symbol of male repression. These are, yet
again, differences of meaning, of beliefs, attitudes and values. They create
problems when one culture tries to deal with another.

There are also often sub-cultures co-existing within one nation. Here
again the ways that people communicate with one another both define and
are defined by the sub-culture to which they belong. What is meant by culture can be quite complicated. It could be about being black Afro-Caribbean,
but also male, and young. It could be about being Bangladeshi, but also
female, and third generation born in Britain. It could be about being Irish,
but Northern Irish, and Protestant. It could be about being Scottish, and gay.

The ways that people talk to one another in cultures imply what they
believe as part of that culture. The conventions of social interaction will be
different.

## 2.10 Class

Similar things may be said about **the influence of class on interpersonal communication and the expression of ideas about class through interpersonal communication**. Class is also part of culture and varies from culture to culture. It describes people's status and power in a given culture. In some cultures priests may be better regarded – seen as of a better class – than they are in others. Certainly class and status are recognized nonverbally. For example, high-status people are usually recognized by being given more body space and territory than others. Some institutions actually encourage class differences – or exploit them – through communication. For example, 'high-class' hotels will dress the staff in certain uniforms: these staff are expected to address guests as 'madam' or 'sir', to suggest such differences. Actually, they are trying to massage the self-esteem of their guests. Some public schools still allow pupils to play out class games – for example letting younger boys work for the older ones, and even using classist language ('fag'). Some grammar school teachers may address pupils only by their surnames. This kind of interaction encourages class language and a sense of class/status when such people leave school.

There was a notorious and popular book produced by Nancy Mitford many years ago, which identified what she called 'U' and 'Non-U' uses of language and general behaviour. 'U' stands for 'upper'. For example she identified different words for lavatory – toilet, loo, bog – and pronounced on their properness and classness. These different uses of words are still with us, as you could work out for yourself. It has also been suggested that there are different kinds of language for what people describe as the working class and the middle class. These have been called restricted and elaborated codes. Research in this area suggests for example that elaborated-code users ask more questions and give more explanations for what they do and say. This is especially seen in parenting behaviour. Restricted-code parents are more inclined to simply tell their kids what to do.

## 2.11 Conventions

These keep on coming up when one talks about communication because 'rules' for encoding or decoding are pervasive. They are everywhere, even though we may not realize that they exist. They are also in interpersonal communication, sometimes referred to as **social interaction.**

**These 'understood' rules affect how we deal with people under all circumstances** – meeting them, carrying on conversations, interviewing them, arguing with them, trying to be friends with them. We have talked previously about conventions in a more formal sense, with reference to codes and signs. Here, we are referring to them in a more social sense, though not simply as rules for behaving 'properly'.

So this section is not about etiquette, but it is, for example, about having learned when to speak and when not to speak. This could be affected partly by rules relating to the status of the people involved – 'Don't interrupt your mother!' There would also be general conventions about taking turns in conversations, regardless of who was talking or what the occasion was. We have learned not to talk over one another the whole time through using and noticing little bits of non-verbal behaviour, such as people glancing at the person they want to speak next just before they have finished speaking.

These conventions of social interaction are very much connected with the idea of skills. People who are good at communicating really know the rules, whether they realize it or not. Skilled use of conventions would also be another way of defining appropriate or effective communication.

---

**Do we say what we mean?**

Hint: when do people try to cover up their true feelings?

---

**When does regulating communication become nothing but manipulation?**

Hint: think of ways in which you can try to get what you want or can help other people to feel OK.

---

## 3 Perception – of ourselves and others

### GEORGE'S STORY

*George Moorcroft had worked at a precision instruments factory for twenty years. He had graduated through an apprenticeship to assembly work, to building proto-types for new instruments. He was a careful man who took a justified pride in his work. There were three other men of similar age and skills who shared the same workshop with him. Between them the men had tackled many exacting tasks, from building a miniature control arm which could pick up a human hair, to making a device for measuring the effects of pressure on any piece of material.*

*George was a perfectionist, with a well-regulated life. He was a neat man and a creature of habit. In fact, the only unpredictable thing in his life was the time he would take to do a job. If his work was going perfectly, George would clock out at 5.30 pm on the dot. But if he was not making the progress he desired, or the projects manager was up against a deadline, then George would work all hours to finish the job.*

But the management of the company also knew that George and his work-mates would not be there for ever. And they wanted to train up some younger men as replacements. However, George was not pleased when, one day, he was faced with his new trainee, Alan.

For a start he was suspicious of Alan because he hadn't been through an apprenticeship. In fact, the old apprenticeship system had gone anyway. But, worse than this, Alan had an HND qualification and he had only been with the company for two years. George seemed to forget that by the time he was Alan's age – 24 – he had completed his own apprenticeship.

But it was when George actually first saw Alan, one Monday morning, after he had been warned of Alan's arrival, that he decided the lad wouldn't do. And he went straight to Ron Dowling, the projects manager, to tell him so.

'I mean,' said George, 'you give me a chap who doesn't even turn up in proper overalls. I'll bet he can't even use a slide-rule.'

'Ah,' said Ron. 'But you can't say that yours is exactly a dirty job, George. He doesn't need overalls to do the job.'

'But you know that's not the point. It's a matter of attitude. The chap didn't even look as though he'd combed his hair this morning. What do you think I'm to make of that?'

'I don't know. You tell me.'

'I will tell you. It means he's not careful. Not going to take care with his work if he doesn't take care with himself. And another thing, he's a sight too familiar. Calling me George at first meeting. But anyway, it's not just that. It's the little things. He doesn't look you straight in the eye. He was lounging on the edge of a bench when I came in. And so far, he doesn't seem to be paying attention to anything I say.'

'But you left him working?'

'Oh yes. I left him with a small calibration job.'

Ron Dowling appeared to lose interest in George's problems, and turned his attention to a small metal component lying on his desk. It was a complex valve, which immediately distracted George too.

'A nice piece this. Not our work, of course. So it must be the opposition. How did you get hold of it, Ron?'

Ron Dowling looked at George without a smile.

'Alan Lovat made that, George,' he said.


## ABOUT GEORGE'S STORY

This tells us that we shouldn't judge people by appearances. But we often do. George had a view of the kind of person who should be doing the kind of job that he was. This view was based on himself and his experience. He made assumptions about Alan, what kind of person he was and what he was able to do. And all this from a few signs. From signs of untidiness he perceived Alan to be untidy in everything that he did. And in making this assessment of Alan, George was much influenced by his own view of himself.

When we talk about perception and interpersonal communication it is all about how we assess ourselves and other people; about why we do this; about the results of this assessment.

Perceiving is very much about communicating because it affects what we say to other people and how we say it. George perceived Alan mainly through what he heard and what he saw. All signs must come in through our senses.

But the important thing was the meaning that he made from these signs. Especially as he was wrong about Alan.

And you may have noticed that the idea of perception is very much connected with the idea of feedback, which we have just been talking about. It is feedback messages which we perceive when we are talking to other people. And so, of course, it is the non-verbal signs which are extremely important to the way we perceive others, because they are also important in feedback. In each case we need to look at the signs, their meanings and their effects. But, where feedback refers to the ways in which a conversation can be regulated and adjusted, perception goes further. We perceive people before a conversation has even started. And we perceive ourselves.

## 3.1 Perception of self

This is rather important, because how we see ourselves very much affects how we communicate. For example, if we see ourselves as quiet, shy people, then we aren't likely to be very positive in talking to others. We won't start conversations. We would be especially poor at talking in public situations.

And yet we weren't born as quiet, shy people. There is no law of nature that says we have to be like that. We could learn to communicate in a more positive way and then perhaps get a more positive view of ourselves. And perhaps we could learn to take a more positive view of ourselves, concentrating on what we know and what we are good at, so that then we end up communicating more positively.

There are two main aspects to the way that we perceive ourselves: we have a self-image and we have self-esteem (see figure 11).

### Self-image

**This is a view of ourselves as we think we are.** This always contains a mixture of optimism and pessimism. We may think that we are taller than we really are. But then we will also probably think that some spot or blemish on the face is larger and more noticeable than it really is. This self-image includes, therefore, a notion of our physical selves, but also refers to our

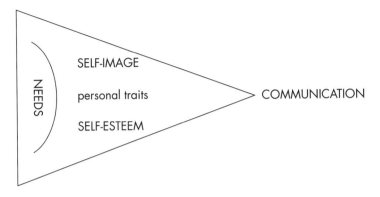

**FIGURE 11** We communicate out of who we are, who we think we are, how 'good' we think we are

personality. Of course, we do not see ourselves as others see us. Again it is probably easier to prove this in the physical sense. Have you looked at yourself in a snapshot lately, or listened to yourself on a tape-recorder? Do not despair! It can be a shock, but once you stop to think about it, what you see and hear is not bad.

This self-image is developed through our relationships with others. Other people's attitudes towards us may affect our self-image. For example, a child in a lower-stream class at school may have a rather negative self-image. This would be because the child would see other people's attitudes towards 'lower-stream children' as being rather negative.

In many ways it is the personality aspect which is more important. The kind of character which we think we have, and the kind of qualities and abilities which we think we have, must obviously affect how we get on with others. If we see ourselves as being good at a particular sport, or as knowing quite a lot about that sport, then it is likely that we will talk well when it comes up as a subject.

In very general terms, one can also talk about having a positive or a negative self-image. Those people who see their skills and qualities in a positive light are likely to be more positive about talking and listening.

**We also have an ideal self-image. This is an image of ourselves as we would like to be, and as we would like others to see us.** Some people try to make their self-image match up to this idea by behaving in certain ways. It can be a good thing to try to be a 'better person'. But it can also be a bad thing to have ideas which are impossible to achieve. Failure to match up to ideals can be destructive to the personality. Parents may expect a lot from their children at school. A child can build these expectations into their ideal self-image. But then there may be a problem if, for example, the child fails examinations.

## Self-esteem

In effect we have already referred to this. Esteem is about the good or poor opinion one has of something – in this case, ourselves. Whatever picture we have of ourselves, it is esteem which affects our interpretation of that self-image. For example, we may see ourselves as being bad at passing exams and getting paper qualifications. But we don't necessarily have to have low self-esteem about this. We could shrug it off because we know that we are good at other tasks. Or we might think that it is actually a bad thing to have passed too many exams because that would suggest that we were the kind of person that we don't want to be.

Esteem is about the attitude that we have towards ourselves. By looking at ourselves more objectively, it could be argued that we could improve our self-esteem, and so improve our use of communication.

One could visualize self-image as in figure 12.

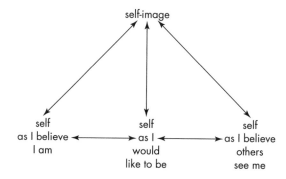

**FIGURE 12**   Elements of self-image

## 3.2 Perception of others

**We assess other people by looking at and listening to them.** This happens when we first meet others, and while we are talking with them. Our judgements are mainly about what they are thinking and feeling and are made mainly on the basis of their non-verbal cues. In this sense, perception is like a series of guesses about the other person, based on our previous knowledge and experience of them, or of people like them. We start weighing up and passing judgement on people as soon as we set eyes on them. So we cannot help perceiving others. The real question is whether or not we perceive them accurately – quite often we don't.

The longer we are with someone, the more we are likely to find out and notice about them. So the better our judgements are likely to be. But in fact, many of our contacts with other people are quite brief – like interviews

– so we are likely to have to make judgements on the basis of limited information. In this case, we should be careful about looking and listening, and then about making our minds up. Too often this is not the case. For example, for a while at least, we are inclined to think that because someone is wearing glasses, they must be intelligent. It may take a while to find out otherwise. And by this time we may already have acted on the mistaken impression that we have formed.

**What we say to others and how we say it is significantly affected by the way we perceive them.** If we see someone else as threatening and dominating, then we may try to back off, or be rather negative in what we say. And the point is that they may not see themselves like that at all. Indeed, they may not be like that – it could be that our perception is faulty because it has been careless.

So, where other people are involved we are continually monitoring their non-verbal signs in particular. From things like their tone of voice and their gaze we hope to find out what they really mean when they communicate with us. This is not just to do with what they mean by words which they may be using. It is to do with meanings about themselves and what they may be thinking, especially about us!

One thing that is well evidenced is the way that people try to make very rapid judgements about others. They try to sort out the kind of person that they are dealing with before they know them very well. This is called **impression formation**. An example of the kind of error this can lead one into is explained in section 3.4.

## We perceive their personality

That is to say, we form an opinion on what kind of person we think they are. There has been much discussion about questions such as do we have a fixed personality or have we a variety of personalities? Looking back at the idea of the various personae that we present to other people, it seems that the second idea is more likely to be true. But in any case, one can agree that we usually assess others' personalities in terms of a few major concepts such as friendly or hostile, dominant or submissive. We build a picture of the person we are dealing with and, according to our view of their personality, as well as our perception of ourselves, we decide how to communicate with them.

For example, if a normally quiet and retiring person gets into conversation with someone who they perceive to be very confident and outgoing, then they would probably end up doing more listening than talking.

You should also remember that there are always a variety of factors such as context, or knowledge of the subject of conversation, which should be taken into account when explaining what is happening and why.

## We perceive their emotional state

That is to say, we form an opinion as to what their dominant emotions are at that time. Again, this matters because it affects how we carry on talking to them. We will decide what strategy to use. We will choose the most appropriate signs. We will use our communication skills.

And it should be remembered that it is a skill to perceive accurately what is going on. The other person might be pretending that they are calm and content, when they are not. We may notice signs like eye blinking, tensing of face muscles and slumped body posture, which suggest that all may not be well.

The other person's emotional state matters because it affects how they communicate with us, as well as how they will receive our communication. We know that. That is why we pay attention to how they are feeling. It probably isn't much good asking an employee to check a book-keeping error if you know that they have just heard that they have won the Pools!

## We assess their attitude towards us

That is to say, we try to work out what the other person feels about us. We know that they will form an opinion of us, as we do of them. So we try to find out what that opinion is. That common phrase, 'It's not what you say, it's your attitude', tells us just how important attitude is in our dealings with others. Perceiving is an active, searching process, so we look for attitudes in others. We need to evaluate their position in relation to ourselves before we feel confident about talking with them. But, as with the other instances discussed, it is very possible to make mistakes. For example, signs of emotional state can easily be misread as signs of attitude. Someone who is tired and drained emotionally can easily be thought of as being negative in attitude. We should also beware of reading our own attitudes and emotions into others. For example, if we are feeling pleased and happy about something that we have achieved, then we are likely to see others as having a more friendly attitude towards us than may in fact be the case. If we show a friendly and caring attitude towards the other person and they return that attitude towards us, then there will be a good flow of communication. There will be sharing and understanding.

## We make assumptions about attributes of the other person

That is to say, we make guesses about who they are, about their background and about their lifestyle. We do this from their appearance in particular. We like to be able to place other people in a role or a job. We like to be able to define them in various ways so that we can fit them into our scheme of things. So, we would guess their age from clothes, hair, face.

We would guess their job from clothes or perhaps from possessions that they have about them. Uniforms are actually meant to define people's jobs to others.

We would certainly want to guess the other person's sex, from things like clothes and hairstyle. Some fashions of the young, at the moment, confuse the traditional signs of sex (or gender). For example, make-up is no longer the exclusive sign of being female that it once was. This can be confusing and threatening to some people because it breaks the conventions, or rules. It also shows that the meaning of signs is not fixed.

We would try to guess someone's status. This could be in terms of the class that we suppose they belong to, or in terms of their rank within the type of job we think they do. For example, we might assign someone to a certain slot in society if they were wearing expensive clothes, or drove a Rolls-Royce car, or were addressed as 'my lord' by another person.

We would guess the other person's role in a given situation. For example, a female who appears to be between the ages of 18 and 45 and who is seen pushing a pram is likely to be placed in the role of 'mum', in the minds of onlookers. She could be the aunt of the child in the pram, she might be childless. But still, she will be seen as a mother.

All of this tells us that perception is not only about recognizing signs and making assessments of others. It is also about placing other people in categories. We need to define the kind of person they are so that we can decide what is the best way to communicate with them. Unfortunately, we are often too hasty in placing people in categories because we are too hasty and careless about reading the signs.

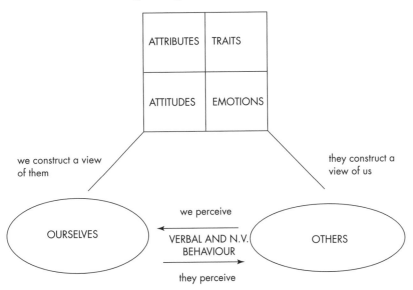

**FIGURE 13**    We construct views of ourselves and of others, in our heads

This placing in categories has its plus and minus points. It is useful to be able to organize our understanding of the world. Such categories in our heads are called **perceptual sets**. If we have a 'set' such as *creatures with claws*, then this can be useful in learning to avoid creatures with claws if they have proved dangerous in the past. Equally, there is a danger that we will put everything we know in 'boxes' in our heads, and not make connections between the categories.

**Stereotyping is another kind of categorizing.** Here too, it is quite useful to organize our understanding of people in our heads in terms of types and characteristics (see figure 13). It is a mental function that can increase the probability of our sorting out the attitudes of others towards us quite quickly. If you like, this is another example of communication coming from survival mechanisms. Older short female with smile is likely to seem less threatening to a child (to anyone?), than is older tall male with frown.

### Attribution and motivation

One approach to perception is known as **attribution theory**. There is much research in this area which is in effect about perception, as we are describing it. However, one major aspect of it has not been properly brought out. That is to do with how, **when perceiving people, we attribute motives to them**.

We make guesses as to why they are doing or saying what they are. These guesses will come from our close observation of how they act and talk, as well as from our observation of the consequences of their behaviour. We want to understand people's motivation because we want to work out what are their real attitudes towards us, and perhaps towards others.

For example, if you see someone lose their temper, shout at someone else and cause that person to cry, then you will not only want to work out why they did this, you will also think rather carefully about how they might treat you.

## 3.3 The basis of assessment

So perception is about 'reading' signs and seeking the meaning of those signs. Our judgements are based on those signs and our ability to notice them and then to make sense of them. The way we make sense of them is itself based on our previous knowledge and experience. People can become nervous in strange social situations precisely because they don't have previous knowledge and experience. They don't know 'how to behave'. That is to say, they don't know what signs to look out for and what the rules are for making sense of them. To take another situation, this is why some magazines can continue publishing successful articles on the subject of 'what to do on your first date'.

It is also important to realize that our assessment of others is based on all the information available. That is to say, our judgements are based on all the signs operating, verbal or non-verbal. Or at least they are based on a number of signs. And the information that we have could include a relationship with the other, or things that we have already heard about the other.

Perception is a continuous process. The more we interact with another person, the more information we have to go on, and so the more accurate our judgements are likely to be.

## 3.4 Problems with perception

### Projecting our wishes onto our view of others

To some extent we see what we want to see in other people. For example, if we think that other people like us and we like them then we are inclined to think that they have the same sort of views and opinions that we have. This isn't necessarily true.

### Making assumptions about others

In this case, it is as if we fill in missing information. We would assume that someone carrying a sports bag and a hockey stick is a hockey player. We assume that someone who 'looks us in the eye' is sincere. We have learnt probable meanings of signs and tend to assume that these probabilities will always be true.

### Making categories of people and the signs associated with them

In one sense, it is a useful skill to be able to put labels on things. But it is dangerous to do this too quickly. Just because a man is wearing a straight white collar round his neck does not prove he is a priest, and it certainly doesn't prove that he is sweet-tempered and forgiving. The worst kind of categorizing is called stereotyping. This is when we (or the media) use a very few familiar signs to place people in jobs or roles in an uncritical and simplistic manner. And when we have placed a person in such a slot, then we assume that they have all kinds of qualities or attributes. Usually the key signs of stereotyping are those to do with appearance. For example, someone wearing a suit is usually assumed to have status and some kind of white-collar professional job. Assumptions may also be made about this person's character and lifestyle.

## *Allowing first impressions of others to influence us*

In particular we tend to pick on one or two characteristics of the other person and let these influence our opinion of that person. This is called the 'halo effect'.

For example, at a business meeting one could be unduly influenced by the fact that the other person was wearing expensive clothes and an expensive watch, and using an expensive pen. We might assume that they were rich, successful and worth listening to. That might be what they wanted us to think. So we shouldn't be too influenced by these first impressions. Nor should we jump to conclusions taken from a few details. Indeed, usually the halo effect fades away as one gets to know the other person better, gets more information about them. But we still need to beware because it isn't always possible to get to know that much about someone else.

Figure 14 illustrates key elements in the process of perception.

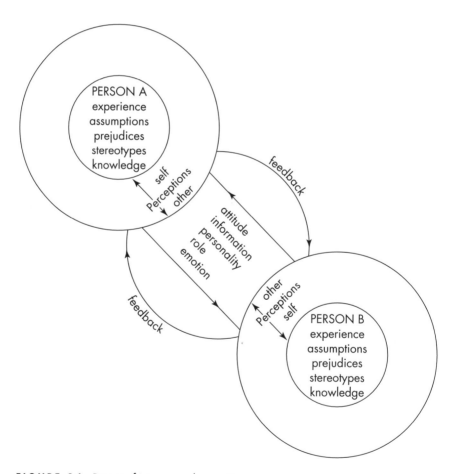

**FIGURE 14**   Process of interpersonal perception

> **Do you think we underestimate ourselves as communicators?**
>
> Hint: think of times when you have surprised yourself by what you have said.

## 4 Barriers to communication

ANGELA'S STORY

*Angela didn't like the early morning turn with the patients. It was hard work if you took it at the end of a long night. It was hard work if it was the first thing that faced you at the beginning of a day. It was especially hard with the old people. Many of them were so lively at six o'clock in the morning. That wasn't always a good thing.*

*There was old Mr Cummings in the bed at the far end. For a start, he wore a deaf aid. It was so old-fashioned that it looked like a sea shell stuck in his ear. No wonder he couldn't hear anything. Besides, she suspected he turned it down deliberately. After he had shouted 'What?' a couple of times, then Angela would lean over him to yell into his ear. That was when he came up with his favourite line, 'Give us a kiss, love.' In one week, Mr Cummings had got more kisses out of the nurses than the doctors had in two years. It was all a laugh, really. Just irritating at six o'clock in the morning. With that wonky deaf aid, you never knew if you had got through to him or not.*

*Of course Angela felt sorry for him as well. It was no joke having an artificial hip joint put in you at the age of 71. But then it was no joke looking after someone like Cummings. People had this idea that old folk grew light like sparrows. Cummings was still a big man. And it took two of them and a lot of effort to shift him around for bed changes.*

*When Eric Cummings opened his eyes he knew it must be six o'clock. He always woke up at that time. A habit from years of having to get up and out to beat the factory clock. The dull ache in his side was still there. He wished that he hadn't woken up. There wasn't much fun left in life nowadays. In fact there wasn't much life left. But he didn't like to think of that, even though this hip business had given him a shock.*

*The nurses were a starchy lot. Rather stuck-up young misses he thought. The girls in the factory had been different. Always larking around and not minding the occasional cuddle. Times had changed. He blamed it all on this women's liberation stuff. These nurses all took themselves too seriously. They wouldn't even call him by his first name. It was all Mr that, and Mrs this. He liked to feel comfortable with people. And he didn't feel comfortable here. The doctors were the worst. They would come round, look at their sheets of paper. Whisper about you with the nurses. And then when you asked what was happening, you got a mouthful of long words. Talking about . . . whatever it was . . . micturition or something like that. If they meant a Jimmy Riddle, why didn't they say so?*

*Anyway, it was terrible, being surrounded by all these old people. Eric sighed, jiggled his deaf aid to stop the buzzing, and tried calling for the nurse.*

*Angela sighed. There he was again. Probably wanted another pan or something. Her feet ached as she set off down the ward. Silly old devil, she thought. He probably didn't need her at all. Just wanted to chat. And she didn't feel like it now, especially after last night. That was the trouble with some of the old people. They didn't seem to think you were human, had a life of your own. After all, she did have a job to do.*

## ABOUT ANGELA'S STORY

This tells us about some of the things that get in the way when we communicate with other people. If interpersonal communication is meant to be about understanding between people, then it seems that Angela and Eric Cummings didn't entirely understand one another. The problem is that there are many things that can get in the way of saying what we really want to say to others, of putting over our feelings. Because of course there is more to interpersonal communication than just exchanging messages of fact. And even the facts of his condition were not being put across clearly to Cummings by the doctors.

The factors which get in the way of free and full communication between people are generally called 'barriers'. A more accurate word is 'filters', because there are rarely total barriers to understanding. You may also come across words such as 'noise' or 'interference' in some older texts on communication. It all adds up to the same idea of obstruction. And often the most important barriers are in the mind. For example, it is clear that Angela and Mr Cummings had different attitudes towards one another, coming out of their different experiences. This also meant that they had rather different beliefs and values, partly to do with their ages and partly to do with their backgrounds. We need to recognize such barriers and filters for what they are before we can do something about them. Then we may improve our communication with others.

## 4.1 Perception and filters

We have already discussed how poor perception filters communication (in section 3.4, 'Problems with perception'). The types of problem are also types of filter.

You should also make a link with the idea of psychological barriers because the filters are in the mind. And it is in the mind that the coding and decoding aspects of communication take place. This is where we make sense of the information about the other person that we see and hear. So we may filter before we say something or after we have heard something.

**The basis of this filtering is in the assumptions that we make about other people.** In one sense it is a useful skill to be able to make intelligent guesses about another person's character or behaviour. We want to know how to deal with them. But on the other hand, it isn't much of a skill if we simply jump to conclusions. It is important to learn to perceive accurately and thoughtfully. Consider the following examples. As a general instance, what about those occasions when adults talk about children in front of them, as if they are not there? Somewhere there is a filter operating which cuts out awareness of children as people and as part of the same world as the adults.

A rather more particular example of a filter could be to do with reactions to accent. It has been known for people to think that users of regional accents have less credibility and authority than those who use so-called middle-class accents. People are put through perceptual filters, and in this case the regional-accent users could come off worse. At one time the BBC demonstrated the existence of this filter and the belief behind it in their reluctance to allow regional accents in newsreaders, presenters and correspondents. This is a useful example because it also suggests that the media play some part in constructing our beliefs and values. These beliefs and values in turn become filters through which we perceive the world. We shall discuss more of this in chapter 5.

## 4.2 Mechanical barriers

**Communication may be blocked or filtered by physical factors in the communication process.**

Noise around those talking can create a filter within the context of communication. A physical problem like deafness could block the reception of communication. A physical problem such as a lisp could impede the production of communication. Any breakdowns in equipment involved with communication would also count as mechanical barriers.

## 4.3 Semantic barriers

**Communication may be filtered by the careless use of words.** Semantics is to do with the meanings of words. If words aren't used appropriately they can't produce meanings which are likely to be understood. This comes back to the idea of codes and conventions. If we break the agreed rules of grammar or spelling or use of individual words, then we are likely to set up a semantic barrier.

'Dot cre wot yuo is ezier when fergetting' is more or less gibberish. It breaks the conventions agreed by the users of the English language code. The meaning is filtered or blocked.

Of course the meaning depends entirely on the code, its conventions and other factors such as the context within which the code is used. For example, 'drop-out' means something particular and technical to a video user or engineer. It is part of a secondary code of language to do with that technology. More generally, we use it as a piece of idiom to describe a certain kind of person.

So, another definition of this kind of barrier is useful.

Communication is blocked when we cannot attach meanings to words used because the conventions of the code are broken or because we don't know the code and its conventions in the first place. If someone talks to you in Italian, and you don't 'know' Italian, then there is a semantic barrier.

As we suggested in the first chapter, words are only signs to which meanings are attached. **Meanings exist in the mind, not in the words themselves.** So if we cannot attach a meaning to a sign, even if we know it is a sign, then there must be a barrier to communication.

## 4.4 Psychological barriers

**Communications may be filtered or blocked by attitudes, beliefs and values.** Attitudes are particular views of people, situations and events. They are based on beliefs.

These are the most common cause of difficulties with interpersonal communication. These filters shape what we say before we say it and affect how we interpret what others say to us.

Since it is inevitable that we have beliefs and opinions of some sort, some kind of selection and interpretation within the process of communication is also inevitable. But the question is how conscious are we of what we are doing to messages when we talk to other people and listen to them? We shouldn't jump to conclusions about what other people mean by what they are saying. We should think about what we are trying to say before we speak. If we don't do these things, then once more we are making assumptions. We are not perceiving ourselves and others clearly.

The effect of these barriers in the mind rather depends on who is talking to whom about what and with what intention. But obviously, these fixed assumptions that we call prejudices need to be taken seriously. And these prejudices lurk just below the surface of the mind in many of us. There has been much talk about racial prejudice in recent years. Clearly, it matters a great deal to an applicant for a job if that person is black and the interviewer has a subconscious prejudice that black people are unreliable or bad time-keepers. It isn't the most blatant examples of prejudice which necessarily cause the most problems. It probably wasn't rigid male chauvinism that kept females out of newsreading jobs in broadcasting for many years. Rather, it was a kind of ill-considered prejudice which suggested to the controllers of broadcasting that this wouldn't be 'quite right'. And there was evidence that quite a few people in the audience felt the same way! More recently, there has been the case of two French owners of a British company coming to terms with national prejudice. In fact, they took on the mildly prejudiced jokes about 'Frogs' and were sensible enough not to take them as deep insults to their nationality and eating habits. They made a point of getting to know their work-force personally and built a good relationship with them, which proves the point that effective communication can create mutual understanding and banish assumptions and prejudices.

Some books on communication refer to factors such as religion or culture as separate types of barrier. We don't, because in the end it is the beliefs and values in the minds of people involved that set up barriers when, for example, culture is a factor in a given situation. Again, the barrier is psychological. If a Sikh suffers abuse to do with his wearing a turban, or an Australian is the butt of jokes about kangaroos and beer, then it is no good blaming the turban or the kangaroo. The barrier to free and friendly communication is in the mind of the person offering the abuse or making the joke. Once more it may be seen that meanings are in the mind, not in the sign.

## Comment

It is useful to visualize how these three types of barriers, or filters, affect the communication process (figure 15). Mechanical barriers in particular exist in the context and the coding processes; semantic barriers in the formulation and interpretation of the message; and psychological barriers in people's emotional processes.

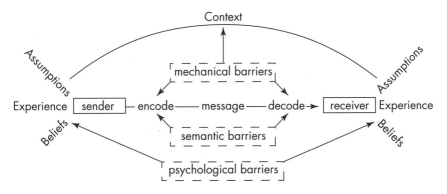

**FIGURE 15**   Barriers to communication

---

**How open is your mind?**

Hint: be honest about times when you put up barriers against other people and their ideas, or even say things just to please other people.

---

## 5 Interpersonal skills

**Communication skills used between people depend on recognition of and good use of verbal and non-verbal communication.** When people are talking to one another they are not just talking. They are using body language, among other kinds of non-verbal communication. They are also in some kind of social relationship – friends, employer and employee, parent and child. For this reason you will also hear the phrase 'social interaction' used by people interested in communication. So too the phrase 'social skills' is often used instead of 'interpersonal skills'. These social skills of communication can be described, learned and used successfully.

## 5.1 Social skills

**Social skills are used to make communication with other people effective and satisfying to those involved in the interaction.** For example, if you are talking with a friend about holidays that you both have had, then the conversation will be enjoyable and both of you will feel happy with it if you show that you are listening to each other and that you like each other. This listening and liking is something that you both learn to communicate.

When you communicate such attitudes and feelings you are making a response. Your response is based on how you assess the other person – in other words it is about perception. It is a skill to notice aspects of someone else's behaviour and to judge these accurately. But one also has to do something about what one has noticed. We call the reactions which we notice and assess 'feedback' (see figure 16). We have said that the idea of feedback includes our reactions to feedback. Our reactions should include an adjustment in our own communication. When we adjust and give out our own feedback we are doing something positive. This positive response can take different forms. For example, if you are talking to someone about their work and that person shows signs of unhappiness you might then respond by steering away from the subject or by trying to find out what is wrong. Such responses depend on exactly who is involved and on what the situation is. Either way the feedback has been noticed and some kind of positive response has been made.

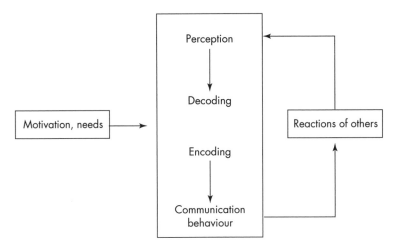

**FIGURE 16**   Social skills model, after M. Argyle (*Psychology of Interpersonal Behaviour*)

**It is a skill to recognize feedback and to make a positive response to this feedback.**

Interaction with others goes well if they feel that we have noticed what they are trying to say about us and what we are saying. It doesn't mean that one has to agree with everything that someone else says. But it does mean that the other person has to feel that basically we are paying attention and that we like them. Feedback in interpersonal communication means that each person is recognizing the other person. People like to be liked.

If someone comes along with a personal problem – say, they have quarrelled with a friend – then there isn't going to be much real communication if they feel that you aren't listening or aren't interested. You don't have to even approve of their quarrel in order to recognize the problem and to talk it over. To show signs of recognition is part of communication. To do it well is a skill. So one can also say that:

**It is a skill to be able to give signs of recognition and approval to others.**

Getting on with people isn't just a matter of talking and acting in a socially correct manner. It is also a matter of using feelings and intelligence in order to try and understand them. When dealing with other people it is important to be able to 'put oneself in the other person's shoes'. This involves a sympathetic understanding of the other person's views and of their experiences and of their place in the situation in which you are both involved. This understanding and ability to take the view of another is called empathy. The act of understanding in this way is called empathizing.

**It is a skill to be able to empathize with others.**

In order to achieve this empathy one also has to pay close attention to the other person, to their apparent needs, to making sense of those needs.

This attention which we pay to others when talking to them is in fact listening. It is surprising how often people do not listen to others. These are the conversations where someone's response to a comment leads away from what the speaker is talking about. Or it might be a response which starts talking about personal experiences and 'ignoring' what the speaker has been trying to talk about. In these conversations an exchange of words is taking place, but there isn't much listening going on. It is also worth pointing out that there are actually two broad types of listening experience. The one we are talking about here has to do with everyday conversation. There is also the listening that one does in a lecture or classroom. We will say more about this in the last chapter, and more about 'social listening' in section 5.2 of this chapter. But either way one has to make a positive effort to listen. The proper receiving of information (listening, reading and the like), which involves decoding, is as important as effective creation of communication.

**It is a skill to be able to listen to others.**

Of course all these ideas about communication and skills are linked together. For example, if one shows that one is listening then one is also giving feedback to the other person. In the same way it is possible to say that such listening and feedback are also part of self-presentation. We have already explained what this is. What is worth emphasizing is that effective presentation is something that we can learn to do. As with listening, it is possible to say that there are two broad types of presentation. The more formal kind involving presentation to a group will be discussed in chapter 6. But the kind of presentation which we make in everyday life, which includes strategies, is the one that we are now interested in. Some performances are more conscious than others. If you are working in a shop at the end of a hot Saturday and are tired, then you may make a deliberate effort to keep up a polite and interested performance for a customer. You will use your skills to do this. On the other hand, if you are trying to talk to a friend about something that you have decided to do then your performance may be fairly unconscious. Still, the point is that you want them to see you in a certain light, to see you perhaps as a decisive and cheerful person. It will take skills to do this. It takes control of those skills to do it successfully.

One particular expression of listening is the skill of what is called reflective listening. Quite simply, one shows that one is listening by asking follow-up questions. The best kind of questioning is that which picks up on the word or phrase of the topic that you want to know more about, and uses it in the form of a question.

'. . . and the coach stopped at this really weird place on the way back.'

'Oh? So what was weird about it?'

As well as showing that you are paying attention to people who are talking to you (and not just thinking about what you want to say!), this is a good way of getting people to talk, of getting to know them.

**It is a skill to be able to offer self-disclosure in a manner appropriate to the occasion.**

In this case the skill is about you being able to talk about yourself – but not endlessly! In fact it is rather more about revealing something of yourself. If you are having – or trying to start – a conversation with someone, then it helps to tell them something about your background. If you are prepared to 'give something away' then others will feel that you are more trustworthy. Anyway, it is likely to provide a starting point for more conversation. This is not about telling the story of your life as soon as you meet someone. But it could be about revealing some of your likes or dislikes – places you like to go, favourite things to eat, and so on. It sounds trivial, but once people feel OK about sharing small secrets then they may (but only *may*) want to share bigger ones.

This idea of having 'hidden' information about yourself has been expressed through a diagram called the Johari Window (see figure 17). The diagram has its explanation attached, but you will notice that it is not just about things you know about yourself, but choose to keep to yourself. It is also about things that you do not know, or see, in yourself, though others do see them. Obviously this idea is both about our self and about our ability to communicate effectively.

**It is a skill to control self-presentation, with a sense of what is appropriate to the situation.**

| | |
|---|---|
| OPEN PANE<br><br>What I know about me which is what others know about me | BLIND PANE<br><br>What others know about me, but which I don't see |
| HIDDEN PANE<br><br>What I know about me, but which I am keeping a secret from others | UNKNOWN PANE<br><br>What no one knows, not even me, but which I may discover about myself one day |

**FIGURE 17** The Johari Window describes the hidden and known self, which affects how we talk to others and they to us

We have also talked in this chapter about perception and about the problems and barriers which relate to this in particular. We will say a little more about these in section 5.3. However it is important to realize that such perceptual skills are part of social skills and are used in everyday life. We learn to make judgements about other people. We ought to be careful about how we do this. It can take an effort to avoid the kinds of problem referred to in section 3 of this chapter. And it is worth remembering that perception is about the communication we make after the judgement as well as about making the judgement itself.

**It is a skill to perceive carefully.**

Finally there is one social skill which one might say is the basis of all good interpersonal communication. That is the effective use of verbal and non-verbal communication. It can be said that all the other skills depend on this. Ultimately interaction between people depends on verbal and non-verbal signs, how we make sense of them and how we use them. This is not to say that things like judgement and feelings are not important. But the fact is that we guess their existence from our words and deeds. We express our ideas and feelings through external signs of communication. The quality of our expression will define what other people think of us and how well we get on with them in conversation and in all situations. When we try to say what we mean or to say the 'right thing' we are trying to control our communication so that we do just that.

**It is a skill to control and use non-verbal behaviour effectively.**

## 5.2 Listening skills

It follows that effective listening is tied up with effective use of verbal and non-verbal communication. The latter is especially important because it is often not noticed, and because we have already seen that messages about feelings and attitudes are largely carried through this channel.

When we are talking to someone, they 'know' we are listening because of signs such as the head tilted to one side slightly, direct gaze, a certain amount of nodding and even some noises that we make to punctuate what they are saying. The importance of this might be shown by the trouble which television producers go to when shooting the 'noddies' showing an interviewer apparently responding to what the interviewee is saying (these listening signs are recorded after the interview is over!)

Just try a conversation in which you deliberately make no response at all to your friend and watch how they dry up and ask you what is wrong! These responses show them that you acknowledge that they are there and talking, that you are keeping up with the main points that they are making and usually that you go along with what they are saying – that you approve. Like all the other skills, you have learned to do this; some people have not learned to do it very well – and so may not get on with others. But again, one can still learn such listening skills and improve them. Of course one should not be too deliberate. If one ends up looking like a nodding toy dog with a daft smile on one's face then this is as disconcerting as showing nothing at all. So of course skills have to be tried and practised and adjusted to the person and the situation concerned.

**It is a listening skill to acknowledge the person who is talking.**

**It is a listening skill to help keep the conversation going.**

**It is a listening skill to show some approval of the other person and what they are saying.**

## 5.3  Perceptual skills

It is also useful to elaborate on these skills. We have seen that essentially there are three phases to perception. There is the first stage where one actually notices the appearance, behaviour and words of the other person. The second stage happens in the mind where one makes judgements about the other person, perhaps using previous knowledge of that person, or knowledge of people and situations which we believe are similar to the situation that we are in. There are internal decisions made from those judgements about how to carry on the conversation. Then the third stage is where we actually talk back, respond and give feedback.

It is possible to say that perceptual skills are also to do with avoiding the kinds of perceptual error which we have described. One can summarize key perceptual skills as follows.

**It is a perceptual skill to make accurate observation of the other person's words and behaviour.**

**It is a perceptual skill to avoid jumping to conclusions about the other person.**

**It is a perceptual skill to make careful judgements about the other person.**

**It is a perceptual skill to make an appropriate response to what they have to say.**

---

**How skilled are you as a communicator, and in what ways?**

Hint: talk to your friends!

---

## Review

This is to help you check on the main points of this chapter, 'Interpersonal communication'.

First we said that interpersonal communication is about communication between people, usually face to face. It is about making contact with others and about how and why we do this.

### 1 MEANS OF CONTACT

1.1   Non-verbal communication is one channel which carries messages to and from other people. It includes three codes, called body language, paralanguage and dress.

1.2   Speech is the other main channel of communication between people. It is a code, composed of signs. It includes secondary codes. The signs can be used selectively, as when we choose a register. Our verbal and non-verbal signs are special to our culture.

1.3   Contact is for exchanging messages and meanings.

### 2 DEALING WITH OTHERS

This is about how we use the means of contact that we have.

2.1   We use strategies when choosing our words and non-verbal signs in order to achieve some purpose through communicating. Some strategies are used so often that they become habits, even rituals.

2.2   Games are strategies for manipulating other people.

2.3   We present ourselves through a persona when we deal with other people. We stage a performance. We have different personae for different situations.

2.4   We can learn a variety of communication skills, some interpersonal, some requiring use of a range of media. Interpersonal skills help us make contact with others. Skills help create and confirm various kinds of relationship.

2.5   Relationships are defined by the ways that we use communication, for better or for worse.

2.6   There are various categories of social situation, which affect how communication is carried on.

2.7   We regulate our contact with others by giving and receiving feedback. This comes through non-verbal signs in particular.

2.8   Communication with others is affected in many ways by gender. There are discourses of male and female, which include meanings about male-ness and female-ness.

2.9   The way we talk is affected by our culture and its beliefs.

2.10  The way we talk is affected by our sense of class, and expresses our ideas of class.

2.11  There are conventions of social interaction which we use unconsciously to manage how we deal with others.

## 3 PERCEPTION – OF OURSELVES AND OTHERS

Perception is about noticing signs that tell us about ourselves and another person, and then making sense of them.

3.1  There are two main elements in the self that we perceive: the self-image and self-esteem. What we think of our self will affect how we communicate.

3.2  When we perceive others we make an assessment of them. This assessment is concerned with personality, emotional state and attitude. We also make assumptions about attributes of the other person: job, sex, status, role, age. We attribute (suggest) motives to people when we perceive them.

3.3  We base our perception on what we see and what we hear, especially on non-verbal signs.

3.4  But we perceive others imperfectly because of certain problems:
     that we project our wishes onto our view of the other person,
     that we categorize people too readily and too simply,
     that we make assumptions too easily,
     that we are inclined to be influenced by first impressions.

## 4 BARRIERS TO COMMUNICATION

When we communicate with others there may be factors which filter our messages when we are putting them together, or which cause us to filter the messages of others when we are making sense of them.

4.1  In the process of perception, the most common kind of filtering happens because we make inaccurate assumptions.

4.2  Mechanical barriers are to do with physical obstructions to communication.

4.3  Semantic barriers are to do with problems in conveying, receiving and agreeing about meaning.

4.4  Psychological barriers are to do with assumptions and prejudices which cause the message to be filtered. They would affect encoding when communication is given and decoding when it is received.

## 5 INTERPERSONAL SKILLS

Interpersonal communication skills are also social skills which are used in various social relationships.

5.1   Social skills can make communication with others effective and satisfying. It is a skill to make sense of others' feedback and to make appropriate responses.

Key social skills are: to show approval to others; to empathize with others; to listen effectively; to present oneself appropriately; to perceive ourselves and others accurately; to control verbal and non-verbal behaviour to good effect.

5.2   Listening skills use non-verbal communication.

Key listening skills in social situations are: to acknowledge the person who is talking; to maintain the conversation effectively; to show approval of the other person.

5.3   Perceptual skills are present in the three stages of perception, recognizing, reflecting and acting.

Key perceptual skills are: to make accurate observations of the other person; to avoid jumping to conclusions; to make careful judgements; to make appropriate responses to what is perceived about the person.

## Debates

### Is it true that females are more socially skilled than males, and if so, why?

- One issue raised is to do with exactly what we mean by social skills (see the social skills checklist).
- Another issue is to do with why this might be so. Here, you need to look at socialization and upbringing, at what girls do that boys don't do, at what is valued in female behaviour.
- You'll probably want to question the relevant view held by some that females are somehow naturally better at dealing with others, at caring, even at getting their own way! (see gender and ideology)
- One other issue related to this debate is whether or not it matters anyway (see uses of communication and values).

WHAT DO YOU THINK?

### Why do some people seem to be better at communicating than others?

- One point is to decide what you mean by 'better' (see communication skills).
- Another point is that it is often easy to confuse how much a person

says, or how freely they speak, with 'good' communication (see purpose and audience).

- Another point is that people's communication performance often varies form situation to situation and from audience to audience (see basic concepts and their significance).

WHAT DO YOU THINK?

## Assignments

### Assignment One

Draw up a grid with the categories of body posture, body proximity, touch, gesture, gaze, down the left, and with two wide columns for situations 1 and 2 along the top. Then fill in the grid boxes in note form to explain how you would:

Situation 1 – express disapproval of an elderly man who is jumping a queue that you are in

Situation 2 – express approval to a 5-year-old child for a drawing that she is showing you

### Assignment Two

Either through discussion or role play work out and write down strategies for the following tasks. Your description should cover verbal, paralinguistic and body language signs.

(a) making an excuse to a friend for not meeting them
(b) encouraging someone who is shy to come out with you and your friends
(c) persuading the boss where you work part-time to give you extra hours' work

### Assignment Three

Arrange to observe someone whom you don't know for about five to ten minutes, by inviting them into your group to talk with you, perhaps about their job.

Use a grid which you have previously copied (see figure 18) for people in your group to fill in two copies – one after one minute, one at the end. The grid rates a person in terms of attitude and personality, on a scale of points. You could add other opposed pairs of qualities to the grid if you want to.

At the end of the exercise add up points or check ticks, and compare your scores. See if there are any changes from the first to the second

| | 6 very | 5 fairly | 4 not very | 3 not very | 2 fairly | 1 very | |
|---|---|---|---|---|---|---|---|
| hostile | | | | | | | friendly |
| dominant | | | | | | | submissive |
| extrovert | | | | | | | introvert |
| unsympathetic | | | | | | | sympathetic |

**FIGURE 18**   Personality assessment grid

assessment. Discuss what you may learn about perception both from these changes and from whatever overall agreements or differences there are.

## Assignment Four: Case Study

Refer to the copies of a letter and a doctor's note, to answer the tasks below.

You are a tutor working at Prestwich College. Andrew Johnson is one of your tutees. There have been complaints made and concern expressed about Andrew's frequent absences from college. He has broken two appointments to talk to you about his situation. He has made various excuses to staff, but has not talked to anyone about a medical problem. Some staff think that

---

### CHESTNUT PARK SURGERY

Prestwich

Tel : 01865 774131

Drs. M. Banks, J. R. Keppel, R. C. Staunton

8 April 1998

This is to confirm that Andrew Johnson has been suffering from depression and has been taking medication for the last month. Under these circumstances Andrew is unlikely to perform to the best of his ability and may need periods of complete rest.

Dr J R Keppel

63, Hampton Road,
Prestwich,

01865 - 748371

SK14 3TN

18th April, 1998

Dear Mrs. Woodlard,

I have received your note about Andrew, and I understand why you are worried about his progress at college. I didn't know that he had missed so much time. It is a pity that you didn't contact me before. You may not know that I am a single mother. Also Andrew has been under the doctor. I enclose a note from doctor Keppel explaining how Andrew has not been well.

Anyway I agree that we must talk about Andrew's situation, with his exams getting closer. I can't take time off work but I would meet you any time after 5.30 if that is possible. You can ring me at work on 01865 - 748494.

I hope to hear from you soon.

Yours sincerely,

Shirley Johnson.

he should not be taking his exams in six weeks' time. You have written to his mother before, without getting a reply. You have now received this letter, with a doctor's note, from Andrew's mother.

It is urgent to take action on Andrew's case. Unfortunately you are due to be away for a week, at a conference, at the very time when you would like to see Mrs Johnson. You decide to ask a colleague, Roger Sturton, who also teaches Andrew, to meet Mrs Johnson. He agrees to this. You will contact her later, after their meeting.

Now complete the following tasks.

(a) Make some notes for yourself about this case, which cover the following:
- comments on how you think the staff and Andrew's mother may see the situation differently;
- a list of factors to take into account in dealing with Andrew's case;
- a brief list of points to make to Roger Sturton (but diplomatically!) about how you think the interview will need skilled handling.

(b) Draft a letter to Mrs Johnson, explaining the situation and inviting her to come to talk to Roger Sturton at 6.00 pm on Thursday of next week.

(c) Write a note to Roger Sturton covering a copy of your letter to Mrs Johnson, and describing the main points you would like him to deal with in the interview.

(d) Draft a short memo to staff, discreetly explaining that there is a problem and that it is being dealt with.

## Suggested reading

Burton, G., and Dimbleby, R., *Between Ourselves*.
Hartley, P., *Interpersonal Communication*.
Marsh, P., *Eye to Eye*.
Patton, B., and Giffin, K., *Interpersonal Communication in Action*.
See also the resources list at the end of this book.

# Chapter 3

# Communication
# in groups

A group of people is considerably more than the sum of its parts.
Judy Gahagan, *Interpersonal and Group Behaviour*, 1975

This chapter deals with some aspects of communication in and between groups. We provide insights into why people form and join groups and how people behave in groups. Such knowledge can help us to express ourselves more effectively in social situations.

Forming groups

# 1 What is a group?

ANDY'S STORY

*Andy was bored with his Saturday job. Perhaps it would be more truthful to say that he was frustrated by it. He wanted the money, and the people he worked with were all right. But it messed up his social life on Saturday nights, and he had had to give up football when he took the job, six months ago.*

*He had really enjoyed the football. It was only a little local club but they all took it quite seriously. They practised as well as playing. People in the team were his friends, or the older guys were people's brothers. And he reckoned they were quite good – Mike Wilson, their captain, had been playing for a minor league before he got married and decided to cut down his commitments. He had a way of getting you to do things without bossing people around. They all had a good laugh, and would often meet in the pub on Sunday lunchtime. Andy felt awkward about doing that once he had left the team, though everyone told him to come along. He didn't feel part of it any more.*

*It had been a hard decision, dropping his game. But he had to have the money. He had gone back to college after messing around for two years, and money was tight at home. Mum had a part-time job. But Dad had lost his job over a year ago when one of the divisions at the works was closed down completely. He just couldn't find anything else. Certainly nothing like what he had before. Privately Andy thought his Dad was being a bit fussy what he did for a job, but he could see why he felt like that, having had a decent job before. It was his Dad being made redundant that had jolted Andy into taking a look at his own life. He had just taken family life for granted and the money that came in. Then all at once his elder sister Jo had left home to live with her bloke – and she had a job. His Dad was out of work and around the house. He couldn't tap his Dad for the odd fiver any more. They hadn't had a family holiday since, though Andy hadn't been that fussed anyway.*

*But it had disturbed him that the family seemed to be drifting apart. So after a serious talk with his Mum he had decided to go for a course, and she had got him a job at the toy warehouse through a friend of hers.*

*Now he was finding it tough going. He didn't finish work till eight. Sometimes he even felt too shattered to go out, what with college work as well, and made some excuses to his mates. He was fed up about this because they had a good crowd going. The main people had all been to the same school as Andy, and they got on well together. Andy knew where he was with them, and they always looked to him to make people laugh. They would go to the same clubs. He felt easy with them. Not like the people at work, who were all right, but it was different. The one positive thing about work was this girl he fancied, who'd started there recently. So maybe he would stick it out after all.*

ABOUT ANDY'S STORY

This story shows how naturally social we are. We all belong to groups of one sort or another, and these groups are important to our lives, to our happiness. We often spend our days moving in and out of one group or another.

Some of these groups are reasonably stable and long-lasting, like our family. In other situations one may meet groups of people, like on a bus. However, we would argue that such sets of people are not a true group, where there is interaction and bonding. You can share a purpose with a set of people on a bus – to travel somewhere. But that is all. There isn't much contact. You don't form any relationships. Whereas even at work Andy formed some relationships. And his friends were very important to him. He felt at ease with them; they shared interests and accepted behaviours. They had their own things that they liked doing, and places that they liked to go to.

In established groups like this people know their place in the group and how to relate to one another – they have their roles. Andy made people laugh. It was a different situation at work. He belonged to different groups and had a different place in each, had to behave differently in each one.

## 1.1 Groups we belong to

Each of us inevitably belongs to a variety of groups.

You could list those groups you joined from your own choice, for example, a youth club or a pop group. You could also list those groups you joined without a free choice, for example, your family or your school. There are many different sorts of groups with different sorts of purposes. They cater for our different needs. These needs may be short-term (an evening party) or long-term (a club that we belong to). It is interesting to consider why we join and form our various groupings (see figure 19).

The word 'group' can carry many different meanings and associations. **It is helpful to describe different types of groups according to their functions and qualities.** We have just noted that some are short-lived gatherings of people and others are more permanent gatherings. Some are formal, others informal. Some are small (say, five people), others are large (say, several hundred). Some are local, others international. People in a group have some interest or purpose in common which brings them together.

Although **individuals in a group share common interests**, these people may not always share all of themselves. Having agreed on some pur-poses, people may disagree fiercely about how these purposes should be achieved. They might disagree on how the group should be organized. Some members may want all members to be equal, but other members may prefer to have a designated leader for others to follow. When people gather together there is usually some sort of struggle for power.

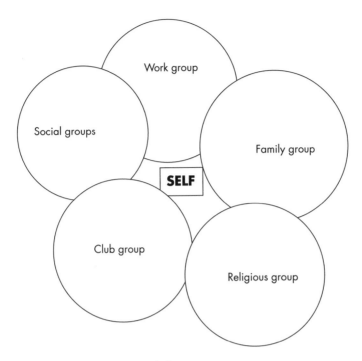

**FIGURE 19** Our self and groups we belong to

Relationships and patterns of communication have to be developed for the group to function. **If there is no interaction between the individuals then a group cannot be formed.** A college or school class is a collection of individuals; it rarely becomes one group, but usually consists of several sub-groups.

## Family groups

The first group which most people join is the family group.

As babies we have no choice about this since we are born into a particular situation and depend on those around us for physical and emotional support. Domestic groups, whether in the form of a traditional family, single-parent family or commune of several adults and children, serve to provide security and an environment in which people can develop and grow. A vital part of this is learning how to use the languages of human communication.

The first relationships we form are with our blood relations – a phrase that indicates the prime importance of these contacts. Our needs as growing individuals must be met by these people close to us who form our primary group.

## Informal friendship groups

These provide important needs of belonging. Everyone recognizes that children develop through playing with other children and with adults. But people of all ages continue to benefit from relaxed contact with others. An atmosphere in which we can communicate ourselves freely and share with others comes from a secure friendship group.

Such groups are often called *peer groups* because the relationships of these groups are between equals. These groups are most evident amongst adolescents at a time in our lives when we especially need to be with other people we like. We are often seeking to redefine our individual identity, to seek our own concept of what we are like and what we want to become. We therefore tend to seek out others who we believe are similar to ourselves. As we change so we change our group memberships. Our family relationships often undergo strains as we experience and make these changes.

## Formal organized groups

These are an element of all societies. They include school and college groups, voluntary organizations such as Brownies, Cubs, Guides, Scouts, youth clubs, church groups, sports clubs and work organizations.

These organizations have stated aims and some of these we are required to join by the state, for instance school groups. Membership of groups helps each of us to develop his or her individual characteristics. We also develop our relationships with other people and the society in which we live. This process of development is often called *socialization*. This term describes the progress of becoming an active participating member of the society into which we are born. Being a member of many groups is necessary to develop as a person able to relate to and communicate with other people.

The functions of an organized work group may be to produce goods, produce a service or to make some sort of profit. In addition to these functions an organized group of human beings will also inevitably fulfil other functions for its members, for example functions such as developing relationships, developing images of the self and personal identity, and enabling or preventing fulfilment of people's potential talents.

More will be said about communication in organizations in chapter 4.

## 1.2 The nature of groups

So far we have sought to provoke some thinking about yourself and the different sorts of groups you encounter.

The rest of this chapter will concentrate on the ways groups operate and on the individual's behaviour within them. Before we go on to this, however, we wish to focus our previous comments by drawing up **a list of qualities that define what a group is**:

(a) To become a group the individual members must exist in some sort of **relationship** together. There must be some form of communication between them and the group develops some sort of cohesion in order to stay together. Not all the members of the group may like each other, and they may not always find it easy to co-operate, but these tensions will not be allowed to break up the group.

(b) Group members must share **common goals, purposes or interests** and recognize these. A crowd at a bus stop shares the goal of hoping to catch a bus, but they may not interact together at all and, therefore, do not form a group.

(c) Members of a group accept a system of **common values or norms of behaviour**. Some of the groups we have mentioned earlier, such as the Scouts or some schools, indicate such norms by requiring obedience to a set of rules and the wearing of a uniform. Often, however, the pressure for group conformity is less obvious.

(d) Members of a group develop **set roles of behaviour** in a particular situation. These roles can be assigned, as for example in a committee when one person is elected as chairperson, one is secretary and so on. Alternatively in a specific group one person may become the silent one, one becomes the joker, one the show-off and so on. But that same person in another group may adopt a quite different set of behaviours.

With a family group and other groups that exist over a long time these set roles may change. A lifetime may take the same person from being the baby of the family to an independent child and then an adult who takes responsibility for other members of the family.

(e) This **conformity to norms of behaviour does not mean that everyone in a group behaves in the same way**. Not all relate to each other in the same way. The stability of a group usually depends on people accepting different roles and sometimes there can be a clear identification of status in which one person is openly the leader and others are followers.

(f) Members of a group have an **identity** that may be represented through their dress and pattern of behaviour.

---

## Which groups do you choose to belong to?

Hint: think of groups that you could choose to walk away from or to change.

## 2 Why do people join groups?

### 2.1 Reasons for forming and joining groups

There are two main reasons for people wishing to join themselves into a group: (a) to achieve a shared goal or oppose a common threat; (b) to have a sense of belonging and security.

### (a) To achieve a shared goal or resist a common threat

On your own you may not be able to wield much influence, but if you can persuade others to join you, then the influence of the group can be greater than the separate efforts of lots of individuals. There are countless examples of pressure groups formed to apply pressure on decision makers to make or change a decision in their favour. Can you think of some local and national pressure groups? They could be concerned with environmental issues or the rights of a particular section of society.

For the group to perform effectively it has to achieve the group qualities that were listed in the previous section.

*   What sort of uniting relationship can be built?
*   How will the group ensure that its supporters really do pull together?
*   Will everyone want the leading roles?
*   Will no one actually want to do the donkey work?
*   Can such a group work informally or does it need a stated structure, for example chairperson, secretary, treasurer, publicity representative?

A group of people which is formed to achieve a set task assumes at least one common interest in its members, but there may be many more differences between the individual members which will make their relationship and communication difficult.

In such circumstances group members normally seek a formal structure which all are required to agree to. Aims have to be agreed. Responsibilities have to be assigned. The group must present a united front.

At the heart of these issues is the need for group problem solving. An individual can weigh up the evidence, formulate alternative courses of action and then select the most desirable one. However, for a group to follow this problem-solving process is less easy.

One dominating individual may be seen to wield excessive influence or the opposite may happen and the majority, who may be looking for the easy way, dominate the discussion.

The communication skills outlined in chapter 2 – of using non-verbal communication; of careful listening; of taking note of barriers to communication – all these are needed to influence a group in coming to the appropriate universally supported view.

We have concentrated on a 'pressure group' example. But these ideas are appropriate to the workings of committees, working parties set up to perform a specific task, and indeed to a total organization or association.

People in all of these sorts of group may have only one thing in common. They would not 'naturally' join together as a result of similar backgrounds, closeness of age, or a spontaneous interest through which members of a group might just drift together without any conscious intention to do so.

## (b) To have a sense of belonging and security

In this case there may not be any particular task you wish to achieve, but you simply enjoy being part of the group. You may enjoy dressing and behaving like other people to show you identify with them. In saying this people often think of mods or punks or romantics, who are obvious groups of people who have some things in common. But the same comments could be made about company executives who adopt accepted patterns of dress and behaviour at work and in their social lives. Simply wearing a certain sort of tie or a particular badge can show group solidarity. The use of communication skills to form relationships has been noted as one of the main functions of communicating in chapter 1, section 2.1.

Many groups form accidentally, simply from people with like interests gathering together. The purposes of such groups may not be formally stated, but the members simply enjoy being together and enjoy the social contact the group provides. The image of the traditional English pub satisfies these sorts of group needs.

Many people recognize in themselves and others a desire to be 'sociable'. To be able to speak to and mix with other people they identify with. **We create our own personal identity through membership of groups.** We define ourselves by a list of 'I am . . . ' statements.

We feel secure in the knowledge that we share values, attitudes and beliefs with others, so that to say 'I am a punk . . . a member of CND . . . a student . . . I play football . . . I live in . . . ' gives us a feeling of security, even if the security of the group may seem to be in opposition to other groups that other people belong to. Such statements will lead others to react in different ways: some favourably and some unfavourably.

For each of us they can provide an important reference for what we are and how we see ourselves. As children our reference group will be primarily our family group, but as we mature we choose other groups to align ourselves with. We are prepared to give up some individual freedoms and accept some imposed norms of behaviour because such conformity gives advantages. One of the main advantages is ease of communication with like-minded members of the groups to which we belong.

The opposite of this of course is that a person who shares the norms of the Rotary Club may well not find it easy to communicate with and share the norms of someone who belongs to a pop group, and vice versa. Their attitudes, values, beliefs and perceptions of each other will strongly affect how each interprets what the other says and does.

Membership of groups is very much concerned with how we perceive ourselves and other people. We assign status to various groups although there may not be universal agreement on which groups confer which status. One person wears a uniform with pride which another person 'wouldn't be seen dead in'.

## Comment

In this book we are seeking to make our processes of communication more conscious. Being aware that our opinions, our attitudes and our beliefs have been learned from the reference groups to which we belong can help us to see why we hold them. We tend to join with people who confirm our existing beliefs or offer us beliefs we wish to develop. We tend to reject ideas from people who challenge our beliefs.

Labelling people with group identities can prevent communication happening. Angela's story in chapter 2 (pages 77–8) illustrated some of the barriers that labelling and placing people into stereotypes can produce. Stereotypes often result from our perceptions, even if false and prejudiced perceptions, of group memberships and identities.

We need to be aware of what group membership does to us and to other people's perceptions of us. In the final sections of this chapter we are going to look at how people communicate in groups.

---

**Are you a group kind of person?**

Hint: have you said or done things to 'stay in with the crowd'?

---

## 3 Three key factors in groups

MARY'S STORY

*It was the monthly meeting of the St Joseph's Youth Club – Jo-Jo's as everyone called it – and Mary felt pleased about being secretary. They had something important to discuss, so she read out the solicitor's letter carefully.*

*Jack Smith had been the youth club leader nearly twenty years ago, and he had left £500 in his will for the club to spend on whatever it wanted. Mary had her own ideas about what was needed. She had already talked to the two youth leaders.*

*But she knew that she wasn't supposed to push her views straightaway in a meeting like this, so she kept quiet in the first place.*

*In fact there was a stunned silence for a short time, while everyone took in the news. But then there was quite a buzz. Of course it was Joanne who put her oar in first.*

*'There's only one thing we really need and now's our chance to get it. The club has got tatty and the bar is disgusting. I think that five hundred would let us redecorate and put in a proper bar.'*

*'Just a minute,' said Nick, 'I thought we had already planned to do the place up with volunteers. I reckon we should buy some decent chairs and a new TV.'*

*'I'll go for that,' said George. 'After all we can do decorating ourselves. But we can't make furniture or build a TV.'*

*George's girl friend, Mandy, chipped in. 'Why do we need a new TV? We can watch telly at home. I don't think that people come here much to watch it. What we do need is a snooker table and a tennis table. The ones that we've got are crap.'*

*Mary saw her chance. 'Well, I must say, that's what I thought.'*

## ABOUT MARY'S STORY

Mary had a role to play in this particular group, which was at least a semi-formal one – put together to help run the youth club. She rises to the situation of being secretary and takes it seriously, whatever she is like in other circumstances.

But this story also shows a typical activity of many groups, which is to make decisions. There is usually a pattern to decision making in groups, and of course it does involve a kind of compromise in which individuals may have to suppress their own wishes in favour of the collective feelings of the group. At the same time the personalities of individuals, their communication skills, very much affect the way communication is carried on, and what decision is reached in the end.

If you knew more about the personality, the status, the relationships of people in this story then you would understand more about how they inter-act and how they might reach a decision. You can know more about groups that you see in real life. You can observe them.

## 3.1 Roles

We adopt roles in our lives which help us to form relationships with other people. **A role is a way of behaving which is considered to be suitable for a particular situation.** From an early age we learn to play parts according to unwritten scripts provided by parents, brothers, sisters, teachers, friends and so on. There are times of course when we prefer not to play the role which others try to assign to us.

**We accept to a greater or lesser extent the goals and expected behaviour patterns of a group to which we belong.** There are often tensions between individual wishes and group pressures. Hence we join and leave many groupings during our lifetime. We join or form groups to serve our needs; in return for this we may have to be prepared to sacrifice some individual freedom of action.

As communicators it is helpful to identify the roles we play. A great deal of our education and our socialization consists of us learning what are considered to be patterns of appropriate behaviour in different situations.

The majority of our lives is spent with groups of people and we learn how to behave in those groups. If we attend an orchestral concert at a hall such as the Festival Hall in London, we are expected to sit still and quiet and listen. If we attend a pop concert at the Hammersmith Odeon in London, then we are not expected to sit still and quiet and listen in silence. If we attend a BBC Promenade Concert at the Albert Hall in London we are, by tradition, allowed to sing and dance at particular moments. If we attend an open-air pop concert then the freedom of movement, of sound, of eating and so on is again quite different. In each case we are part of an audience listening to music, but in each case we accept the role of a different sort of audience in which the patterns of behaviour are quite different.

This concept of role in communication is difficult to define, but it is useful to help explain why people behave as they do. At one extreme it may seem that if we are playing a series of roles, or merely taking on ourselves a number of dramatic characterizations, then where is the 'real me', the real person and personality within these different roles? To reconcile this apparent contradiction it is important to realize that a role is an expected pattern of behaviour, but that each person will bring to it their own personality, attitudes and experience. Within the broad framework of a role there is a lot of room for individual interpretation.

For example, if we were to compare two formal committees they would both have a chairperson and a secretary. Each of these roles is defined; however, each person that fulfils these roles will fulfil them differently. One person may be a firm authoritarian chairperson, whilst a second person may be content to let the committee discuss issues in an open way with each committee member's views being equally valued.

Another example might be to observe young children. Especially at the pre-school age from 3 to 5 years children are often trying out roles. Their play will include being mother and father, or maybe playing at being a farmer, a policeman/woman, a shopkeeper or some other occupational role which they have encountered. It is through trying these out and interpreting them for ourselves that we develop our own self-identity and our own personal approach to the roles we shall play.

In order to manage the many relationships which we enter into and to

Roles we adopt

communicate with other people, we have to assume some predictability of behaviour. Hence we tend to predict that people will behave in certain ways according to categories of roles. The following list of types of roles is one which we often consciously, or less consciously use. There is an example of these for a man in figure 20.

## Professional roles

If someone is labelled a farmer, a social worker or a teacher you have certain expectations of them. You would allow a doctor or nurse to do things to you that you would only allow other people to do if they were very intimate with you. A nurse or a doctor in a hospital wears a uniform to signal their role and to decrease their human individuality and personality.

## Age roles

Different sorts of behaviour are considered appropriate to particular stages of your life. You can get away with things, for example a display of tantrum, when you are a young child. A 40-year-old throwing a tantrum would be viewed differently.

## Gender roles

Even though the differentiation of sexual stereotypes is rightly being challenged, there still presently remain some expectations about appropriate behaviour for men and women. If you see a man crying do you react differently from how you behave when you see a woman crying?

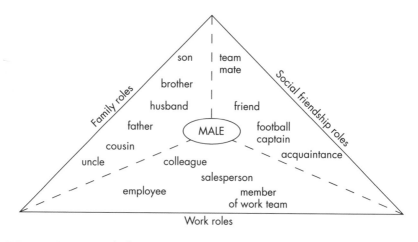

**FIGURE 20**  Types of roles in groups

Look at the illustrations in this book: do they seem to support or contradict traditional gender roles?

## Class roles

Again this role is changing, but in many people's perceptions, whether they are acknowledged or not, there still remain expectations about upper-, middle- or lower-class behaviour. For some people to label another person as bourgeois or working-class or aristocratic can have quite different meanings according to the perceptions and the tone of the person who says it.

Whilst these four categories of role – professional, age, gender and class – can be helpful in understanding other people's behaviour, they are not in any way fixed and we are free to choose the way we play our roles. Although we may not be able to change our gender and age, we can change out of the expected behaviour patterns of a 50-year-old male. Do you have expectations of a 50-year-old male who is a solicitor from a middle-class background? What sort of person do you expect him to be? You might like to try to describe your expectation of what he looks like, the people he mixes with, the way he spends his time and the way he behaves.

## 3.2 Groups, teams and roles

When one looks at how people behave in either social groups or work groups (sometimes referred to as teams), it is noticeable that they will fall into various **role types**. Descriptions of these types are almost like personality labels. The words used say a lot about how any one group member helps the group. This help may be to do with helping the atmosphere and mood of the group – jokers and peacemakers. It may be to do with getting things done – ideas-person or organizer. It may be to do with supportive-ness – compromiser and conciliator. You should cross-refer these ideas to the next chapter on organizations, where it is important that people in work teams should be able to contribute to the task(s), as well as to the happy maintenance of the group.

Of course people do not always help a group. Some can destroy it – at work or in our social lives. The backbiters and the complainers are destructive. Those who help groups are said to have **functional roles**. Those who damage groups have **dysfunctional roles**.

## 3.3 Norms

In a group to which we belong we may be prepared to accept the norms of behaviour which the group has developed.

These norms can be stated as formal rules such as laws in a society or rules and regulations for a school or college. Such norms are imposed quite clearly.

These norms can also be left unstated and informal. For example, in a group of people at a café it may be expected that people will be noisy, joking, fast-talking, interrupting each other, and that each person will be treated on equal easy-going terms. However, the same people transferred to their home situations may accept that at the dining table only one person talks at a time, conversation is conducted slowly, politely and quietly. Such norms are developed by the groups themselves, not externally imposed.

This development of norms usually results from the processes that have formed the group into a stable entity. It has been suggested by B.W. Tuckman and repeated by Michael Argyle (1969) that groups usually go through four clear stages in their development:

(a)  **Forming** – anxiety, dependence on leader (if any), members find out about the task, rules and nature of the situation.
(b)  **Rebellion** – conflict between individuals and sub-groups, rebellion against leader, resistance to rules and demands of task.
(c)  **Norming** – development of stable group structure, with social norms, conflicts are resolved, cohesiveness develops.
(d)  **Co-operation** – interpersonal problems are solved, the group turns to constructive solution of problem, energy is directed to the task.

The third stage of development is significant and the point at which the individual members are prepared to forgo some of their own personal demands in favour of the solidarity of the group. This solidarity may be considered desirable in order to fulfil the task which the group is set or in order to fulfil the social processes of the group in supplying supporting relationships to each other.

If an outsider enters the group he or she will feel the pressure to conform to these norms. A famous study of this was carried out by an American researcher named Asch. He formed a group of people in a room who agreed to deceive outsiders who were brought into the room. The outsiders were shown several lines such as those in figure 21.

The members of the group were told to give an obviously wrong answer about whether the standard line was the same length as line number 1, 2 or 3. The outsiders were therefore faced with a conflict between what their eyes were telling them and what they heard from a majority of those they thought were their fellow group members. Were they to believe what they thought they saw or were they to believe what they thought the other people must be seeing? The results showed that 37 per cent of the outsiders conformed to the judgement of the inner group and were thus in error. In other words quite a significant proportion of the outsiders were prepared to

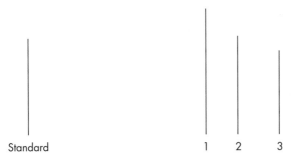

**FIGURE 21**   Comparisons of lines

conform to the group pressure rather than rely on their own observation and judgement.

You might like to try a version of this experiment amongst some of your friends.

In order for it to work there must be an amount of trust amongst those taking part. The group must be prepared to keep together. Such group thinking does, of course, show that if we completely subdue our individual judgements in favour of conformity to the group this does bring dangers. The Asch experiment indicates how group norms can lead to conformity. But it doesn't have to be like that. 'On the one hand a group can develop norms which restrict its members' behaviour and communication: on the other hand a group can provide support and understanding for its members and allow them to express themselves in ways that they otherwise would not have done' (Hartley 1993). The protection afforded by groups can either stifle you or support you. Families can do this as much as work groups. The kind of family which imposes expectations on its young members in terms of their careers can be stifling: the family which gives them space to discover their abilities and convictions is supportive.

## 3.4 Leadership

The final aspect of behaviour in human groups which we wish to note in this section is the question of what is often called leadership. The example of Orwell's novel *1984* indicates a leadership principle that is totally dominating, totally controlling and totally autocratic.

There are, however, other styles of leadership. In societies that wish to perceive and portray themselves as democratic, the autocratic style, whether adopted in families, in friendship groups or in work groups, would be frowned upon. In groups with hopes of being democratic or equal, decisions are not imposed by one member.

Four major styles of group leadership are usually described as auto-cratic, *laissez-faire*, democratic and collective.

### Autocratic

Here one person imposes his or her will on the rest. Often hostility and lack of personal commitment are the result among the other members of the group. However, in groups with formally stated hierarchies, like the uniformed services, such a style is accepted as the norm.

### Laissez-faire

Here no one person or sub-group takes responsibility for decisions. In consequence little is usually achieved and there is a general state of confusion.

### Democratic

Here the group welcomes initiatives from all members and no one person dominates the group. Usually there are more united common efforts and group members consider themselves to be 'we'; i.e. decisions are perceived to be group decisions, shared by all. There may be an 'elected' leader or the role of leader may be rotated.

### Collective

Here the group seeks to avoid the concept of a leader and operates as a team of equals. Each person is assigned equal status and power. Actions and decisions require the agreement and support of all, hence there is need for lengthy group discussion and persuasive communication skills. 'Collectives' can be slow to decide and act, but they can create a very solid and committed group.

Can you apply these broad categories of leadership to groups you know? Are you a member of an organization that seems to be autocratic or *laissez-faire* or democratic or collective?

The autocratic style is sometimes seen as being the most efficient. Decisions are often taken fast and implemented fast. The comparative loss of personal freedom and satisfaction may be accepted for the good of the group. More will be said about groups working as organizations in chapter 4.

To conclude chapter 3 we wish to explore specific examples of how communication operates in small groups.

---

**Are you a team player?**

Hint: think of how often you work with others and how often you get impatient with other people.

---

# 4 Communicating in groups

## 4.1 Observing group communication

We hope that from reading this chapter you now have a clear notion of how human groups exist on two levels: (a) the goal, task or purpose which brought the group of people together and (b) the social, communicating processes that enable the group to work as a group.

In Mary's story we merely indicated the words each person spoke in deciding how to spend £500. If we videotaped such a meeting we could observe a good deal of non-verbal communication, for example tone of voice, nodding of heads, facial expressions, gestures, body posture. These signs of non-verbal communication would indicate what feedback each speaker was giving and what attitudes towards the topic and towards each other the speakers wished to show, or indeed what each was showing unintentionally. Without speaking, each committee member would be likely to express a reaction to each proposal. Maybe some members were not very interested at all in what others had to say, only thinking of their own ideas.

It is possible to observe communication in groups, which is often called *group dynamics*, in two ways.

## 4.2 Participation and interaction patterns

We can observe the participation and interaction of people in the groups. We can see who talks most and least. We can also see who talks to whom.

### Participation in a group

You can record levels of participation by drawing a circle to represent each member of the group and placing a mark in the circle for each time the person speaks.

For example, in a group of five people, labelled A–E, we could record the participation of each person, as in figure 22. In this figure we can see that person A spoke 5 times, person B spoke 10 times, and so on.

### Interaction in a group

To record the interaction between people in the group you can draw the same circles with the same labels and then indicate who talks to whom by linking the circles by lines with arrows indicating the direction of speaking. This sort of diagram is called a *sociogram*. For example, the discussion which we recorded in figure 22 might have indicated interactions such as those in figure 23.

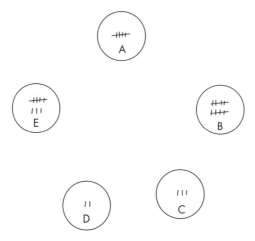

**FIGURE 22**   Participation in a group – how many times each person speaks

In figure 23 we can see that person A spoke generally to the whole group twice, spoke to person B once and to person E twice. Person B, on the other hand, spoke generally to the group four times, spoke twice to person A, once to person C, twice to person D and once to person E. The patterns of speaking and interaction between these people can thus be recorded. If one observes a group discussion and records the interactions in this way it can often be seen that the discussion can centre on one or more people with others remaining very much outside.

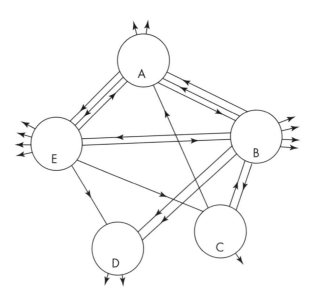

**FIGURE 23**   Interaction in a group – who speaks to whom

## 4.3 Group communication: tasks, relationships, individual needs

Thus by drawing circles to indicate group members we can record the levels of participation and interaction. These sorts of diagrams, however, do not really indicate what the content of these communications is. In order to do this a different method of recording the group processes is needed. We can draw up a grid as in figure 24, which records whether the group members are (a) contributing to the task of the group, and/or (b) contributing to the maintenance of the group relationships, and/or (c) only concerned with their self-centred needs. By using headings for different sorts of communication, some of which are concerned with the task of the group, some of which are concerned with the members of the group contributing to the group, and some of which are more concerned with the individuals working as individuals, we can build a picture of what each person is contributing to the actual discussion or meeting that is being observed.

In this analysis sheet we have not entered any details for the various people, but suggest that you use an analysis sheet like this in order to observe

| Types of group communication | | People | | | | |
|---|---|---|---|---|---|---|
| | | A | B | C | D | E |
| | TASKS | | | | | |
| 1 | giving information | | | | | |
| 2 | questioning/seeking information | | | | | |
| 3 | organizing ideas | | | | | |
| 4 | clarifying ideas | | | | | |
| 5 | summarizing | | | | | |
| 6 | evaluating | | | | | |
| 7 | deciding | | | | | |
| | RELATIONSHIPS | | | | | |
| 8 | encouraging | | | | | |
| 9 | harmonizing | | | | | |
| 10 | sharing/gatekeeping | | | | | |
| 11 | listening | | | | | |
| 12 | relieving tension/compromising | | | | | |
| | INDIVIDUAL NEEDS | | | | | |
| 13 | blocking | | | | | |
| 14 | seeking attention | | | | | |
| 15 | dominating | | | | | |
| 16 | not involving | | | | | |

**FIGURE 24**  Analysis grid for observing group communication according to contribution to the tasks of the group, to the maintenance of relationships in the group and to individual needs

a group discussion. You can, of course, change the headings for the different tasks, relationships and individual behaviours. The headings that we have given provide a range of the types of contributions that people often make to group communication.

From the authors' experience of taking part in such observation exercises we can say that these methods of observing group communication often reveal that how we behave and communicate in groups is quite different from how we thought we had. I may sit in a group discussion and feel that I am making very positive contributions by giving information, summarizing, encouraging other people, listening and relieving tension. However, another observer recording an analysis of the group may have perceived my contributions quite differently. An outsider's view of my contribution may be quite different from the self-image which I have of my group behaviour. We recommend you try some of these observation exercises with groups that you know.

## 4.4 Becoming an effective group member

We spend our lives as members of various groups. In the past thirty years there have been many books published about research into group behaviour and communication. This chapter has tried to provide a brief summary of some of this research. Suggestions for further reading are at the end of this chapter and at the end of the book.

At various points in this book we use the phrase 'effective communication'. By this we mean the ability to express your ideas, to understand other people and to build satisfying relationships with other people, whether in pairs, in small groups or with larger social groupings.

This chapter has tried to provide some insight into aspects of social psychology in order to understand the communication processes that occur within groups. Membership of groups is a fundamental human need. We define ourselves, both for ourselves and for other people, by our group contacts and relationships. We often have unchallenged prejudices and stereotypes arising from our perception of people's membership of groups.

To become effective group members it is useful to take notice of the following points:

> What motivates people to join groups.
> The expectations of roles within groups.
> The relationships between group members.
> The skills of verbal and non-verbal communication.
> Understanding of how groups develop from a collection of individuals to a cohesive force with their own norms of behaviour.
> Understanding of group identities and the labelling of people according to group memberships and roles.

## 4.5 Communication skills in groups

**Group members can use certain communication skills in order to make that group satisfied with group relationships and effective in carrying out group tasks.** These skills – ways of using verbal and non-verbal communication – often draw on interpersonal skills. For example, we have said that good one-to-one relationships depend on signs which recognize the worth and importance of the other person – giving them rewards. The same thing is true for group members. The person who scores the goal in some team sport enjoys praise given by group members. The giving and receiving of this praise also adds to the good feelings about being a member of the team. And if the main task of the group in this example is to score goals, then one can say that the rewarding skill actually helps the group in achieving its tasks. There are certain skills which relate especially to group members as people in a relationship, and others which relate to these people as problem solvers and decision makers: some are personal, some are more practical.

On the personal side, phrases such as 'well done' or 'that's a good idea' offer reward to the group member and help the group. **It is a skill to be able to offer praise to group members for ideas or actions.**

Another personal aspect of group activity that may be underestimated can be described as fooling around or as casual chat. Again, the sense of group solidarity can be reinforced by behaviour such as making jokes. If someone does this then they can help the group to relax which will then help them to get on with their main activity. Obviously too much joking actually becomes destructive – it gets in the way of the business of the meeting or of the play rehearsal – but as with praising others, a certain amount can create group harmony. You may have noticed that news reports of high-level political meetings judge that things have gone well if there are pictures and accounts of smiles and joking as well as of the serious business. **It is a skill to be able to relax group members without distracting them.**

One kind of behaviour which works on a personal level as well as on a practical task level is that which shows agreement. If a group is going to work positively then there has to be a fair measure of agreement anyway. Music groups are notorious for splitting up and re-forming because there is disagreement about musical direction. If a group member positively expresses agreement with some decision or action or idea expressed then this helps the group work together. To say something like 'I'll go along with that' or 'OK and I'll help with the stalls' (a fundraising group) is a positive contribution. Opinion and attitude have been expressed. **It is a skill to be able show agreement with group ideas, actions, decisions.**

It may be noticed that all these group skills require positive action. This is not to say that a quiet group member is not effective. Equally a compulsive chatterer can actually impede a group. But someone who communicates nothing gives nothing to the group. This is true of the more practically oriented examples of skills which we will now look at.

People in groups commonly make plans, solve problems, make decisions. This is true whether one is talking about a formal group such as a council finance committee, or an informal one such as a group of friends deciding what they want to do for the day. To carry out such tasks it is necessary for group members to make suggestions or to give information: 'we could do this or that' – 'why don't we go to that place?' **It is a group skill to be able to offer information and ideas to the group.**

But decisions are also well made on the basis of group discussion. So another skill for any group member is to be able to weigh up suggestions, to evaluate what is being said. Someone might say, 'but would that work if . . . ?' or 'what's wrong with the idea of going into town?' **It is a group skill to be able to evaluate ideas and information offered.**

A good group member is also aware that groups are by definition co-operative. So communication which encourages that co-operation must be a good thing. In various kinds of discussion – and groups do a lot of talking – certain phrases accompanied by appropriate non-verbal behaviour can encourage involvement and make people feel valued at the same time. Someone might use phrases such as 'what do you think, Sue?' or 'how do you feel about going there?' **It is a group skill to invite opinions and involvement from other group members.**

It may be that group leaders are identifiable as people whose opinions are valued. They are the people who are often asked what they think or want to do by other group members. But usually group leaders are also active and positive in their communication. The following two points may relate to any group member, but put together they are also likely to pinpoint a leader. One point about group communication has to do with bringing things together. If there are various ideas under discussion, even if there is disagreement, it is a positive move to help the group to try and reach agreement: 'so how do we all feel about doing this or that?' – 'could we agree on Beth's suggestion for a place and time first?' – and so on. **It is a group skill to bring together ideas and opinions.**

This sort of communication is obviously important in bringing any type of group to make decisions. But decisions also have to be turned into action. Group discussion, and argument, is often about the actions which may be the result of making certain decisions. Again, it can be group leaders who suggest courses of action. They try to wrap up the task and arrive at the goal. In sports teams the captain is the appointed leader and no one argues very much if that person actually gives orders during the game. But in most groups it is more subtle. The positive group member who may be a leader will say something like – 'let's do this or that' – or – 'why don't we make up a list of things to do and share them out?' **It is a group skill to suggest actions involving the group.**

You will notice that we have just emphasized the importance of group involvement. An effective group member talks with the group in mind and always tries to bring in other group members. Someone who says things like – 'I don't know about you lot but I'm going to do this or that' – is actually saying that they are going their way, not a group way. Group skills are used for the group, not for the individual. Sometimes group members will agree to things which they actually disagree with privately, to a greater or lesser extent. They do it for the group.

---

### What's your favourite group?

Hint: there may be differences between who you feel comfortable with and who you most enjoy being with.

---

## Review

This is to help you check on the main points of this chapter, 'Communication in groups'.

### 1 WHAT IS A GROUP?

1.1   It is a collection of people who have some shared interest or aim.
We each belong to many different groups, such as:
      family groups,
      friendship groups,
      work/organized groups.

1.2   Groups depend on relationships,
have common interests,
expect norms of behaviour,
develop set roles of members.

### 2 WHY DO PEOPLE JOIN GROUPS?

2.1   There are two main reasons for forming groups:
      to achieve a set goal,
      to develop social contact and personal identity.

## 3 HOW DO PEOPLE BEHAVE IN GROUPS?

3.1 Each of us plays different roles according to group expectations and our individual personality. Roles are influenced by professions, ages, gender, class and status.

3.2 There are various role types in groups, which affect the success of the group in completing its tasks.

3.3 We follow group-imposed norms of behaviour.

3.4 Group leaders adopt four different styles of behaviour.

## 4 COMMUNICATING IN GROUPS

4.1 Observing group communication for achieving the task of the group and for maintaining the group relationships.

4.2 Participation and interaction patterns.

4.3 Individual functions in achieving group purposes.

4.4 Understanding ourselves and our relationships with others in the groups we belong to.

4.5 Group members can use skills to make the group happy and effective. Key communication skills in a group are: offering praise; helping the group relax; showing agreement; offering ideas and information; evaluating ideas and information; inviting opinions; summarizing ideas and information; suggesting action.

## Debates

### How can groups influence people's communication?

- The first point to sort out is whether those receiving the communication are outside the group concerned, or part of it, or part of another group (see types of group and group roles).
- The next point would be to sort out what kind of group one is talking about, operating in what kind of situation.
- Another point to weigh up would be how far that influence is deliberate and how far it is a matter of how the individual sees the group rather than how the group treats the individual (see group behaviour and group norms).
- Finally one might consider whether that influence, if it exists, is for better or for worse. Groups can give individuals the sense of security which encourages them to be unpleasant, but groups can also moderate the behaviour of individuals who 'go too far'.

WHAT DO YOU THINK?

We are told one way and another both to 'be yourself' and to 'learn to get on with others'. Is there a contradiction here between individualism and groupness?

- One point here is to decide what 'yourself' is (see self image).
- Another point is to decide what 'getting on with others' means (see group co-operation and cohesion).
- Another idea in the debate would be to look at common words and phrases which seem to fit in with individualism or groupness – team spirit, the winner (see ideology).

WHAT DO YOU THINK?

## Assignments

### Assignment One

To separate non-verbal signals from words, videorecord a televised discussion or chat show. Then replay it with the sound turned down. If you have slow tracking, use this to pick out signs. See how many different signs you can identify. Try to work out what they are doing, both in relation to speech and in terms of managing the interaction between members of the group.

### Assignment Two

(a) Make a list of all the groups that you belong to, beginning with family. Write some accompanying notes in answer to these questions:
   - why do you belong to these groups?
   - are they task or social groups?
   - what patterns of leadership do they have?
   - how high a level of conformity does each expect?

(b) Imitating the diagram for roles in figure 20, make a similar chart for yourself. This should indicate the sorts of role which you believe that you adopt in family, work, social groups.

### Assignment Three

Work through the following role play to find out things about role, conflict and conflict resolution.

### Background

Six passengers are trapped at Rome airport in an airliner hijacked by two men from a Middle Eastern country. Other passengers have already been released. The two men are threatening to kill the passengers and blow up the aircraft. They want a quarter of a million dollars, and they want a statement denouncing their country's regime to be printed in major Western news-papers. The passengers want to get out alive at all costs. The two Italian government negotiators on the scene are determined not to let the plane go or to give in to the hijackers' demands. The hijackers are jumpy, and armed with dynamite, grenades and guns. It is hot. Food and water have nearly run out.

## Players

You can make up a number of the characters, including the hijackers and negotiators. But there are the following passengers to play: a mother with a 5-year-old child; a doctor flying to a medical convention; a British military attaché flying to the Middle East; an American actress (not very well known!).

## Task

- To resolve the situation.
- Play it so that each of the three sub-groups get some time on their own to sort out their attitudes and actions.
- The hijackers will spend some time with the passengers, probably trying to frighten them and put pressure on the negotiators.
- The passengers have to stay in a huddle on the aircraft.
- The negotiators have to remain at a distance, but will intervene now and then. They will try to argue and threaten the hijackers out of the plane.

Otherwise you can decide on details of the background and the activities. Give the situation time to develop. See how the relationship of the passengers with the hijackers develops. See who gets their way in the end.

## Assignment Four: Case Study

Refer to the picture of people on the beach for this assignment.

You are writing an article for a school or college magazine – 'Going on Holiday with Friends'. You are going to use the picture as background for this article. You want to look at the good and bad points of this kind of holiday, with some sense of humour. Your main point, or angle, will be to say why this can be a positive experience for friendship.

Part of the article should look at how the roles adopted by people in a group affect how they get on together. Part of it will look at how awareness (or lack of it) of group skills can affect whether or not people have a good time. You'll have to put this across in a 'light' way, showing how 'making an effort', or not, really does make a difference.

Now complete the following tasks:

(a) Write a caption for the photo.
(b) Make a list of three plus and three minus points for this kind of holiday with friends.
(c) Write a headline for the article.
(d) Make a list of positive and negative behaviours which would affect enjoyment of such a holiday (you can refer back to the chapter for ideas).
(e) Write the article.
(f) Design the layout sheet for placing the text and the photo on a page of the magazine.

## Suggested reading

Gahagan, Judy, *Interpersonal and Group Behaviour*.
Myers, G.E., and Myers, M.T., *Dynamics of Human Communication*, chapter 12.
Sprott, W.J.H., *Human Groups*.
Some role play games and simulations for groups can be found in *Interplay*, published by Longman.
See also the resources list at the end of the book.

# Chapter 4

# Communication in organizations

We are born in organizations, educated by organizations and most of us spend much of our lives working for organizations. We spend much of our leisure time paying, playing and praying in organizations.

Amitai Etzioni, *Modern Organizations*, 1964

This chapter looks at a particular sort of social group – organizations. We analyse formal and informal methods of communication used by people in organizations. Our focus is on people and their working relationships.

Industrial relations. *Oral* communication with shop steward, supervisor, personnel officer with ref. to reading works rules, contract of employment, etc.

Social activity. *Oral* communication with colleagues, individual and group discussion.

Quality control with works and customers' inspectors. *Oral and written* communications with ref. to specifications, drawings, inspectors' reports, charts, etc.

**TECHNICIAN**

Operator/crafts re. job analysis, production plan and control. *Oral* communication, with *oral and written* with ref. to drawings, schedules, specifications, charts, etc.

Production planning with production supervisors, planning engineers, draughters, buyer, etc. *Oral and written* communication with ref. to drawings, schedules, charts, etc.

Purchasing with buying department. *Oral and written* communication with ref. to technical specifications, catalogues, brochures, etc.

Responsible to/receive instructions from department manager. *Oral or written* communication with ref. to reading drawings, production schedules, specifications, etc.

Design queries with drawing office and production engineers. *Oral* communication with ref. to drawings and specifications.

**FIGURE 25** An employee's communication activities

# 1 How do organizations operate?

## JANE'S STORY

*Jane Foskett was a determined person. She wanted to go to see the new* Romeo and Juliet *film because it was on their course. In fact she wanted the whole class to go because it would mean some time off school, and anyway that was what she had decided. The only trouble was that Mr Denham, he of the stained tie and an inability to pronounce his Rs, didn't seem to be that bothered.*

*'It's a nice idea, Jane,' he said. 'But the organizing is so much trouble in this place. There are forms for everything. Really it would be easier if you lot went to see it on your own.'*

*'That's all very well, sir. But you know what people are like. Most of them won't do it. My older sister says it's really good. And I think that we should see it.'*

*'You do, do you? Well, I'll tell you what, Jane, if you do the organizing I'll sign the forms and stick them in the right place, and then we can go. But you'll have to get people to sign up, and pay deposits, and book the coach and all the usual things. I'm afraid that you'll find it hard to get pupils to make that sort of commitment, let alone cough up for the coach as well.'*

*He obviously thought that she would be put off. He had underestimated her. This was a young woman who belonged to a largely male Venture Scout troop, had the lads eating out of her hand, and who organized most of their activities. So she was not going to find the school system much of a problem. Jane set about organizing things in her usual pleasant but persistent way. Within twenty-four hours she had chatted up the secretary about the forms and clearances they needed, and had persuaded the cinema manager that if she could get more than fifty people into an afternoon showing then he would give them a group price on the tickets.*

*'That's easy,' thought Jane. 'All we need is two classes, and we can have a big coach full.'*

*Her trip folder grew fat with clearance forms, insurance forms, booking forms, lists of names with ticks and letters to and from the cinema and the coach company.*

*To be fair to him Mr Denham didn't make any more excuses. In fact he backed her up, and put through all the paperwork which she wouldn't have been allowed to. He did check things before he signed them. And she did begin to see why he hadn't rushed to organize the trip himself. They had been handing in a lot of course work. And even though the paperwork was necessary, it really was quite a business getting it all together. Strictly speaking her Dad also helped her a bit. He was a teacher at another school.*

*'A school may not be in business,' he said, 'but we have to run like a business. It won't do you any harm to find out what goes on behind the scenes. I think your Mr Denham has been quite clever in getting you to do all this.'*

ABOUT JANE'S STORY

It is clear that organizations require systems and a range of means of communication in order to go about their business successfully. The people who work in organizations have to know the systems, to be able to operate them. They have to be able to plan. Teachers have to plan their year's work, or plan trips. Schools have to plan their finances, manage their resources, obey health and safety regulations, just like businesses and organizations.

Organizing the trip to the film showing needed a lot of communication. Apart from what was mentioned, Jane had to make telephone calls, conduct negotiations, fill out forms, make lists. She had to do all this in some kind of order, so that she worked her way towards her objective. These activities, this order, can be mapped out on paper. Jane made lists of things to do. But she could have made a flow chart of activities needed. An algorithm is a kind of flow chart. There is a version of one for Jane's trip in figure 26, showing a sequence of decisions and actions.

## 1.1 What is an organization?

This chapter is about communicating in organizations and also about organizing for communication. The word 'organization' can refer to a particular institution such as a school, factory, office, bank; it can also refer to the process of organizing as in a phrase like 'It took a lot of organization.'

In the title of this chapter **we are using 'organization' to mean a collection of individuals who have been brought together to carry out tasks to achieve set aims**. In this sense an organization is of course a sort of group. When we discussed groups in chapter 3 we generally referred to small groups although we made some reference to formally organized groups. An organization is a group that has certain specific characteristics, as follows.

It is **deliberately established** at a certain time by an individual or group of people; for example, it is possible to point to the date when an organization was set up – 'established in 1922'.

It develops **formally structured relationships** and interdependence between people.

It has **set objectives** which the people in the organization are seeking to achieve, for example for a business company to produce goods and services to be sold at a profit, or for a school to enable pupils to learn about themselves and the world in which they live. There may also be 'hidden' objectives which are different from the stated ones; for example in terms of health care for the whole population the medical system in the USA may be inefficient, but in terms of making profits it is highly effective.

It **divides the work to be done** between individuals and groups. There are systems and sub-systems. For example, in a national service

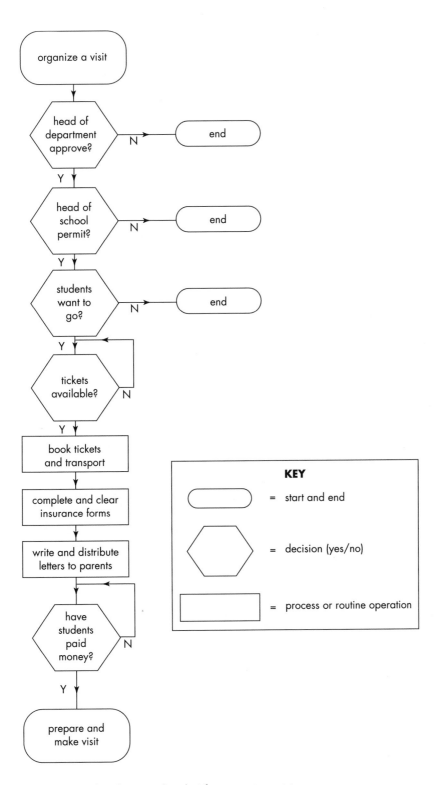

**FIGURE 26** Flow diagram (algorithm) for organizing a visit

industry some have the task of laying pipes, some installing appliances, some obtaining the equipment the organization needs, some selling the services, some dealing with accounts, some coping with taxes, insurance, staffing, safety and so on.

All the various people and their tasks require **co-ordinating into a unified effort** to accomplish the tasks and objectives.

It **manages resources**, both physical (equipment, materials, money) and human (work, ideas, skills). To achieve efficient and effective use of these resources is another characteristic of all organizations. For example if two people are setting up a small company to make and sell computer software, how much of their time and money must be devoted to advertising and selling their products instead of actually designing and reproducing new programs?

Finally **effective communication between the individuals and groups** is essential if the various activities, processes and resources are to fulfil the aims of the organization. This communication takes place both within an organization and between that organization and many other organizations. For example, if the organization is a manufacturing company then it must deal with suppliers of various materials and also with many potential customers. It also has to deal with other agencies concerned with things like taxes, insurance, property and employment.

It is the purpose of this chapter to concentrate on the last of these characteristics. The ability to organize, whether an enormous multinational company or a two-person outfit, depends on effective communication between people.

At its simplest, communication as a part of organizing can be illustrated by a basic organizational task: two persons working together can lift an object which neither of them could lift on their own. But to lift that object the two people must establish a communicating relationship, agree on the objective ('Where's it got to go?'), divide the work ('I'll take this end'), co-ordinate and manage their resources ('Lift when I say go').

Our concern here is not with such small organizational groups but rather with larger-scale business organizations. We are dealing with organizations in the everyday sense of the word, meaning schools, offices, banks, churches, factories, shops and so on.

## 1.2 Relationships and structures in organizations

The traditional shape of organization structures is that of a pyramid which shows lines of authority and responsibility. A typical example applied to a school might look like figure 27.

The head of the school is given authority by his or her terms of employment to make requirements of the staff 'below'. In turn he or she is

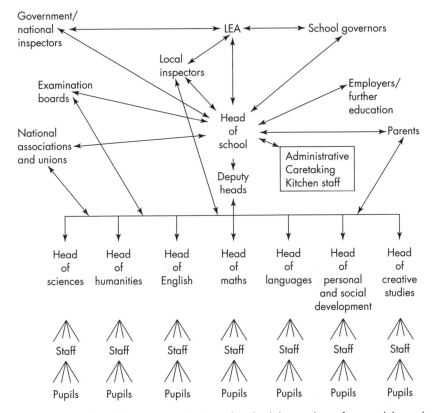

**FIGURE 27** Hierarchical organization chart of a school showing lines of responsibility and agencies outside the school

responsible to higher authorities and involved with other agencies outside the school. The local education authority (LEA) provides the majority of resources including the largest single item, salaries, for a state-maintained school. The LEA appoints and pays the staff – a process in which governors and inspectors are usually involved alongside school staff. The governing body, a group of local politicians, interested people, parents and teachers, is ultimately responsible for the work of the school. In an 'opted out' school a much greater proportion of money comes directly from the government. Also the governors have powers to set budgets and appoint staff, including the head. This type of school is set up more like a business with a board of directors.

The head and other school staff also have regular contact with outside agencies such as examination bodies, publishers, equipment suppliers, professional associations and trade unions, parents and so on. The staff of the school are responsible to the head but also are responsible to other senior staff who may act as intermediaries.

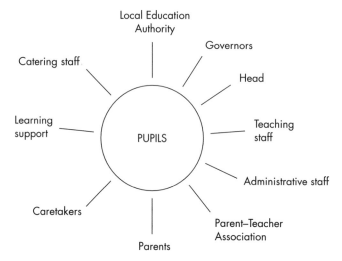

**FIGURE 28** An alternative model for school organization showing various groups in support of pupils and their learning

There are different ways of representing the structure of organizations. For example, figure 28 shows a student-centred model. Our pupil Jane might feel better about this one. These diagrams can not only represent lines of communication, they also reveal something about how the organization sees itself. Hierarchical models are more concerned with status, power and control. They can also reveal that there is too much distance between those at the top and those at the bottom. Effective organizations look for lateral lines of communication as well as vertical lines.

We have concentrated on schools so far in this chapter largely because we can assume that all readers have some sort of direct experience of them.

In terms of structures and networks of relationships other sorts of organizations are often represented in the same way. The divisions of work into units and sub-systems of people will obviously vary according to the size of the organization, the tasks it has to complete and its aims. A manufacturing organization will need to find ways of dealing with tasks like research and development of new and existing products; purchasing of supplies; production of goods; marketing of products; sales; distribution to customers; finance and accounting; personnel recruitment; training and welfare of staff; and co-ordination and administration of all that.

As a comparison with school structures and labels, we indicate how a manufacturing/retailing company might be structured in figure 29.

Within that hierarchical structure we can focus on one department such as Marketing. To show how that department is structured and how it relates to other parts of the company we shall use a spider web diagram (figure 30). A spider diagram focuses on the working relationships rather

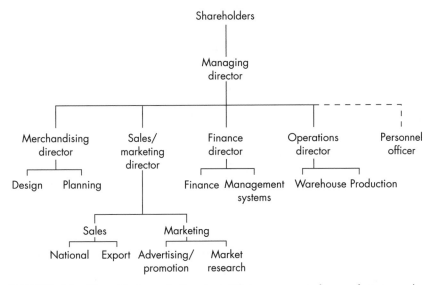

**FIGURE 29**  Hierarchical organization chart of the management of a manufacturing and retailing company

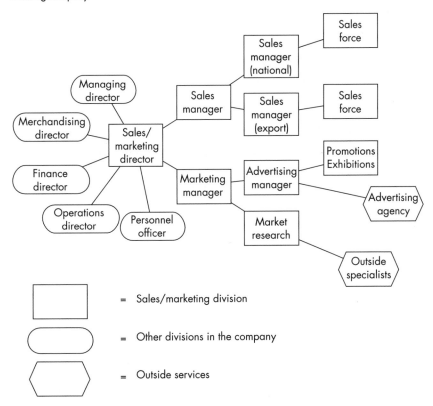

**FIGURE 30**  Spider diagram of a sales/marketing division showing lines of communication in and out of the company

than the status relationships and lines of responsibility of a hierarchical model.

There are lines of communication not only up and down in an organization, but also sideways and diagonally. People will generally speak more freely about their work and themselves and feel more able to initiate contacts with those who are perceived as being of the same status. They will be more cautious in approaching people higher in the hierarchy.

A further point to make is that there are networks of friendship and social contact that can to some extent cut across these matters of status. At lunchtimes, tea breaks or at gatherings like those at churches or sports clubs, people from all levels and sectors of an organization may have personal communication. A criticism of some industries has been the separation of canteen and other facilities according to status within the company. The development of group norms and loyalties which were discussed in chapter 3 is also a strong influence in these matters of open or limited communication: in some companies if you were known to be friendly with 'the Boss' people would be careful about what they told you.

Organizations develop their own norms like any other group of people. An employee who moves jobs from one organization to another within the same industry is often surprised by how different the conduct of relationships between colleagues can be.

There are alternatives to designing organizations as hierarchical structures. One alternative is to design a co-operative structure in which all are working together, with a division of labour, but without notions of superior and inferior status and power. Especially in a small organization it is possible for people to complete the necessary tasks without rigid specialization of functions – jobs can be shared or rotated, communication relationships can be open and equal.

These relationships will be affected by the fact that organizations are very much composed of groups, which are themselves all about relationships. The formal structure creates teams with various jobs to carry out. The informal structure (see 'The grapevine', pages 140–1) is affected by the nature of informal groups.

> It may appear that formal and informal groups are separate. This is not the case. Groups that start off as formal often develop powerful informal relations. Part of a company, as well as being a department, may be a department of friends. Japanese organizations such as Sony deliberately encourage this. Informal groups, such as friendships outside work, can provide useful channels of communication for the company.

> (Chambers 1996)

## 1.3  Networks of communication

Whatever structure an organization takes networks of communication and contact will develop between the people in it. In the spider web diagrams of the previous section we have in fact drawn a network of communication showing the channels by which messages flow. In the final section of chapter 3, figure 23 shows a group of five people where all channels are open; that is, everyone can speak to everyone else.

If we use the same example of five people (labelled A, B, C, D, E) or imagine that these five could represent departments or units in a larger system, we can describe other network shapes in which not all channels are open. A network might be set up in which one person or unit has the key position to channel or withhold information.

There are several network shapes for a network of five in addition to all channels open to all five.

A ———— B ———— C ———— D ———— E

**FIGURE 31**  Chain network

Figure 31 illustrates a very constrained network in which C has an important position because if a message is to be conveyed from A or B to D or E it must go via C. If a strictly hierarchical chain of command were the structure in an organization then the formal network of communication would look like this. If A were the boss he or she might occupy a position at the end of several chains (figure 32).

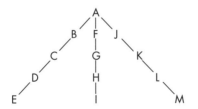

**FIGURE 32**  Pyramid network

Rarely does the network remain so constrained because as we noted in the previous section some sideways and diagonal communication will take place. However, figure 32 could reflect a managing director at Head Office (A) giving and receiving information from regional, area and branch offices.

In the circle network (figure 33), no person or unit holds the dominant position but each can only communicate with two others.

In the wheel network (figure 34), A clearly has the dominant position and is best able to co-ordinate the whole system. A's position at the centre of the network makes all the others dependent on A.

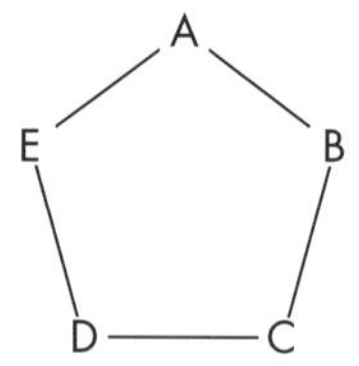

**FIGURE 33**   Circle network

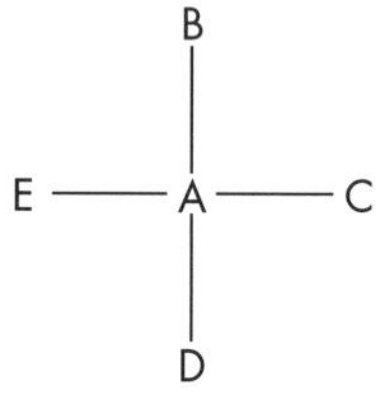

**FIGURE 34**   Wheel network

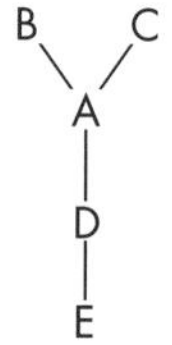

**FIGURE 35**   Y-shape network

In the Y shape (figure 35), A occupies a key position as filter and focus for communication. This shape of network could reflect the information flow between managing director (A) channelling information from shareholders (B) and board of directors (C) to company managers (D) and supervisors (E).

In outlining these possible networks of communication we have not indicated whether the flow of information is one-way or two-way. It can of course be either, depending on the situation. We suggest you try to apply these network patterns to actual situations. With a group of four other people you could experiment by sending messages orally according to different network patterns to see what effects they have on the messages and the people. If during holidays you wanted to organize yourself and four friends living in separate towns to meet for lunch one day, what network would represent the communication tasks?

## Teams and networks

Such networks of communication can be applied to many situations, not only in organizations, but also in social groupings. For example, in an extremely tense family situation it may be that some members of the family will not speak to others so that a wheel or Y network may develop with one person being the mediator. Difficult negotiations may be carried on in the same way.

Additionally such networks show that controlling the channels of communication confers power. In chapter 5 we shall consider the way in which the mass media act as gatekeepers – selecting, filtering and representing the information they receive. The Y network provides a model of this process in which the editor (A) gets information from sources (B and C) and channels it to audience (D) who in turn may discuss it with groups of friends (E).

At first it might seem that the open, all-channel network is the most desirable. But for the purpose of conveying simple information it might be wasteful to have all available people discussing it with everyone else when it could simply be sent out as in the wheel.

Which networks would you use for the following tasks?

(a)   A marketing director has four managers for whom she is responsible and she wishes to decide marketing strategy with them for the following year. Which network would be most appropriate? If the director is A should she use Y, chain, circle, wheel or open?

(b)   The same marketing director has to decide the date of a sales conference which is held annually. Which network would be most appropriate?

There is not a single correct answer, but we suggest that in (a) the director should seek an open exchange of ideas where all of them can speak and listen to each other. If when the director called the meeting for (a) she was also in a position to decide the date for the conference she could do it there. But if when she needs to decide the date the managers are scattered around the country in their own offices she could use the wheel network: obtain from each separately the convenient dates, decide which is most convenient for all and then inform them.

## 1.4 Teams and roles

You should refer back to chapter 3 for much of what is relevant in the idea of role. But it is worth reminding yourself now that work teams are a type of group. They are groups formed by the organization, not voluntarily. People's functional roles (job descriptions) within these groups are also assigned to them. This already provides the potential for conflict (see 1.6) because of differences of opinion about status, for example.

For instance, one common type of organizational group is a quality circle group, formed to get people together who would not normally meet much. The idea is that they discuss at regular intervals the quality of what is done in one broad area of the organization, perhaps in respect of how the public or customers are dealt with. This circle may well have members of different status within it. But this is irrelevant to the work of this team. So the question is whether some members can forget their roles or status, or whether the ways that they communicate are affected by these factors. In this example the receptionist is as important as the personnel manager.

You might also remember the distinction between specific job roles in the team, and performance or personality roles. The sales manager could be a poor chair for progress meetings if they tend to be a Dominator, and won't let others speak enough. On the other hand an accounts assistant might be a positive team member at such a meeting if they are strong as an Organizer.

In terms of effective communication within organizations, one often has to look at the performance of individuals when assessing the capability of teams. And when looking at individuals one often has to look at possible tensions between the requirements of role and the actual skills of the individual both in and out of role. Putting job labels on people does not make them able to do that job. Sticking people together in teams does not make them good team members.

In *Management Teams* (Oxford: Butterworth-Heinemann, 1996), R.M. Belbin describes research which identified an interesting description of team roles complementing one another in a successful group. These may be summarized as:

- Chairperson: good at co-ordinating and working with others
- Team worker: good at putting the team first, at co-operating and being supportive of others
- Shaper: dominant and very involved with the task in hand
- Company worker: good on matters of practical organization
- Monitor/Evaluator: good at analysing ideas and tasks, quite critical
- Investigator: good on research, making contacts and getting along with others
- Plant: good at producing ideas, but not necessarily good with others
- Finisher: good at details and deadlines

A combination of such people should produce an effective team which is good at these things: generating ideas; being clear about tasks and goals; generating free communication and trust between group members; problem solving; helping each other; generating constructive criticism; reaching agreement.

Figure 36 suggests different management styles which a chairperson could adopt. But which do you think is most effective? How do you think that these relate to the network diagrams?

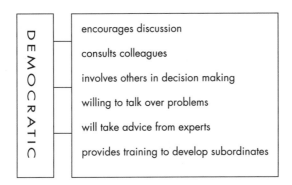

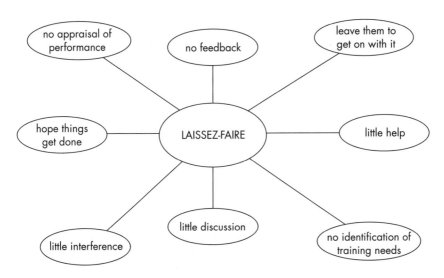

**FIGURE 36** Three different management (leadership) styles

## 1.5 Informal channels of communication

People in organizations may carefully lay out a plan of the structure including networks of communication. They may establish policies for keeping people informed of what is happening through regular meetings, notices or memos. They may establish policies for communication with outside agencies; for example, who is to have responsibility for signing orders and letters to go out. Most organizations do now recognize the need for such communication policies to keep people informed.

However, it is not possible to predict all the informal and personal networks and channels that develop. These informal, to some extent hidden, communication systems are a significant part of the human life of an organization. In a very restricted communication environment, such as an extreme example like a prison, this underworld of communication becomes very active. In a more open communication environment, where people know that there is a systematic way of learning about things that matter from their supervisors and managers, the hidden networks are less active because fear and uncertainty decrease. People have a tendency to consider that secret information is sinister information – 'Why don't they want me to know?'

### The grapevine

The most common term to describe the unofficial, informal network of communication in an organization is *the grapevine*. This communication system based on hearsay, rumour and speculation is sometimes highly developed and fast. It is less concerned with information about how to carry out the tasks and objectives of the organization than with gossip. Gossip can perhaps be defined as information about other people, attitudes, opinions, relationships, interpretations, predictions, values. The grapevine fosters and spreads rumours and is often full of prejudice and partial truth ('Well, they say there's no smoke without a fire . . . '). Rumours spread fast, especially on issues where people are uncertain or anxious. It's often said that on the grapevine the outcome of decisions is known before the decisions are taken.

The effects of the grapevine are usually seen as harmful to the smooth working of an organization, but it does not always pass on malevolent gossip. It can convey good news fast as well and may serve to boost morale through creating interest in developments and innovations.

Grapevines are based on opportunities for communication, probably verbal but possibly written. Common examples of opportunities are before and after meetings, in the canteen, shared journeys to work, even in the toilets. Also, internal electronic mail systems provide the opportunity for gossip. So sometimes opportunities are linked to formal communication situations. But they can also come out of informal situations, such as when workers play a particular sport together, or even when they have relationships which cross over the lines of official company structures.

It is generally agreed that an active grapevine is present when people are kept ill-informed through official channels of communication.

Another aspect of these informal channels is simply personal relationships between people. People have lives outside the organization in which they work. And it is natural to talk about work sometimes when you meet socially.

It is beyond the scope of this book to discuss at length the topics of industrial relations, consultation procedures or methods of employee participation in high-level decision making and formation of policies for companies. However, from a communication perspective it does seem that if people are kept well-informed and involved in the issues and changes facing an organization then there is less distrust and conflict between 'us' and 'them'.

Many companies and other organizations make great efforts to keep everyone informed about what concerns them through methods such as regular newsletters or team briefings in which every supervisor at every level in an organization is required to brief the team he or she is responsible for.

## 1.6 Conflict

**It is sometimes mistakenly thought that all problems and conflicts between individuals and groups can be resolved through effective communication.** Very often the phrase 'a breakdown in communication' is used to describe the cause of conflict. This certainly does happen and misunderstandings and mistrust can develop simply because people have failed to talk to each other. Hostile attitudes can be eased by openly discussing the attitudes and their origins.

However, it must be acknowledged that conflicts do also arise because there are real differences of interest, differences of attitudes, beliefs and values. Certainly open discussion of these can enable all sides to understand and face the conflicts as problems to be solved together.

As we said in chapter 1, communication can have the purpose of changing attitudes and behaviour.

Origins of conflict can usually be placed under three headings:

First, *personal* – within an individual there are conflicting ideas and desires and values; frustrations in achieving one's aims; conflicts of roles between personal inclinations and the expectations of the groups you belong to or the position you occupy.

Second, *interpersonal* – there are differences of experience, perceptions, opinions, values and patterns of behaviour between people; there is often competition for scarce resources, whether for salaries, promotion, new equipment; people can fail to agree on how a relationship should be conducted in terms of status, authority or role.

Third, *in the organization itself* – potential for conflict exists when differences in status and power in a hierarchy are not mutually accepted; different parts of an organization often perceive their needs and interests in opposite ways (see figure 37).

THE ORGANIZATION

CONFLICT OF NEEDS AND VALUES OF THOSE INVOLVED

**FIGURE 37** Three kinds of conflict in organizations

Facing conflict as a problem that can be tackled is the starting point. If two people or two sides in a dispute are only interested in which one is right and which one is to blame then the conflict can only be worsened. If the sources of conflict can be defined and communicated then there's a chance that the problem can be 'managed' with both sides winning.

Ability to face conflict issues does certainly relate to communication abilities and skills in relating to and between people. An understanding of how we share meanings, how we use language and non-verbal communication, how we perceive one another and how we behave in groups can help us in our relationships. And, as we have previously suggested, the quality of personal relationships is a key factor in organizations. **A willingness to trust, to listen, to use and accept different communication styles and roles in different situations are all abilities we need for effective communication.** If you treat people with mistrust and are always on the defensive, only listen to your own ideas, always seek to use the same communication style whatever the situation, then you are likely to experience communication breakdowns.

**How important is 'the system' in an organization?**

Hint: think about people!

## ASHLEY'S STORY

*It was time for his progress interview. Ashley Barnes was nervous. He knew that he didn't really have to be. His supervisor in the insurance company was very fair. But she was also the sort of person who you felt you didn't want to upset. This was the end of his first year, and he had already had two interviews. They always did spend more time on you when you were new.*

*He had hated his first interview because he hadn't known what to expect. But the second one hadn't been too bad. In fact because of that he had been moved around to get more experience. So he couldn't really complain. Sue Clarke was all right, really. She had told him exactly what he was there for.*

*'I want you to talk to me,' she had said. 'I'll ask you some questions. But you have to speak up for yourself, otherwise I may not find out things that will help you enjoy your job more and hopefully make some progress in this company. I get the same thing from my line manager. I find it really useful talking to people like you. It gives me another view of things. It gives us a chance to talk about you and this place, not just the work that you have to do. So tell me for a start, how do you think things have changed for you since the last interview that we had?'*

*Ashley hoped that he hadn't talked too much. But she had asked him about himself and about how he saw himself in the company, so he had told her. At least you felt that somebody cared. Some of the old hands were rather cynical about the process. It doesn't bring you a pay rise, they would say. But there was more to work than money, thought Ashley, even though it comes in very handy. He wanted to end up being a manager because he didn't want to stay stuck doing the same thing for ever. He should get more money if he was made up, but that wasn't the only point.*

*He looked at his watch and realized that it was time. He knocked on the door.*

## ABOUT ASHLEY'S STORY

This story reminds us that organizations are not just about systems and about means of communication. They are actually about people. Companies invest time and money in what is now called human resource management. People are not just cogs in a company machine. They are skilful, useful, communicating beings. Their ability to communicate in one way or another is actually what makes the organization function.

Ashley's progress interview is about recognizing the worth of people in an organization, it is about making people useful to that organization. His story indicates that people may respond to this recognition: that they are not only motivated by money, that they want what is called job satisfaction. Giving them time for talk and self-expression makes it possible to find out what will bring that satisfaction, and helps them work productively.

It is also the case that people at work often have to be part of groups or teams. Again, face-to-face communication skills become very important here, as do group skills. People need to accept roles, to work with others, to co-operate. The game which follows emphasizes these points, as well as the need to be able to communicate clearly and accurately.

## 2 Applications: case studies and activities

In this section we want to bring together ideas from chapters 3 and 4, through material for discussion and activity.

### 2.1 Case situation: a progress interview

This is for you to discuss in terms of why we often feel negative about interviews, and what would have made you feel more positive about interviews that you have had at school, college or work – even those which have been concerned with matters of discipline!

### 2.2 A model-building game

This section takes the form of a game designed to investigate the ways in which channels of communication might operate in a *chain network*. Such a three-level chain network could be the pattern in a small hierarchy. This game will also teach you something about roles and leadership styles.

If you cannot get a group of people together to play the game you can probably try something similar with just three other people. Ideally you need at least ten people and an organizer to set it up and build the original model. You need some Lego bricks or other materials with which you can make something. One version is to give each group a fixed quantity of paper or card, paper clips, etc., as used for the original construction. You need a room, preferably with tables and chairs. You need another private area that only some of the players have access to.

### How to play the game

(a) Groups with at least five people in each group must be formed. We suggest that nine is the maximum number for one group. If there are fifteen people and you have sufficient model-making materials then it is advisable to form three groups of five each.

(b) Each group organizes itself into the following roles:

> *Builder* – two or more people
> *Supervisor/instructor* – one or more
> *Manager/planner* – one or more
> *Observer* – one or more

*Builders* will attempt to construct a model that is a duplicate of the original model built by the game organizer. Builders must not see the model until the game is over.

*Supervisor/instructors* take instructions from the managers to tell the builders how to construct the model. They can ask the managers questions. They act as intermediaries between the managers and the builders. Supervisors must not see the original model until the game is over.

*Manager/planners* go to the private area with the game organizer to look at the original model that is to be copied. The manager's task is to describe the model to the supervisors, who will then tell the builders how to construct it. Managers must not let the supervisors see the model nor let the builders hear the manager's instructions.

*Observers* observe the whole process between managers and supervisors and between supervisors and builders. They can see the original model at the start. They must not communicate with any of the players. Observers are required to write notes about what is happening which are to be used for later discussion in debriefing after the game for all participants. The notes could include comments on things such as: how roles were allotted by the groups at the start; whether leaders emerged; whether too much or too little information was given by anyone; whether the managers' instructions were changed when they were passed on to the builders; what problems or conflicts arose and what were their causes; whether there were frustrations, what they were and why they arose; how they could be resolved.

## The game

During the course of the game, each group has to build a model which is a duplicate of an original. This original can only be seen by managers and observers. There is a time limit set for completion of the game. This must depend on the nature of the model, but about fifteen to twenty minutes is suggested. Nothing must be drawn or written down except by the observers for their own use. Only builders can take part in the construction.

## The debriefing after the game

When the time is up all participants come together to discuss questions such as:

How did they feel about their assigned roles?
Were the channels and techniques of communication effective?
If not, how could they be improved?
Did the observers' views of things differ from the players'?
Did they learn anything from the game about communicating between people?

This game has been adapted with permission from 'Communication in the organization – a simulation', which is published in M.T. Myers and G.E. Myers, *Managing by Communication*. The Laboratory Manual in the book provides many other activities, simulations, case studies and assignments related to communication in organizations.

## 2.3 Case Study: I heard it on the grapevine

Rumours spreading on a grapevine flourish when people are hungry for information or believe that they are being kept in the dark. Even if you are at school or college this case study is relevant, because all organizations have grapevines. There are questions for you to answer. In any case you could discuss how your grapevine works, what kinds of rumour travel along it, where they come from, what effects they have.

Here we present a case of an office grapevine on which there is currently a strong rumour.

### AN OFFICE IN THE CITY

*Brian presently works as a clerk in an insurance office in the City of London. He has been there for seven years and intends to stay because the people are friendly, the work is interesting – dealing with different sorts of claims – and the company gives attractive fringe benefits like cheap loans and mortgages. Brian enjoys working in the City with easy access to shops, concerts, plays and art galleries. His office is a short walk from the station so he can get from home to office desk in forty minutes.*

*Since it's an open-plan office with a relaxed but busy atmosphere there is a good deal of contact between the staff. They talk about the work but they pretty well all talk about their interests outside the office as well. Brian thought there wasn't much going on that he didn't know about.*

*So it came as a jolt to hear a rumour that the company was thinking about closing its City office and opening a new office in the west of England. The person who told Brian said that he'd heard it from someone upstairs who said she'd heard it from a cleaner who overheard a phone conversation one evening.*

*The story went round the office like wildfire. When a few of them talked about it in the pub at lunchtime there were mixed reactions. Some of them would love to get away from London to the country and if the company offered the right terms they'd jump at it. Others certainly didn't want to move and they hoped there was nothing in the story.*

Arising from this situation, consider the following questions:

(a)   Is there anything Brian should do after hearing this rumour?
(b)   Imagine you are the office manager and you hear about the story going round the office. You have been told nothing about any such idea and

it bothers you that such a story is circulating. It is certainly affecting your staff at the moment. What action (if any) would you take?

(c)   Alternatively, imagine you are the office manager in this situation but you have been told confidentially that there is a proposal to move the office out of London. The decision has not been taken yet. What action (if any) would you take?

---

**How does our communication change when we are at work?**

Hint: look back at ideas about context, audience, purpose in chapter 1.

---

## Review

This is to help you check on the main points of this chapter, 'Communication in organizations'.

### 1.1 HOW DO ORGANIZATIONS OPERATE?

We made an overview of organizations and listed characteristics which help us to understand how they work:

> they are created for a purpose,
> they have structured relationships within them,
> they set goals,
> they divide up the work tasks,
> they co-ordinate the separate parts,
> they manage resources,
> they communicate within themselves and with the outside environment.

### 1.2 RELATIONSHIPS AND STRUCTURES IN ORGANIZATIONS

We looked at the formal and official perception of structures. These are often expressed in diagram form as pyramidal or web-shaped. Questions of hierarchy and status arise. Alternatively there can be co-operative equal status.

### 1.3 NETWORKS OF COMMUNICATION

Information flows in several ways and networks are a way of visualizing this. An open access to and exchange of information may be desirable. Or it may be preferable, or more efficient, to restrict the flow.

### 1.4 TEAMS AND ROLES

Work team members have various job roles and personality roles. A successful team contains a particular combination of role types.

### 1.5 INFORMAL CHANNELS OF COMMUNICATION

Alongside or outside the formal structures and networks people develop their own information flows and channels for communication. The grapevine and social relationships are features of this.

### 1.6 CONFLICT

Effective communication takes account of the differences between individuals and groups. People can learn to see the sources of their conflict. These may be

> within the individual,
> between individuals or groups,
> a result of tensions in the organization.

If conflicts are faced they may not disappear but they can be managed as problems to be jointly solved.

### 2 APPLICATIONS: CASE STUDIES AND ACTIVITIES

Finally, we focused the general account of organizational communication with three case studies based on problems and issues:

> A progress interview
> Channels of communication
> I heard it on the grapevine

## Debates

**Why is it so common to hear people talk of 'communication problems' when an organization or company is in some kind of difficulty?**

- One point to discuss has to do with organizational culture, which can put a lot of emphasis on systems and finance, above anything else (see systems and structures).

- Another point to sort out is what kind of communication and what kind of problem one might be talking about (see means of communication and barriers to communication).
- Another point may have to do with communication within the organization in general, within work teams in particular, or with communication from the organization to others.

WHAT DO YOU THINK?

**How is it that communication means different things to different people within organizations?**

- One problem is that different people have different roles in an organization (see roles and functions).
- Another problem is that different organizations place a different emphasis on different kinds of communication. You need to discuss different examples of such organizations.
- Another problem is to do with the ways that people think about communication and ways in which we use the word in our society. You need to discuss the differences between communication as system, as technology, as something that people do (see means of communication).

WHAT DO YOU THINK?

## Assignments

### Assignment One

Make an investigation of an organization that you know about or are part of. We are not telling you exactly how to carry out this investigation. But if you work it out from the tasks below then you will have to do some interviewing and talking to people. It would be good communication practice to present your findings in the form of a report. You could also present them orally to a group, using audio-visual aids. In the list of tasks below we have assumed terms relevant to a school. But you can easily add topics or adapt the tasks slightly, according to the organization that you are dealing with.

(a) Draw an organization chart, with labels for departments and people's titles. The chart should show the whole structure and lines of responsibility.
(b) List the outside agencies which the school has contact with. You may use general headings such as 'suppliers' rather than going into great detail.

(c)    Explain what regular meetings are held and why. Include those which are for staff and pupils within the school as well as those which include outsiders.

(d)    Explain what systems exist for keeping people at all levels informed of what is happening in the school. Refer to examples of the types of written and oral communication which do this.

(e)    Describe what publicity brochures are produced. Describe what has been the most recent publicity in a local newspaper.

(f)    Is there a school newsletter or magazine? What is its purpose, readership, content, style? How often does it appear? Who contributes to it?

(g)    Describe the contents of three noticeboards in the school. Where are they located? Who are they for? What topics are on them? Are they kept up to date? How well are the notices written and designed? Do people take notice?

## Assignment Two

Arrange an interview with someone who works in an organization that you don't know about. Write up a summary of what you find out. Your topics could include the following: means of communication used by the organization; time spent by the interviewee on communicating; what forms of communication the interviewee uses; public relations.

You should prepare your questions in advance, let the interviewee know what they are about, and ask them if you can record the interview. If they have time you would find it very useful to discuss your summary of what you found out with the interviewee at another meeting.

## Assignment Three: Case Study

Refer to the photo of Sophie Sanderson and to the newspaper article about her, for this assignment.

### Extract from article in local newspaper

You are a member of the Local Education Authority Schools Service that is responding to complaints made by Sophie's father, as well as to the increasing public outcry about the case. You already have some knowledge of the school involved. As part of your preparation for bringing people together to resolve the conflict you carry out a number of tasks, among them the following.

(a)    List the people in the school who you think should have been dealing with Sophie's concerns about the quality of her education.

(b)    List those people who you think should now be dealt with in discussing the situation as it is.

15-year-old Sophie has caused an uproar at the school by writing a letter about the staffing situation, which we published in last week's edition of the Post. Now she has been suspended from school by the Head, Patrick Benson, for 'bringing the school into disrepute'.

Chair of Governors, Mrs Molly Bergreen, has backed the Head saying that the matter could have been dealt with internally. But Sophie's father, David Sanderson, disagrees. He has already involved the local education authority, who have told us that they are actively investigating the case.

Mr Sanderson claims that he has previously tried to talk to the Head about the problems with teachers missing from classes and having supply cover, but without success.

'Sophie has as much right to freedom of speech as anyone else,' he said. 'The school has a problem which they are not admitting to.'

Sophie told us that she still believes that lack of proper teaching is going to affect her exam results this summer. The L.E.A. has promised to make a statement in the near future. Mr Sanderson claims that the Parent–Teacher Association is backing his daughter's claims.

(c)   Draw a small group network model covering the people involved in the discussion, which you think would help deal with the situation most effectively.

(d)   Describe how you think the complaints should have been dealt with by the school system.

(e)   Draw a network diagram for the school organization which you think would make sure that such a situation would be dealt with in the future before parents or pupils go public with complaints.

## Suggested reading

Evans, D.W., *People, Communication and Organizations.*
Myers, M.T., and Myers, G.E., *Managing by Communication.*
Sallis, E., and Sallis, K., *People in Organizations.*
Stanton, N., *Communication.*
See also the resources list at the end of the book.

# Chapter 5

# Mass communication

Television pictures tend to be unquestioned; they are accepted as being as 'natural' as gas, water or electricity. They seem to be untouched by human hand.

Stuart Hood, *On Television*, 1983

This chapter concentrates on the mass media and takes examples from the press, radio and television. The institutions, processes and products of mass communication are the focus. The chapter considers what it is like to live in our mass-media society. There is reference to mass-media influence and effects. Advertising, news and visual images are discussed in particular. There is reference to current developments in communication techniques.

Photo: Ray Burmiston

# 1 A mass-communication society

### DERRY'S STORY

*Derry wasn't into computers. She didn't mind video games. And she did like aggravating her brother, Geoff. So the first thing she did on her Wednesday off was to take her cup of coffee into the living room and begin fooling around with the 'Caves of Orc'. Nasty creatures materialized on the screen as she penetrated deeper and deeper towards the Knowledge Stone. She had to zap them or evade them, and the shrieks of dying monsters rose in a crescendo before the door burst open, and Geoff threatened her with an even worse fate if she didn't leave the computer alone.*

*Derry didn't have to summon the dignity of an older sister. She was better at these games than Geoff was, and he knew it. But then, they were all the same. Electronic comics she called them. She shut down the computer and then pointedly put a video cassette in the recorder so that Geoff couldn't use the screen anyway. She munched a low-calorie biscuit while watching the end of the tape that she hadn't seen yesterday. She would have to return it to Caroline today.*

*Derry glanced at the clock on the recorder. She must ring Caroline and Sue if they were all going to meet up in town. The other two were out of work, and would waste the whole day if Derry gave them half a chance.*

*Her father came past while she was on the phone in the hall and put an alarm clock on the window ledge. Derry glared at him, knowing that it was timed to go off in five minutes. It was stupid the fuss he made about her phone calls when he was picking up messages from America on that electronic mail box thing of his.*

*'But,' said her father, 'the company pays for it because it's worth it to them to know that I'm in touch with what's going on over there even outside working hours. They're getting overtime out of me for nothing. And I can get in touch with Philadelphia pretty well immediately. So I think . . . I don't think I have to justify myself to you. You pay your share of the telephone bills and we'll all be happy.' The alarm went off. Geoff made a face at Derry as he went out of the front door on his way to school.*

*Derry left soon after, with a fashionable little cap jammed on over her head-phones, and the rhythms of the Cuban Swing Band dinning in her ears.*

*'If you took those things off you wouldn't have to shout,' said the assistant good-naturedly, when Derry bought her copy of* Heartbreak. *Derry blew him a kiss, and he blushed.*

*She had a quick look at the magazine while she was on the bus. The three girls swapped magazines and tapes among themselves.* Heartbreak *was a favourite because of the photoplay romance stories. At one time they had taken them more seriously than they did now. But they still had a good time laughing at the wooden poses of the models, and making up new captions for the photographs.*

*It was like that afternoon TV programme that they watched or recorded whenever they could. It was some reject from Australia called 'Beach Babies', and it was a real cult with Derry's crowd. They all had nicknames from the series, and had a whole repertoire of 'Beach' jokes which kept everyone in fits in the pub on Friday nights.*

*Derry smiled to herself as she saw Caroline and Sue already waiting for her below the display screen at the bus station.*

### ABOUT DERRY'S STORY

This tells us something about the ways in which our lives, in work and leisure time, have come to depend on means of mass communication. The very reality of our everyday experience is partly an experience of a made-up world, invented by the media.

Derry's lifestyle and common experience is one in which she uses mass-produced communication objects, in which she can receive communication broadcast on a mass scale and in which she can communicate with others via communication systems operating on a mass scale. In other words, the telephone, television, personal stereos are taken for granted by her. So are the more high-tech items such as the world-wide computer link system that her father uses.

Our work and leisure experience is changing rapidly. It is the systems and products of mass communication which are the greatest part of this change.

## 1.1 What do we mean by 'mass'?

We could be talking about a *system* or *product*, or *audience*. We can define 'mass' mainly in terms of *volume*, *scale* and *speed*.

**The system is the organization that does the communicating, such as the postal service or the radio broadcasting network.** We can say that such systems are mass because they operate on a large scale and carry so many messages so widely.

**The product is the object produced or carried by the system.** It could be something physical like a newspaper, or something that is experienced, like a television programme. The use of the word 'product' will be discussed later on. But the point is that these products are manufactured. Whether we are talking about thousands of copies of a magazine or millions of copies of a best-selling record, the point is that we are concerned with massive numbers from a mass-production system.

**The audience may also number thousands or millions.** It may be composed of people who have much in common – or little except the fact that they are all listening to the same programme. But still, the numbers are sufficient that they become significant in any analysis or explanation of the communication process. They affect how and why communication takes place. This communication can be happening on a massive scale (e.g. telephone), and very fast, and in great quantities.

## 1.2  Mass – so what is the significance?

**Mass production of messages also means mass repetition of messages.**
The main feature of mass communication when compared with other categories is that it does operate on such a large scale. Before we look at our media society and the operation of the media in more detail, it is worth grasping the basic fact that we need to look critically at them because they say the same sort of thing in the same sort of way so often.

And, apart from this repetition of messages, there is also the matter of penetration. Radio messages can penetrate right into the home or a car or even some remote holiday spot. Leaflets, letters and newspapers are pushed through our doors. And with these objects, and through these systems, come the ideas and beliefs which they can carry. The messages get right to us, again and again. So it should be clear that we need to look carefully at what the messages are, who is sending them, why and with what possible effect.

The sheer scale of the operation that we are describing means that it is bound to have some effect on things which everyone thinks are important – our relationships with others, what we believe in, how we describe and understand the world around us.

Mass communication is also part of that world. We suggest that there are particular aspects of our mass-communication society which are worth looking at in more detail, as follows.

## 1.3  Systems – availability, but no control

**Our society has been greatly changed this century as systems of mass communication have become available to more and more of the population.** We are more aware of what is going on in the world at large through media such as television and radio, which also use satellite and cable systems. We can keep in touch with people over great distances through a telephone network that allows us to dial direct to the other side of the world. We can buy examples of a range of technologies which can entertain us through eye and ear. There is much available to us, which can make our lives more fun, keep us in touch with others, keep us well informed about events and issues of the day. Systems are available for us to use, even if at a price which cuts out the poorer members of the population. But this view of a society playing and working with readily available mass-communication systems must also be corrected in another way.

We don't have much control of these systems, as individuals. If we don't like the way our television service is run, there isn't much we can do. If we switch off in sufficient numbers, a given programme may be dropped. But that is about all.

These remarks are intended to raise issues about the process of mass communication. The issue of whether or not the system is satisfactory as it now stands is raised when one describes the operation of the system – that is, how communication is taking place. It is our intention to raise issues as a part of communication theory, as we describe briefly these main aspects of mass-communication society.

## 1.4 Information – a contained explosion

**It is true that our society has been greatly changed by our ability to move information around very fast, over wide distances.** It is the various means of mass communication that have made this possible.

Government and commerce have always depended on their ability to handle information. The sheer volume of information to be processed for an ever increasing population has encouraged the development of new technology. Local government could not manage without computer files to store their information. Banks and other businesses could not manage without cable-linked computers connecting branches with their main offices. Our holiday bookings depend on the ability of airlines and travel agents to exchange information about flights and passenger bookings via similar systems. The list of examples is endless. Our society could not be administered without mass communication.

But the population in general is also able to obtain and exchange information on a scale unequalled in the history of mankind. We now take our telephone and postal systems for granted. We are getting used to sources of information such as Teletext. And broadcasting and print media are themselves sources of information about many things, including other places and other peoples.

Mass communication has made all this possible. As a society, we are now used to the idea of giving, getting and using information on a mass scale.

**But we should also realize that there are certain limits to this new information-based society.** These are mainly limits of access, limits of control and limits of cost. We referred to our limited ability to control these systems in the last section. Sometimes this raises very important issues. For example, powerful institutions such as credit-control agencies or the police store information about us.

**The issue raised through such uses of mass communication is to do with who has the right to say what about whom, who controls the system and who has access to the system.**

The question of access to information also draws attention to limitations in mass communication, as much as to the advances in new technology. Ever since the first edition of this book was written there have been promises of, for example, instant access to your local library, to 'look up' information electronically. This has not happened. It is true that many of the cities in Britain are now wired up with fibre optic cable, to enable access to information technology. But what has happened for ordinary people is that these cables give them more access to more TV channels, and new phone lines such as Mercury. There are experiments with local shopping by cable. But this is all. One problem is that people have to be persuaded to invest in new technology to give them access to information, and not everyone really wants it. There is also the concern for copyright and control of information. Those who own information sources want to charge for them. One has to have the technology for charging, and again people have to want to pay.

But there are two means of access to information which are now significantly available. One is the home computer, with its own bought databases on CD-ROM discs. The other means is the Internet, specifically the Web function of this.

## The Internet

This provides genuinely free information to anyone with a link to the Net, with or without their own website. There is a huge amount of information placed in the homepages of various websites. Some of this information is original material – e.g. university departments. Some of it is plain illegal – copyright material loaded onto the Web and untraceable from source. Some of it is commercial – newspapers or film companies wanting to promote themselves by providing some information about their operation, and especially about the latest products.

The Net can be used commercially, for example by estate agents' organizations selling houses. But so far its technological openness has defied attempts to censor its material, or to make money out of it. It is possible to make money by *using* it; for example, there is a music database from which you can buy numbers to download onto your cassette only after making electronic payment.

So access to information on a mass basis is developing via new technology, but not so fast as the pundits promise.

## 1.5 More fun – but less real choice?

We are lucky to have more time and more money to entertain ourselves than previous generations.

It is mass communication that brings us this entertainment. Entertainment has, in fact, become an industry in its own right. Our economy depends on the money spent on entertainment, in the form of things like videotapes, cassettes, television and magazines. These things are mass-produced or mass-broadcast – bought and seen in huge numbers.

Often various means of communication interact to produce examples of entertainment on a broad front. For instance, millions of people have enjoyed the *Batman* film. Many have also enjoyed the book of the film, related comic books and toys, to say nothing of posters and related articles in newspapers and general magazines. They will also enjoy the videotape of the film, or watch it via broadcast or cable television.

The range of entertainment is considerable. It is part of our lifestyle, our culture and our society. Television serials are part of everyday conversation. Women's magazines influence the spending of millions of pounds each year on clothes, make-up and pop music.

Mass communication brings a vast range of entertainment to our society, and so changes that society. But it is also true that the vast range does not offer the choice we may think it does. There are relatively few organizations producing the entertainment that we enjoy. And the types of entertainment are also quite similar in many cases.

For example, one company (Newscorp) owns three major British newspapers, *The Times*, the *Sun* and the *News of the World*. And the last two are pretty similar in look, content and treatment. Much space is devoted to pictures, sport, gossip and sex.

So this raises the issue of whether or not we get the kind of entertainment we want. It also raises the question of whether we tend to want the kind of entertainment that we get because that is all we are used to anyway.

Once more, we can support the idea of our being a mass-communication society by looking at the facts. But then we also need to look at the process of communication in order to understand what kind of messages we are getting and why.

All the concepts described in chapter 1 can be used to examine, for example, a newspaper as a piece of communication. What we are now doing is adding to those ideas. It is, you may remember, basic to the study of communication that one must never take anything for granted, or believe that the way things are is a natural way of communicating.

## 1.6 Mass communications as extensions of ourselves

**We have used the various means of mass communication in order to extend our human powers of communication.**

The kind of society we have is a result of this extension. It is, most obviously, a society in which its members can keep in touch with one another in great numbers and over great distances. It is also a society in which we may scan the world via the television screen. These facts support the idea that our world has, in a sense, grown smaller. This is represented by that much-quoted phrase 'a global village'. To this extent we have tackled the problem of a growing population by using machines to extend our powers of communication in face-to-face contact.

A public address system extends the scope of the human voice so that it can address an audience of hundreds. The telephone system extends the range of the human voice across continents. A magazine page stores words more accurately than human memory. A television image represents non-verbal language across great distances and to millions at a time. And now it can be argued that computers extend our abilities to think and make decisions (activities that are behind all our communication behaviour).

In our society, work activities and social activities depend, to a greater or lesser extent, on systems of mass communication. It could indeed be argued that those who do not have items such as a television and a telephone (and a computer terminal?) are socially disadvantaged. They are not fully in touch with society as a whole. And this raises further issues about what we think is essential to a healthy society in the mass-communication world that we have created.

## 1.7 The media and social reality

**The media are part of the reality of our world. They also help create that reality.**

We are a mass-communication society because mass communication is a part of that society and its activities.

We have invented new kinds of communication to do jobs for us, in work and leisure. The driving force behind these inventions is often commercial – to make money out of communicating or to help business perform its internal communication tasks more efficiently and more cheaply. But the effects of mass communication go beyond companies and their achievement of profit.

For a start, communications businesses, including advertising, are worth so many billions of pounds, and keep so many people employed, that the economy would collapse without them.

But also the media, in particular, shape society through their ability to mass-produce messages. If we think that we are a 'modern and affluent society', for instance, then that view is partly a result of what the media show us. In this way, the media help invent our view of the world, of ourselves, of our whole society. Just as we partly base our beliefs and opinions on what friends and parents tell us, so also to some extent we base our views on what the media tell us.

To this extent, the media are, for example, part of the political process, whether they like it or not. They can show us political events as they happen. They can raise political issues. So they also help define what those events and issues are.

This in itself raises many issues about the uses and effects of mass communications. What view of the world do the media represent? How accurate is this view? How is it put together? By whom?

Once more, all of these are questions which are basic to any analysis and explanation of the process of communication.

## 1.8 The media as institutions

**The media are made up of, run by and controlled by organizations which are described as institutions.**

In general, any organization like Viacom or the Westminster Press, which owns TV channels or newspapers, is an example of an institution. But it isn't just about owners. United Artists UK owns a cable system, but not TV stations. W.H. Smith owns Waterstones bookshops, but not a publishing house. The Independent Television Commission controls commercial television operations in certain respects, but it does not own a TV company. There are lots of media institutions that are not owners, but which are powerful in one area of the media or another.

Such institutions, not least those in advertising, are behind our entire mass-communication systems. They run the means of distributing information and entertainment. They run the production systems; they sell the product. The influence and span of control of these companies is made greater by the fact that many own shares in similar companies, and they own similar institutions in different countries.

The predicted pattern of media ownership is that fewer and fewer institutions will own more and more of the world's media/communication systems. One implication is that powerful institutions will control the ideas contained in their media products. Another is that there will be less and less real competition, and so less and less real choice in the types of magazines, programmes and other products that we have available to us (see also section 2.8 on ownership, finance and control).

## 1.9 The media – power and influence in society

**The media have power and influence because of the extent of their communications operations.**

We have also referred to their characteristics of repetition and penetration, which contribute to their power. It is a power to communicate on a scale unequalled in the history of mankind. The precise effects of this power and influence are not to be simply measured. This book is not designed to take on the detailed analysis and reference available elsewhere.

But the broad thrust of influence is pretty clear. We may refer back to the last section, in which we noted that the media shape our view of the world. Later we will also examine the idea that they tend to reinforce a view of the world as it is, rather than looking at alternative views.

In terms of media effects, major issues are often raised about the representation of violence or of political affairs, for example. Any general election is now largely dominated by media presentations, so far as the public is concerned. More specifically, the politician, as a media personality, has come to stand for political beliefs and attitudes. Party politics are represented through party personalities. The influence of such politicians depends, to a great extent, on the influence of the media. The precise effects of such an influence are, however, something which is much disputed. This is true, even though the notion of the power of the media is still accepted in general.

In the United Kingdom television has the power to reach 18 million viewers at peak viewing times. The two most popular UK newspapers each have the power of 3.5 million identical sets of messages, every day. And if the precise effects of such power are harder to measure than some communications analysts are prepared to admit, it still remains a quantifiable fact that, for example, television advertising does increase the sales of a given product.

Again, the quality of media power is marked out by the range of media through which messages may be passed at the same time. An election campaign can use posters, radio, mailshots, for example, as pure advertising. And it can orchestrate free publicity through news and magazine programmes. So the messages are being duplicated and reinforced across the media. This point also reminds us that while it is true that those producing media material have the power of access to huge audiences, other interest groups may have the cash or the influence to be able to use the media to exert power. The power of the media lies in who uses them and to what effect. For example, politicians believe that radio and television can influence the opinions of people. The political parties have a right in law (Acts of Parliament by which they created commercial and public broadcasting) to put out party political broadcasts. Exactly how such broadcasts affect people's opinions is open to argument. But still the power of the media lies in such use by politicians to say what they want to say to millions of people.

If, then, there is some kind of power and influence available through the use of these media of communication, certain issues obviously appear. These may be expressed in terms of basic questions, such as who should be given control of this power? Who controls the controllers? What should the power be used for?

## Conclusion

So we are indeed a mass-communication society. This means that we use the different kinds of mass communication in various ways to conduct business and leisure in our society. It means that the use and experience of various types of mass communication have today become a normal everyday occurrence for members of our society.

But it also means that the nature of our society has changed significantly from the experience of the last century, and it is still changing now.

Mass communication is part of our world, but is also helping to define how we see and understand that world.

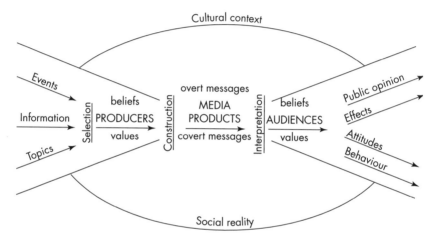

**FIGURE 38** Model of mass-media communication process

---

**Where do you draw the line between information and entertainment in the media?**

Hint: don't worry if you can't!

---

## 2 Interpreting the media

ALEX'S STORY

*Alex was aware that something was wrong as soon as he woke up. But it was nothing he could put his finger on at first. The flat looked the same. The noises of Saturday morning were the same as usual. But there was something disturbing in the air, like the first faint odour of leaking gas which alerts the senses to threat.*

He made it down to the front door just as the milk was arriving. That was one custom he had approved of since arriving in England several years ago. Doorstep delivery. But he wasn't prepared for the neat-looking girl who gave him a distinctly inviting grin as she slung the bottles down. Alex adjusted his dressing gown more tightly and wondered what had happened to Whistling Charlie who usually made the delivery. He switched on the radio while he made breakfast. The news was charting the course of a trade union dispute, and Alex listened absent-mindedly while the offer made to the employers was discussed and a trade unionist was asked whether he thought they could bring management back to the negotiating table.

As Alex was leaving the building for his Saturday shopping round, he was startled to bump into a large and hairy young man wearing motor-cycle leathers. As he backed off apprehensively, noting the tattoos and heavy boots, the woman from the downstairs flat came out.

'Hallo, Alex,' she said cheerfully, 'I see you've met Don. He's our baby-sitter. Reg and I came back so late last night we thought he'd better stay.'

'Pleased to meet you,' said Don, as he loomed over Alex.

Alex was pleased to get on with his shopping. He prided himself on the speed with which he could get round the supermarket, and come away with everything that he really wanted. So it was rather annoying to be held up in the checkout queue by two children in front of him. They were disputing the price of some item with the cashier. Alex noted with some surprise that they seemed to be in charge of the shopping for a whole family. But they also appeared to be well organized, and the boy won his argument when he told the cashier firmly that, old stock or not, the price on the label was what he was going to pay. Alex frowned. He felt uneasy.

He went for his usual cup of coffee, where he often met Steve and the rest of the crowd. At the table next to him a group of young men were laughing together over some magazines, and Alex leaned over to take a look while pretending not to. True Life Romance, he read on the cover of the magazines. He frowned again.

'Mandy's very good-looking, but you know girls like that. They're only after one thing,' he heard one of the young men say seriously. Alex paid his bill and left.

Of course he didn't see the car, or he wouldn't have tried to cross the road in the first place. As it was he found himself lying in the gutter with a severe pain in his right leg. He lay there, very calmly considering, believing that he now knew what it was his seventh sense had been trying to warn him about. In his detachment he even found time to admire the calm efficiency of the female police inspector who had turned up to direct operations. Alex was the only person who was badly hurt. But he had caused three vehicles to crash into one another. It was bedlam. And two male passengers were crying quietly by themselves with no one taking any notice.

'Rotten men drivers!' he heard a bystander say indignantly, before he fainted.

Once in hospital, Alex found that boredom was more of a pain than his leg. The nurses were very pleasant, but they had a job to do. And under the circumstances he hadn't had time to plan for his stay in bed. For some of the day they were able to watch a communal television set, placed at one end of the ward. The trouble was that the *programmes weren't much good. Alex watched bemusedly as one drama or comedy after another rolled before his eyes. The only programme he enjoyed was a comedy involving a family with a blind son who had the end of the ward in hysterics with his perceptive remarks about the rest of his family. But at night, there was nothing to amuse Alex, and he couldn't sleep, or suppress an increasing sense of anxiety.*

*On one particular night a friendly blond nurse named Michael turned up with a book for Alex. The trouble was that Alex had nearly got to sleep on this occasion. He peered blearily at the book's title.* Alex Through the Looking Glass, *he read. Panic gripped him. All was not right with the world. Alex knew that the only way to deal with his problem would be to go to sleep. Then he would be safe.*

### ABOUT ALEX'S STORY

You will not be surprised to hear that this story was not meant to be taken too seriously. But it does have a serious point. Much mass-media material, especially the entertainment side, tends to communicate a rather limited view of people. It repeats certain types of programme and types of people in these programmes. This is where the concepts of genre and stereotyping come in. We will say more of these a little later.

The main thing is to recognize that these limitations are there, and do mean that our view of the world is, to an extent, limited and distorted. Recognition of this problem is, in fact, a good way of correcting it. Alex's alternative experience was one in which men, women, young people, did not behave as they do in the media.

The media represent a world in which nurses are usually angels and female, and young men are rarely interested in romance and love.

You will recognize other points that the story tries to make. You will probably not agree with all of them. And certainly the media do not have the monopoly on generalizations about people and groups. We utter some of them in our everyday observations and opinions.

But then, what we say has a limited audience. This is certainly not true of the media whose messages can, we have noted, reinforce through sheer repetition.

There is more happening than meets the eye, in the process of communication through the media. We must interpret this process, to find out what is going on. We use certain terms/concepts to do this interpreting.

## 2.1 Texts

**Any example of media material or media product may be described as a text.**

So just as books are texts, so are music tracks, radio programmes, book covers, and so on. The point of using this formal term is to get into **textual** analysis – **the decoding of texts to discover their possible meanings**. Most people have been in classes which talk about books, which analyse characters or what the writer is getting at. The same thing can be done for all media texts, visual as well as verbal.

Any kind of analysis, whether it is about how the story is put together (see 2.5) or deconstructs the image (see 3.2), or talks about the use of camera and editing in films (see 2.4), is trying to get to the meanings of the text. It is useful to have the understanding and ability to describe the style of a magazine article. But what really matters is how that style contributes to what one thinks is the message of the article: how it contributes to the effect on the reader, intended and otherwise.

So in a film an unexpected cut to an extreme closeup of a gun firing into camera can be described as just that. But what it is also about is shock, an assault on the viewer, a sense of violence. That is what the text means, rather than how it does it. **Textual reading** is another word for analysis, for getting at the meanings. It has been suggested that there are three kinds of reading of text.

An **agreed or preferred reading** is one where the audience makes sense of the text pretty much as its creators meant them to – a lot of genre material is like this, very predictable.

A **negotiated reading** is one where the meanings are not so obvious, and one has to think about it. For example, the hero of a story might not be so perfect, perhaps a bit of a bully as well as being brave. So we have to negotiate what we think of them.

An **oppositional reading** is one where for whatever reason we take a different meaning from the text than the one that was intended. For example, the heroine might have been set up as seductive and attractive to a certain kind of male audience, whereas a female viewer might read her as pathetic and foolish.

## 2.2 Mediation

**'Mediation' is a general term used to describe the transformation of original material (scripts, events, etc.) when it is processed through any one of the mass media.**

Any form of communication is only a set of signs standing in place of some original event, object, idea, etc., and so a kind of mediation must always take place when communication takes place. A film showing tigers in the wild is only showing tigers. It is not bringing us the real tigers or the original experience.

But the term 'mediation' is usually taken to mean more than just 'standing in place of' and so transforming. We use it with reference to the media because they often actively transform all that they represent.

Again, it is convenient to leave out fictional material in any discussion. It is obvious that fiction does not pretend to present factual experience. Such material may mediate the author's intentions. Or again, one could look at the way in which a television version of a novel like *Mansfield Park* mediates that original novel. But in either case, we are pretty sure that a transformation has taken place.

However, much media is factual, or purports to be so. It is here that we should look most carefully at the idea of mediation.

This idea should cause us to ask what kind of change has taken place from the original to the media version. And how that change has taken place, why and with what effect. All the points that follow in this second section of the chapter build on the concept of mediation, and confirm the fact that it really does matter that it happens .

For example, sport is mediated in the way that television represents its various events. On a mechanical level, football matches are repackaged by the editing process: they have the illusion of being seen as they happen, but time is compressed until only the drama and the goals remain.

Even when a match is shown live, the football is very much a mediated event. The viewer becomes a god through the mediating power of the camera, which can survey the entire pitch from above, or the details of play as if we are out there on the pitch. Video discs permit the mediators to control time, giving us an instant flashback of action replay on the goals scored. And the commentator is actually heard as mediator, producing explanations and interpretations of events on the field which might never have occurred to us if we had been at the match itself.

For another example, the events and the very clothes of the fashion world are mediated through magazines. In this instance, we note two things: that different media can work together in the mediation process – creating a notion of what is fashionable at any point; and that there can be creation as well as transformation in the mediation process. The idea of what is fashionable for summer wear, for instance, is not just the result of articles on fashion shows or what is available in certain shops, but also of opinions coming from the people who write the articles and take the pictures. At the time of writing, the 'V-back' look is fashionable in a wide range of women's clothes. The magazines are not just mediating what is 'out there'. The fashion articles become a source of information and ideas in themselves. In this way the media can be an active part of our cultural life. Mediation is an active process.

**In this way the media help create culture, as well as our social reality.**

## 2.3 Realism

Within media texts our sense of reality, or their quality of realism, is valued by audiences, but is entirely constructed. **Realism is nothing but a set of conventions.**

Audiences are interested in the quality of realism of a media text for several reasons. One is that we want to believe in the story, at least while we are watching or reading it – it is as if we really are in an American city with exciting things happening. Another may be that we want to believe in the truth of the message behind the story – that true love really does win through every time. Another may be that we want to feel personally involved – have a sense that we really are there in the spaceship. Another is that we expect certain kinds of text to have certain kinds of realism: we don't mind if Bugs Bunny gets blown up but miraculously survives; we do expect documentaries to give a sense of actual events, places and people. All these examples, associated with different reasons for expecting realism, can involve different conventions for producing that particular kind of realism.

You'll remember that conventions are kinds of rules to make sense of codes. So for instance to make sense of documentary as just that, there are rules for how the film or video material is handled. You might expect real locations and real people, the use of natural sound and lighting, single camera setups, and so on. In fact there are various types of documentary which use different combinations of convention – you could work these out for yourself. One interesting one is the kind of documentary which is about historical events.

We expect our film to seem real at least when we are watching it, even if we criticize it afterwards. The fact that we are inclined to criticize material on grounds of realism – 'I don't believe anyone would have been so stupid as to go down that cellar!' (probability) – is due to western culture having developed an appetite for realism through the growth of visual arts in particular. Photography has given the illusion of 'capturing' life on film, since it started over a hundred years ago. Now computer games are having more and more memory devoted to making them seem real – with naturalistic characters and places on screen.

## 2.4 Media language

**Media texts may be described through specialized language, or may use special language, spoken and visual.**

It is useful to pick up some of that language, especially as it relates to visual texts. You have already been doing that, in that some special terms have been formally explained – the word 'text' itself. Other terms are assumed to be sufficiently well known – 'closeup'. Others acquire meaning in the context of our explanations – 'double page spread' (DPS) for a magazine.

It is useful to know what a layout is, or a press release. The last chapter will elaborate some of these points, especially in relation to film and video. Here, it is useful to be able to use language which accurately identifies what you are trying to describe – there is a difference between a pan and a track right.

## 2.5 Narrative

**'Narrative' is a formal term describing the structure and sequence of a text.**

It is what we call casually 'the story', but is more than that. Certainly narrative is about what is 'told' and the order of its telling. But you need to remember that this does not just apply to fictions. Documentaries and news articles also tell us something in a certain order. What is put first, second and last matters, in fact or fiction. An article on floods in Bangladesh can lead up to what the government agencies are doing about the disaster, just as a story about a murder can lead up to discovering the identity of the murderer.

This 'lead up' is partly about **plot** – what happens in what order, and partly about **drama** – how excitement and reader involvement can be created by that order and by the way the story is told, by the language used. It is argued that many, if not all, narratives are organized around ideas of **conflict and resolution**. The storyline sets up a problem for the characters, develops conflict between some of them, but eventually resolves that conflict in some way – as with 'happily ever after' endings to romances. The drama in such stories works up to a climax of excitement, and then the denouement is where everything is sorted out. Narratives where everything is wrapped up neatly at the end are said to have **closure**.

It is worth remembering that the story is not just 'out there', waiting to be discovered in the pages or on the screen. We actually make the story in our heads from cues which the text gives us. Some texts direct our understanding more than others. Genres are much more what are called **closed texts**, because they are so bound by conventions that they are fairly predictable. If what is happening and how is not so obvious, is not so predictable, then the narrative is more open – indeed one has an **open text**.

The **cues** referred to are really signs (referred to in chapter 1). Lots of them can come together to help us make the narrative in our heads. For example, think how you could be told that two people are going to fall in love in a TV drama. One obvious way to do this is to cut together medium closeups of the two apparently looking at one another, and to hold the shots for longer than you would with characters who 'didn't matter' to the story.

Cues can also bring about **narrative positioning** (see also 2.3). This is all about how you relate to the film or story. This positioning of the reader or viewer is most strong and obvious with fiction. For example, a writer can use the 'I' form to make you think you are being talked to by the person to whom everything really happened. You'll see that this could also be counted as a device of realism. Don't worry about finding overlaps between our sections, especially conventions which seem to apply to different topic areas. They do! And a film-maker can use a moving camera or a particular camera position to make you think that the camera is one of the characters, and that you are that character. This is called **subjective narrative**. You have been positioned – manipulated in fact – to be part of the story.

## 2.6 Selection and construction

**The content of any programme or newspaper is the result of a process of selection and construction.**

Any example of media material is an example of a piece of communication that has been produced from a number of possible sources, and put together from only some of these. What is more, it has been put together in a certain way. What has been left out may be as important as what has been put in.

The way the material has been constructed will depend on a number of assumptions made by the media makers – assumptions, working practices, habits, conventions, to do with the 'normal' or 'proper' way to handle a given subject or a given type of programme, article, etc.

In this book we tend, by choice, to look at examples from television and newspapers. But the terms used, and the ideas they contain, could be used in any one of the media.

For example, a pop single is constructed from a number of tracks laid down in the studio. Some of these are selected from different takes and put together (mixed) to create a number that never existed in this form in the first place. And indeed, there may be several numbers which could have been chosen for this single release. Only one is chosen. The studio (and a record company) have selected and constructed this piece of communication because they think it will entertain a mass audience and will sell.

For another example, a typical radio news-magazine programme is constructed from many pieces of material available – tapes, live voice, cable links with foreign places. And all these pieces of material may be on a variety of subjects, treated in a variety of ways. In the end, the programme editor will preside over a selection process which leaves out some material, reworks other pieces, sets up a running order and a time for each item. He has made decisions about that piece of communication which we call the programme.

We notice that, in the category of the media especially, it is very obvious that communication is not a 'natural' process. It is an activity that is performed in certain ways for certain reasons. In the end, the media are usually trying to chase audience figures and profits. The ways in which they communicate become more understandable when one remembers these two basic facts.

We may also notice that the media are distinctive in that items of media communication are produced by a group of people, working collaboratively, rather than by individuals. The idea of an individual creator is attractive to us because our culture leads us to believe in individualism – personalities, stars. But the facts are different.

For example, this book is the result of collaboration between two authors, an editor, a secretary, photographers and artists, printers and others. It is constructed by a number of people. It didn't just happen. You are reading these words because we decided that we wanted to communicate about communicating.

## 2.7 Product

**The term 'product' draws attention to the fact that the media manufacture 'goods' which are bought by the audience as 'consumers'.**

The term is used to draw attention to the fact that most pieces of communication coming through the media have to be promoted and sold in a marketplace.

Routledge is not producing this book only because it believes it can be useful. The company also believes that it will make money and enable them to produce more books.

The concept of product includes the ideas that the communication is produced in quantity and is sold. It is useful to an understanding of how and why communication takes place because often these facts are obscured.

For example, television series are made on a production line, called a studio, just like a make of car. They will be sold through publicity work, trailers on television, possibly newspaper ads, just like the car. The television company is also trying to please its consumers, called the audience. (Even the BBC must chase the ratings and compete, in order to justify its licence fee.) The consumers in this country also pay for the product, through this licence fee, or through that proportion of the price of other products which is set aside by advertisers to pay for advertising. To say all this is neither to praise nor to condemn the end result. It simply illustrates the how and why of the communication process. And perhaps it will stop some people from pretending that there is either art or commerce in mass communication, when often the truth lies somewhere between these two ideas.

## 2.8 Ownership, finance, control

**Media messages come from somewhere, and must be paid for by someone.**

We can interpret the media and the way they communicate with more understanding if we understand their sources – of ownership as well as finance. It is clear that the cost element, as well as the ability to own all this message-making technology, distinguishes a film, say, from a conversation, or a note put through a friend's door. People see communication in a different light when they have to pay for it.

Other books can give you more factual detail than we are able to offer in the space available to us – but we think it is worth giving the main picture of what is going on.

**Our media of mass communication are largely owned and run by corporations, a few of them state corporations, most business.** Many of these corporations work on an international basis. All of them own pieces of a variety of media industries. The immediate result of this is that they often (but not always) think in terms of large audiences and large profits. And the result of this situation is that they will often produce material which, in order to have a mass appeal, works to a formula. In particular, there is a desire to appeal to the American market, for two reasons. One is that the USA spends more money on communication products (especially entertainment) than any other country in the world. The other is that the Americans have such a well developed system for distributing and marketing communication (among other products) that it pays to keep in with them. Events such as the Cannes Film Festival or the London VideoCom Fair are used by corporations to sell communications products on an international basis.

For example, in Britain S.C. Pearson has interests in television, film, books, newspapers and other industries. It owns the Westminster Press, which in turn owns among other papers the *Financial Times*. It owns 56 weekly magazines including *The Economist*. It owns, among other publishers, Longman books and Penguin books. (Penguin also owns other publishers such as the Viking Press.) It owns Goldcrest Films, which also owns 25 per cent of Yorkshire Television (Yorkshire itself has taken over Tyne Tees, and both are now owned by Granada). It has stakes in the Premier and Music Box cable channels. It owns companies outside the media world such as Royal Doulton China, Lazard Partners merchant bank and leisure attractions such as Madame Tussauds, Wookey Hole and Warwick Castle. Pearson also has interests in oil and large estates, and it owns various American companies.

Clearly this network of alliances and of ownership not only typifies the source of communication in the mass media, but also says something about their power. It helps us interpret as well as describe. It helps explain why the media sell a lot of entertainment product – it is profitable. As we have said, it helps explain a certain lack of variety in the types of communication product. It helps explain the ability of these owners to market and promote their products as heavily as they do.

Current developments in communication and technology do not

change this overall pattern of centralized control and concentration on entertainment formats. New satellite channels across the world are owned or controlled by existing media corporations. This is not least because only they have the cash to finance such developments and perhaps carry the losses involved in starting up such ventures (a million pounds a week loss for Sky channel in its first year). In British commercial television, when contracts come up for renewal for the existing companies, potential new owners are still dominated by media interests – for example, the Virgin company, which is heavily involved in the music industry. In the American film industry Japanese household names like JVC and Sony own major corporations such as Columbia. Those same Japanese companies dominate the production of equipment for broadcasting. They are now trying to corner the market for new high-definition television and new video formats.

Public ownership, exemplified by the BBC in Britain, does not change the situation. The BBC does not make a profit, but it does chase audiences and ratings like any commercial organization. If it did not show that it was, in general, pleasing mass audiences then there is no doubt that the British parliament (which sets the licence fee) would question whether it should go on getting the fees that it does. So the BBC sells its programmes in world markets, and it sells spin-off products. It also retains an enormous power over what we see and therefore what messages are incorporated in programmes. This is because it and the commercial companies still have 90 per cent of the audience. The satellite alternatives are no real alternative in that they are geared even more to mass appeal – sport, music, films. The bottom line is that any kind of system has to be paid for.

This leads naturally to considerations of finance. Who pays, and how?

One simple answer is that the audience always pays – at the box office, through the cover price, at the counter, through the licence fee, through the goods they buy.

That kind of financing represents no control, other than in the crudest terms, over what is bought. But the immediate financiers may have a powerful control over the communication that we buy. This is why, once more, it is worth describing the situation broadly, so that one can then interpret it in terms of consequences. There are two immediate sources of finance for most examples one can think of.

One is the direct finance that comes from the owning company or its backing bankers. And the cost of media operations is so huge that it is not surprising that the owners have to be what we would call 'big business'. It costs an average of £250,000 to produce one hour of drama for television. Hardly surprising, then, that Granada obtained American co-production money to finance the twelve hours of the famous drama serial *The Jewel in the Crown*. And the effect of this is to concentrate power further in the hands of those producers who do have money (and so reinforce their kind

| | |
|---|---|
| **BOOKS**<br>× value of sales | REED/ELSEVIER (e.g. Heinemann)<br>NEWSCORP (e.g. Harper Collins)<br>PEARSON (e.g. Longman and Penguin)<br>HOLTZBRINCK (e.g. Macmillan) |
| **MUSIC**<br>× volume and value<br>of sales | PHILIPS (Polygram)<br>SONY (CBS)<br>EMI<br>MATSUSHITA (MCA – Time/Warners – WEA)<br>BERTELSMANN (BMG) |
| **FILM<br>PRODUCTION and<br>DISTRIBUTION**<br>× investment and<br>returns | SONY (Columbia and Tristar)<br>VIACOM (Paramount – and Blockbuster video)<br>NEWSCORP (20C Fox)<br>DISNEY<br>TIME/WARNER<br>MATSUSHITA (Seagram/MCA – Universal) |
| **COMMERCIAL TV**<br>× hours output/<br>programmes | GRANADA (and Yorkshire/Tyne Tees)<br>CARLTON (and LWT & Central)<br>UNITED NEWS & MEDIA/MAI (HTV and Anglia) |
| **MAGAZINES**<br>× sales | EMAP (e.g. *Elle*)<br>REED/ELSEVIER (e.g. *TV Times*)<br>UNITED NEWS & MEDIA (e.g. *Music Business*)<br>NATIONAL MAGAZINE COMPANY (e.g. *She*) |
| **DAILY<br>NEWSPAPERS**<br>× sales | NEWSCORP (e.g. *Sun*)<br>MIRROR GROUP<br>DAILY MAIL and GENERAL TRUST<br>UNITED NEWS & MEDIA (e.g. *Daily Express*) |
| **COMMERCIAL<br>RADIO**<br>× listeners | EMAP RADIO (e.g. Kiss FM)<br>GWR GROUP (e.g. Brunel Classic Gold)<br>CAPITOL RADIO (e.g. Southern FM)<br>CHILTERN RADIO GROUP (e.g. Galaxy) |

**FIGURE 39** Media ownership in Britain. The chart indicates where, in different media, 70 per cent or more of the market, defined in terms of sales etc., is dominated by specific companies. It will be seen that a number of the 'owners' are multinationals based outside Britain, and that a number appear more than once.

of material), and to lock out anyone with ideas about doing something different. Lest our picture looks too desperate, it should be pointed out that, for example, Channel Four in the United Kingdom has been set up in such a way as to allow smaller companies to get some of their productions onto the screen. Similarly, American public-service channels also serve minority audiences. They provide some sort of alternative to the mass commercial product.

But then there is the second main source of finance – advertising. Advertisers pay heavily for a special kind of communication, and expect to see results. They may themselves be large companies, with a good deal of financial muscle. And, for example, a magazine advertisement for lipstick sells not only because of the persuasive skill of the advertisement, but also as a result of the communication in the rest of the magazine. So one obvious effect of this source of finance is that the magazine producers tend to produce the kind of material that will please the advertisers – material which sells to the target audience that the advertisers are aiming at. No one needs to twist the arms of the magazine owners. If they don't sell copies then their marketing division cannot prove to the lipstick manufacturers that it is worth paying to advertise in their magazine. No income, no magazine.

So the matter of who pays for the communication does affect the content and treatment of the communication that we get. Our magazine example is bound to put in feature articles about make-up, which, like the advertisement, suggest that lipstick makes you more attractive.

This in itself reinforces a certain way of looking at things, a certain sense of what is 'normal'. And so it would seem that, in our example, the communication is about more than lipsticks and the idea of what is attractive.

## 2.9 Media and audience

You will see that the word 'audience' appears often in this chapter, not least in relation to advertising.

In the first place the audience for the various media may be described as those who view, read and listen. It is also common to refer to **mass audience** to make the point that media such as cinema and magazines have viewers and readers whose numbers run into hundreds of thousands a week. However, it is also important to realize that in fact **the media have many audiences**.

**Audiences are targeted** by the advertising and circulation managers of newspapers, television and all the other media. There is an audience for a magazine on American football, there is an audience for a TV programme such as *Friends*, and so on. All these audiences have slightly different characteristics, measured by the usual markers of age, gender, socio-economic grouping, etc. Audiences with such characteristics can be targeted by producing material which appeals to them. This raises an interesting question as to whether the audience is found or made. Does a TV programmer have an audience in mind and put on material to suit? Or is the material put on, which then finds an audience? Obviously after many years radio producers and journalists, for example, do have a fair idea of what their audience is like and what they want. But still it brings one to another point.

**Audiences may be constructed.** This idea points to the fact that it is possible to 'find' an audience for a media product and to build it up. For example, *The Golden Girls* is a TV comedy which has a pretty broad appeal, but which is still biased towards the older viewer. The American production people had cottoned on to the fact that an increasing proportion of the population was elderly. Or one can look at a British up-market magazine for males such as *GQ*, which again has constructed an audience for its product by appealing to a section of the population through a type of magazine that did not exist ten years ago.

Audiences are crucial in any model of the communication process in the media because, after all, they pay for the existence of the media one way or the other – cover price, box office, licence fee, and the like. The response of the audience to media product is carefully checked through continual market research – hundreds of people are interviewed every week by BARB, the broadcasters' research organization. So we should not look at the audience as a lot of gaping mouths to be fed with whatever pap the media choose to throw in. In fact this raises another point.

**Audiences are active.** This means that audiences actively select what they want to read or view. A certain type of audience will actively choose between a range of computer magazines. Another type will choose whether or not to switch on the news. It is still common to hear the mistaken view that the media, especially television, make us passive. This is not true in many ways. First it takes a great deal of attention activity to watch and understand TV. Then again there is research evidence to show that people do not sit still and watch TV anyway – they do some surprising things while the set is on. And there are other points about activity, such as the well evidenced connection between increased participation in certain sports and the amount of exposure they are getting on television. The notion of an active audience also ties in with ideas about how we may or may not be affected by media messages.

**The uses and gratification theory of the connection between the audience and the media suggests that we use the media to gratify needs that we have inside us.** It suggests that we can be quite active in trying to satisfy those needs. So we select music to satisfy moods, we select magazines to satisfy interests, we select TV channels and programmes to satisfy whatever we think it is we need at the time – excitement, romance, the need for security, social needs, personal needs and so on.

**Audience profile refers to the description of the audience for a particular media product.** It isn't very hard to work out the profile for a magazine by looking at the content and style. One can describe the readership in terms of age, gender, occupation, interests and possibly role and location. It has also been common to identify audiences through socio-economic descriptors labelled A to E, where A stands for the wealthiest top management people, and E stands for those with little or no income – students and the unemployed. In all cases what industry is really interested in is disposable income – how much you have left over to spend after your main costs are covered. The profile which identifies gay people is used to target what is called the pink pound. Gay people generally are not parenting, and have more money to spend than many others.

**Audience lifestyle refers to the interests, spending habits, relationships, activities, values of a given audience.** This has developed as a refinement of profiling over the last ten years or more. Lifestyle recognizes that some groups of people will spend a lot of money on their lifestyle, almost regardless of whether or not they can really afford it. It also recognizes that people generally can be persuaded to consume if it fits with their lifestyle. This affects the media in two ways. Directly it has to do with media products fitting in with lifestyle. So magazines for specialist music tastes can succeed if they become part of the lifestyle that goes with the music. This kind of specialist media product has found a **market niche**. But secondly, because the media are generally paid for by advertising income, identification and use of lifestyle also affects the media indirectly. Many television ads clearly represent some way of life which audiences have or would like to have.

**Audiences can be primary or secondary.** That is to say, the primary audience for a film is the one that first sees it in the cinema. But then there are many in the secondary audience who rent the video or even buy it, as well as those who watch the film when it is screened on terrestrial channels or on satellite. *City Slickers*, a comedy crossed with a Western, actually made more money on video than it did at the box office. This distinction between such audiences applies especially to print media. It is the difference between readership and circulation figures. More people read magazines and news-papers than actually buy them. Market surveys are interested in these 'lost' purchasers – why do they read but not buy?

## 2.10 Scheduling

A particular method of focusing on audiences is **to schedule your media product so that its timing suits a certain audience.** Usually, scheduling is a term applied to the placing of TV programmes at certain times. So, programmes for young people are scheduled for screening in late afternoon to early evening, to catch the after-school audience. Others are placed on

Saturday morning to catch the same audience in its free time. Programmes with certain degrees of sex and violence are scheduled for after the 'watershed' – nine o'clock in the evening – in the hope of missing the young audience. The allied concept of programming – choosing types of programme as well as their timing – is seen in the scheduling of sports programmes in the summer. So many people are on holiday or out and about at this time of the year that programmers for the channels will not put out expensive material at these times.

The idea of scheduling obviously applies to radio, e.g. particular slots for news programmes. In principle it is also what release patterns are about in the cinema. Here, they actually try to release blockbusters that will appeal to children and families in the summer – because they are free and in the mood to go out. The same thing is true of the Christmas slot.

## 2.11 Overt and covert values

**The media often communicate messages about beliefs and opinions.** These stand for values – notions to do with good and bad, for and against, proper and improper, and so on.

These values may be very obviously stated. The 'Vote Labour' headline on the front of the UK *Daily Mirror* a few elections ago let one know pretty clearly the opinions of that newspaper.

But some of these values are not obvious or overt. They may be hidden or covert. Just how hidden is a matter of opinion, depending on a particular piece of communication, and on how perceptive its receivers are. But still the idea of covert values is a useful one for interpreting the media. It should cause us to look more closely at what is really said, and how.

It should also be said that those producing the piece of communication may or may not have intended to conceal certain messages.

In the example of an advertisement, it is likely that there is an intention to conceal. Those who construct advertisements are skilled communicators. They are aware that a product can best be sold on the back of an idea, and that idea should fit in with the audience's existing beliefs and values. But the idea mustn't be too obvious. For instance, there are at the moment a number of advertisements selling food products in association with the idea of health. So far, this is fairly plain: the value of good health is expressed as an overt value, in the case of all those advertisements for items like butter, bread, orange juice and yoghurt. But you now may recollect that many of these advertisements also show the product being consumed by families and, even more specifically, being served by the wife or mother. The covert value and message is that families are OK, and a good family buys and consumes the product. Also, advertisements for food, like many others, trade in covert messages about guilt and pleasure.

To take another example, crime thrillers are always popular – *NYPD Blue* on TV, *Lethal Weapon* on film, *V.I. Warshowsky* in novels – because they are presented in an exciting way. So the first message one can get is that crime is adventurous. Whereas the police will tell you that a lot of crime fighting is very boring and bureaucratic. Crime stories may also imply that violence happens but the cop hero will come out OK. This is almost a suggestion that violence is 'safe' – for the hero at least. This is nonsense. People don't recover easily from even a crack on the head. More bothering still is a suggestion that acts of violence are somehow OK if they are being committed by the police in the cause of law. We the audience may be set up to accept this covert message because the violence is being done to the 'baddie' who is a pervert, psychopath or whatever. The overt values may be about the importance of keeping law and order. But covert values can suggest that this is a more exciting activity than it really is; that law-keeping methods are not to be questioned.

Equally, we are suggesting that such covert messages do need to be looked for, debated and condemned if they are presenting values which are unacceptable to ourselves and/or to our society.

And in this process of analysis and interpretation we may also come across interesting contradictions in the covert values – and in our society's values in general. For example, in the case just given, we might assume that everyone would say that they believe in the rule of law. This is meant to protect us from the behaviour of unsocial individuals – those we might call criminals. But at the same time, we also believe in the right of individuals to 'do their own thing', and to preserve their own sense of what is right and wrong – a sense of 'natural' justice, perhaps. The works we referred to present a contradiction between natural justice and legal justice, between an individual's needs and the needs of society.

So there are covert messages in most examples of media communication. These messages are dominantly about values. The values are to do with the meaning of the communication. These meanings have more or less significance according to obvious factors like what is said, who says it, who is receiving the message, and how many times it is repeated.

## 2.12 Representations

The media re-present our world to us. They are not a window on the world. They are not a mirror for reality. They reconstruct our world and ideas about it. Even news does this. (Here you should refer back to the section on mediation (2.2), which explains how the media transform what they present.)

The media represent all aspects of our world. So one can look at how they represent, say, schools or criminality, as much as how they represent women or the disabled. However, it is common to look at representations of people by groups or types. The media tend to represent us to ourselves as if we all belong to one group or another. And then they represent those groups as having certain characteristics. What is more, this representation includes value messages about what that group and those characteristics stand for. Common groupings are by age, gender, sexual orientation, job, roles – the same sets indeed as may be used for audience profiling! The value messages are basically about approval or disapproval. Sometimes they seem to be downright contradictory – girls can be either prissy virgins or promiscuous tarts – boys can be either violent yobs or cool and gorgeous.

These kinds of simplistic representation are referred to as stereotypes.

## Stereotypes

**A stereotype of a person is based on repeated description and ideas. A stereotype stands for a set of people, like women or businessmen, and is supposed to typify that set.**

A stereotype is a simplification. It is not only about appearance, but also to do with relationships and beliefs connected with the type of person. In effect, it adds up to a snap description and an uncritical judgement of that person.

There are many well known stereotypes of women, such as the so-called dumb blonde. But people are also typed in terms of things like race and religion. Some stereotypes are actually meant to be insulting – the image of the mean Scotsman or Jew. In fact, most stereotypes are insulting in some way, and all are a kind of evasion of the real complexity and interest of complete human beings.

The media use stereotypes of people as a kind of shorthand for getting their messages across. It is easier to represent a stereotype than to describe and build a full character. But while the media are guilty of reinforcing stereotypes, they have not invented them. They use them because it is known that they are used and understood by society in general. They offer an easy point of contact. The worrying thing is that stereotypes are also often a collection of prejudices. In this sense the power of the media becomes destructive because in repeating stereotypes they are repeating prejudices on a grand scale.

For example, comedy is full of stereotypes. We are certainly not in the business of damning all comedy because of this. But we are saying that much comedy communicates through stereotypes, and that this is not always a good thing. There are arguments about comedy releasing tensions and helping people come together. But some comedy around the stereotype of the mother-in-law is likely to create tension in those ladies, rather than release it. Similarly, if one belonged to the Chinese community then the exaggerated voices in some radio comedy could be rather irritating. And on television, if one was male and gay, then the exaggerated limp-wrist style of some comedy stereotypes would also be pretty infuriating.

Stereotypes predominate in fictional material. But they are by no means exclusive to comedy. Boys' comics represent stereotypes of square-jawed war heroes. Horror movies represent swooning female stereotypes in nighties. Romantic novels represent stereotyped heroes. One type, for example, is middle-class, male and masterful. He has the power that comes from his work and social position, and can sweep the female off to exotic places. In short, he represents a fantasy, but a fantasy with a narrow range of ideas.

So, in one sense stereotypes are a device for sketching in a character quickly. In another sense they may be a device for appealing to the audience's existing attitudes and beliefs, and indeed, prejudices. They certainly do communicate values to the audience and appear to have the effect at least of reinforcing those attitudes and beliefs.

Because they are so recognizable stereotypes are commercial. They help material become popular and profitable. When Robin Williams created *Mrs Doubtfire* he drew on the stereotype of the middle-aged female battleaxe with a heart of gold. He also borrowed a bit of the bossy governess, and he topped it off with a Scottish accent. The process of recognition and understanding goes round and round. People's awareness of such stereotypes is reinforced and set up for the next example by the very fact that the media repeat them and have large audiences.

## 2.13 Genres

**This same process of repetition also reinforces the popularity of identifiable forms of media product called genres.**

The main idea of genre incorporates a story form in any one of the media, including repeated elements like stock characters and situations. Science fiction stories or cop thrillers are genres. But the idea of genre may also be extended to identify other repetitive types of media product.

For example, television quiz shows may be said to be a genre because they also work to a formula. They are always about competition, often for a prize. They always have the same hero figure – the ever-smiling compère. They often have young, glamorous women as stock characters, usually to give away prizes. The backgrounds are frequently the same – garish, theatrical sets. And they even have a kind of repeated storyline which involves the compère as narrator raising the tension until the climax at the end, when a winner is announced and rewarded. At the time of writing, a UK quiz show, *Family Fortunes*, hit peak viewing figures of 13 million. Ask yourself why this happened. What is it about such shows that makes them so popular?

The word 'genre' helps us to interpret the media because it helps identify a dominant type of media product. It leads us to the repeated elements and then to the messages that are within the stories of genre. For instance, the quiz show's message is something about the importance of competing to get what you want, and about wanting to have material possessions. The media often communicate through the genre formula.

But it is no accident that genres develop. They are popular. And it is not surprising that they also use types and stereotypes in their characterization. Genres are a dominant type of media entertainment because they are popular, and therefore profitable. Stereotypes are part of that popularity.

In the case of either the genre or the stereotype, the point of contact through the communication is immediate and powerful. This is especially true with what are called **icons** of a genre. These are elements of the formula, perhaps the background, more often an object like the Tommy gun for gangster films. Decades of films, of publicity, have engraved the image of this eighty-year-old weapon on our cultural consciousness. Even if we have never seen a gangster movie, we may well recognize this gun – and all it stands for. Any communication sign that can achieve this degree of recognition across such a wide area of the globe must have power. Such power suggests influence as well as popularity.

The significance of the influence of a piece of genre material depends on what one believes its messages to be, as well as on one's point of view. But in particular, genres often represent the main beliefs and values of the culture that makes them at a given time. And in turn the genres also confirm those values as they represent them. The problem is to be objective enough about the communication process to be able to stand back and see what is going on. For example, it is now fairly obvious that those spy, Western and science fiction films of the 1950s that were about invasions and threats to American society were actually about the high degree of anxiety about communism and Russia at the time. Not so many people saw this then. But when we bring together terms like genre, repetition and covert values as tools for opening up the meaning of examples of media communication, then we have a better chance of working out what that meaning is.

The unwritten rules of what elements are expected to be in a given genre and of how they are expected to be used are called **conventions**. We have used the same word to describe the rules which bind the use of signs within codes of communication (see figure 40). So it is a word which is strongly applicable to genre, but not unique to it. What is useful about the term is that it promotes the idea that there are rules. This draws attention to the fact, once more, that we do not make and understand pieces of communication by chance. We can control our production of communication if we choose to. We can also be more precise about understanding the meaning of what is communicated, if we make the effort.

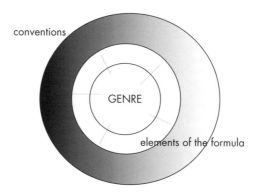

**FIGURE 40**   The conventions of genre bind its elements together into a formula

One example of a convention which works on genre material is that which says that the hero must appear within the first five minutes, if not sooner. It is a way of getting the audience to identify and possibly sympathize with the hero at an early stage of the story. But of course it is only a convention. It is not an absolute rule or law of nature. Conventions in genres change and adapt as the genres themselves are used again and again. Try watching a genre thriller serial with the sound down. You should still be able to identify the heroes and villains. Why and how?

## 2.14 Censorship and control

The mass-media corporations cannot print or broadcast whatever they like. But still it is a matter for great debate as to whether they are or are not controlled enough in terms of what they say and how they say it.

**Most censorship of British media is voluntary.** What this means is that the content and treatment of newspapers, films and television is monitored by organizations set up by the media corporations themselves – the Press Council, the Advertising Standards Authority, the Video Standards Council, the British Board of Film Certification and television committees, which produce codes of practice for the producers. Commercial television and cable standards are monitored by the Independent Television Commission. The media industry decides who will be members of such organizations. These groups decide on what is acceptable for young viewers, or on what constitutes excessive sex and violence.

**There is some direct censorship.** The two examples in Britain are these: the Broadcasting Standards Council has been set up by the government to view all television, cable and video material. If it recommends changes, or, say, the withdrawal of a video, then this would happen because of the unspoken threat of further government intervention. So far, however, it has said or required nothing that is different from the standards of existing broadcasting bodies. The other example is legal intervention. There is one instance of direct interference, in which the government passed a bill forbidding the voices of organizations described as terrorist (Sinn Fein) to be broadcast at all.

**Indirect censorship** could occur if types of legal action are threatened or carried out. For example the government can use or threaten to use the Official Secrets Act or the Prevention of Terrorism Act to stop, or try to stop, material being produced about military matters or about Northern Ireland. There is a long list of programmes about Northern Ireland which have been changed or stopped altogether. There are many similar examples relating to the Secrets Act. The most recent and famous one in the late 1980s was when the British government tried to stop the book *Spycatcher* being printed in countries around the world.

There is an important media debate here involving **the public right to know versus protecting the public interest**. The government lost most of the various *Spycatcher* court cases because the courts decided that the book did not reveal any great secrets that affected national security.

There is no easy answer to the questions raised by these debates and examples. Many people do not like the idea of censorship in any form. On the other hand many people would not want to see hardcore pornography being broadcast at 6 o'clock in the evening when children might be viewing. These are questions and problems which you should discuss when looking at what the media puts out and when considering the nature of media power.

**Codes of practice** that have been set up and written down by various media organizations could also be regarded in some ways as a form of self-censorship. The Advertising Association, the BBC, the Independent Television Commission, all have codes of practice regarding what should or should not be shown, to whom, and how. How far you would want to use the word censorship about these rules is another matter. You might well

**FIGURE 41**   Points of censorship in the stages of making a film

agree that it is OK to have a rule which does not allow advertising aimed at children to ask them to ask their parents to buy them something.

## 2.15 The effects of the media

**Many people believe that the output of the media does affect us in various ways, but this is in fact very hard to prove.** The general view would be that the value messages in media material affect us by becoming part of our personal system of values.

There are particular views that, for example, media output has the effect of encouraging violent or anti-social behaviour. Research has been done into this, as it has into the idea that the media affect voting habits at the time of general elections. Other views of particular effects include the idea that media stereotypes encourage sexist attitudes.

If one looks at each of these ideas briefly it is possible to illustrate **problems with measuring media effects**. In the case of violence it is just as easy to prove that violent scenes in cinema or television have the effect of putting people off such behaviour. In the case of voting habits, as with any effects research, it is impossible to separate clearly the influence of the media from the influence of other factors such as the opinions of friends and family. In the case of media stereotypes the problem, it could be said, is to do with allowing for how the stereotype is handled. A female stereotype in a comic strip is unlikely to affect the audience in the same way as a scene in an action movie. But how does one measure that difference?

This is not at all to dismiss such research. Much work has been done to try to allow for the kinds of problem described. We are learning a lot about factors which influence whether there is an effect or not. It is possible to suggest certain effects under certain conditions. Research has caused people to think more carefully about the types of effect they are looking for.

**Common types of effect** which have been suggested and investigated are: long- or short-term effects, effects on behaviour, effects on attitudes. Generally, media research has moved from an interest in short-term behavioural effects to an interest in longer-term effects on attitudes. In terms of violence this is like saying there has been a move from trying to prove that people go out and commit violent acts after watching violence on TV, to trying to prove that over many months or years people may come to accept or even approve of violence.

This view, that one has to be concerned with effects on people's thinking, fits in with a concern about the media messages which make value-statements, most obviously seen in advertisements or genre material. Examples might be – put a big value on appearance and spend money on clothes and make-up – put a value on being tough and macho as a male and don't be sentimental with women.

**The repetition and reinforcement of such messages is what, it is believed, gives the media such power to affect our attitudes and values.** This is to say, similar ideas are repeated across different media over months and years: 'increasingly today it is believed that the most significant naturally occurring influences of television may be long term ones' (Gunter 1987). So the effect of the media may be made possible through the fact that, for example, messages about Germans, for some people at least, start with comics, and continue through cinema films and TV comedy. The same messages about what Germans are supposed to be like, what we are supposed to think of them, are repeated in different ways. Such messages, perhaps about Germans being humourless or violent, are remarkably persistent and go back to media views formed in wars that finished fifty years ago and more. This persistence is also part of the power of the media and their effects. It forms attitudes and values which become part of the way that we see the world.

## 2.16 Ideology and the media

The attitudes and values which we have just talked about affect our view of everything that we experience. They are part of our beliefs. They apply to our view of people, and to our views about everything from class to sex, good laws to bad behaviour (see figure 42). In fact they add up to **a view of the world**, especially in relation to **ideas about who should or should not have power** in the world. This is **ideology**. The main view of the world held by most people in a given culture is the view which dominates – a **dominant ideology**.

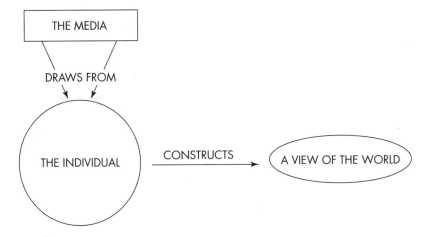

**FIGURE 42** Every person draws messages from the media with which to construct a view of the world

Media messages are part of that ideology. The way articles are written and programmes are shaped partly comes out of that dominant view because the journalists and programme makers are part of it. But then once the messages are there, coming through the programmes and articles, they go back into that ideology. In most cases they serve to reinforce it. Sometimes media material challenges it. Media students need to look for the challenge in the text. In this sense, decoding or textual analysis is about looking for value messages. So it is about uncovering ideology, describing it and testing the validity of what it 'tells' us.

The major topics that we have views about tend to have those views implied through the kind of verbal and visual language that is used when talking about them: topics such as romance or parenting. The tricky thing about ideology is that it is like chlorine in the water – it's there, but difficult to detect. This is because your views on romance and parenting are probably in general the views of everyone else, which are the views of the dominant ideology. Because most people, growing up with the views of friends, family and the media all around them, take them in with their corn flakes, as it were, so these views become naturalized. **It is this process of naturalization which makes ideology invisible.**

And we are certainly not saying that such views are wrong. We are only saying that they could be. We are saying that the phenomenon of naturalization works against questioning what the media 'tell us'. We are saying that being a communication student requires that questioning.

You could think about what your views are on the subjects of romance and parenting, for example, and where you think these views come from. Is romance depicted as a good thing? Do the media confuse romance and sex? If they do sometimes, what follows from this? Do you believe that all adults should become parents? What do you think about adults who don't have children? Are adults naturally able to be parents? What views of parenting are put across in TV programmes? In some of your answers to these questions you may find a difference between what you know is the accepted view and what you yourself think.

These 'topics' which have value messages attached to them are more formally known as **discourses**. One has a discourse when in a given topic area you can recognize particular ways of using communication about the topic – language and codes. And this particular language gives out particular meanings. There are in fact many discourses within ideology. For example – and you would say quite naturally(!) – the verbal language we use about babies is very approving and affectionate. People will say things like 'isn't she sweet!' and 'you're so lucky' and 'they're so cuddly at that age'. People use words like 'sweet' and 'cuddly'. They don't say things like 'what a bald smelly lump!' and 'you're in for some rough nights'. The trouble is that babies are smelly as well as cuddly. But you won't often find the media presenting its audience with alternative views to the dominant ones. This is partly to do with giving people what they want to hear. But it also has a lot to do with selling baby products, and so also an idea of babydom. Take a look at magazine adverts for baby products or those containing babies for some other reason. There is clearly a dominant view, a particular discourse, a certain set of values.

---

**Are we victims of the media?**

Hint: ask yourself how helpless you are as a consumer.

---

## 3 The media: particular examples

### 3.1 Advertising, publicity, marketing

A great deal of money – over two billion pounds a year in Britain – is spent on these three activities. They depend on communication. They use forms of communication, notably the media, as a way of persuading people to think or behave in ways that they might not otherwise have done.

**Advertising is not a form of communication: it is way of using forms of communication.**

*Advertising* has a clear price on it. The communication is charged for, whether it be through posters, radio slots or magazine advertisements.

*Publicity* is not charged for up front, though it may have hidden costs. A popular star may actually charge the media a fee for appearing on a television chat show. On the other hand, a launch lunch for that star's recently published biography could cost the publishers a lot of money to feed the journalists and personalities whom they would like to attend and to review the book well. There again, a film company may get free coverage of some location work because the press believes this will help them sell newspapers.

*Marketing* is the calculated promotion of goods, services, or even an individual. It combines advertising and publicity through a campaign. In the last twenty years the overall concept of marketing has come to dominate the advertising world. Even political parties will employ a marketing agency to help with everything from market research to the promotion of policies and of a public image.

## Finance

Communication carried on in the name of advertising has enormous financial implications. It isn't just that advertising is an industry in itself which creates jobs and turns over huge sums for making adverts and buying media slots. It also fuels the other media industries. Newspapers depend on their income from advertising to keep going. Commercial television couldn't exist without advertising. Magazines depend on advertising. To this extent the needs of the advertisers and the companies who use them shape media material. We get a lot of popular types of programme not just because they sell but because they sell the adverts around them.

## Stereotypes

We have already explained the concept of stereotypes in the previous section.

Advertising tends to exploit the use of stereotypes because it has to communicate very quickly with its audience. As we have noted, stereotypes are immediately recognizable. If the advertisement has to sketch in a situation rapidly, then it helps to be able to slot characters into instantly recognizable roles. Stereotypes are all about instant roles.

Advertisers also like to identify their target audience as a group in the advertisement – 'busy housewives', 'Martini people'. So again, stereotypes help do this.

It is also arguable that advertising is especially responsible for maintaining and fixing stereotypes in the public consciousness. Very simply, advertising campaigns work across a range of media. Advertisements are repeated many times. Apart from genres they are the most repetitious use of communication in the media. So anything that they say, many times, is likely to get known. Even something as unglamorous as a National Savings Certificate scheme becomes indelibly printed on our consciousness as 'Grannybonds'.

And remember that the stereotyping is not just about role and appearance, but also about relationships and situations. There are no unmarried mothers in advertisements, no arguments between parents and children, and people are mostly at home or at play. There are a lot of large, well-appointed cars and large, well-appointed homes.

## Covert messages

Indeed, these stereotypes of people and their situations also stand for messages about values, about a way of life and a set of beliefs that we in turn are invited to believe in. We have already given an advertising example for this concept. And we said then that the degree of covertness or overtness in these messages is a matter of observation and opinion.

But consider one more example. There is the value of 'newness'. Think of the number of advertisements which sell the product using the word 'new', or by emphasizing this is the 'latest model', or by emphasizing the glossy new appearance of the product, or by giving some space age context to the product. All this adds up to the covert message that newness is OK. If it is new, it must be good. This is, of course, convenient to manufacturers competing in markets that are already saturated with a given product and where there isn't much new to offer the public. But it does also mean that we may come to believe in newness for the sake of it. Something new is not necessarily a good thing. It is just – new.

## Alternative realities

Apart from covert values, advertisements often communicate to us an idea of alternative realities. These are other situations and lifestyles. Some commentators have talked of an alternative world of the media. The idea of something manufactured is still there. But it is most accurate to recognize that what advertising communicates to us is a set of complementary fantasies.

These alternative realities are best recognized through the backgrounds in the advertisements. For instance, there is the 'beach in the sun' fantasy, including tropical islands, which has been used to give a context to the sale of products like holidays, crisps, drinks, sweets. Not all advertisements fit the patterns, but enough to make the patterns valid. Again, there is the alternative 'ideal home'. This home has its downmarket and upmarket versions, and is usually shown in separate, disconnected rooms. But it is there, behind cleaning products for kitchen and bathroom, or types of fire and drinks for the living room, or furnishings for the bedroom.

Look for these alternative realities yourself. Construct them for yourself from magazine pictures. You will find other versions such as 'action in foreign parts', the traditional English countryside, the high-tech office, and so on.

The point is that the advertisements promote the illusion that these alternative backgrounds and situations are real. They are not. They are mostly myths about different worlds that the advertisers (and perhaps ourselves) would like to exist. The communication is the result of a careful process of construction, to enhance the illusion. Once more, it carries messages about values which are artificially enhanced by advertising. For example, the English countryside world is also about nostalgia for another way of life (which in any case never existed as it is depicted). We buy the dream of a lost world when we buy the product.

## Advertising as communication

This is to underline the fact that an advertisement is no more or less than another piece of communication. It has an opening tease like any story to gain attention. It develops its own ideas and message in its main part, like a story. And it concludes with a punch line or a twist, like a story – anything to make its message memorable. **Advertising is an example of communication that is very consciously planned.** It is presented with the intention of affecting the audience.

Television advertising is an example of communication that is notable in terms of its costs. On British television a twenty-five-second advertisement can cost £30,000 or more to make, and £60,000 or more to transmit on peak time slots over the whole TV network for a week. In terms of campaigns, covering a range of media for, say, two months, it would cost at least £1 million to give a major new product in the domestic consumer market a proper launch.

But still, advertising is only communication. The process by which it communicates is susceptible to analysis, as with any other example.

When we examine the **source** of the message we notice the interesting fact that it is in three parts. The advertising agency, or creative consultancy, may create the message. But the client for whom the advertisement is made also pays for it, and has some say in what goes into the advert. And the media that present the advert are also a source, so far as the audience is concerned. Their time slot or page space has to be paid for. And indeed, local display advertisements (the boxed ones with pictures) in local newspapers are mostly produced by the paper's own team. Similarly, local television makes solely local advertisements for local businesses.

If we examine the idea of **audience**, then we notice that advertisers, while bearing in mind that they want to communicate with fairly large numbers of people, still try to specify a typical member of their target audience as tightly as possible. The agency will produce an imaginative description of such a person. This will include all the attributes that we perceive in others – age, occupation, status and so on, as well as ideas about their lifestyle. They are careful about who they think they are talking to, and adjust their communication style accordingly. Ineffective communication is expensive.

In the same way, the advertiser thinks about the characteristics of the **medium** that he is using, about its possibilities.

And he is well aware of the social **context** within which he is operating. Advertisements fall within the consensus of our beliefs and values. They exploit them. They would never oppose them. In addition, they are sensitive to cultural nuances within the social mix, especially as they apply to particular groups of consumers. Advertisements for clothes for young people, for example, are alert to changing habits and fashions out in the real world. They follow at a safe distance behind, but they are there.

## Categories of advertisements

Advertisements are usually divided into two broad categories: classified and display.

**Classified advertisements** are those lists of small ads in columns at the back of newspapers and magazines. They are used for recruiting staff as well as for selling and publicizing products and services.

Job advertisements usually include the job title, duties and responsibilities, expected qualifications and experience of the person wanted, some idea of salary, conditions including any fringe benefits.

**Display advertisements** include all press, radio, cinema, TV and outdoor advertising which seeks to display the product or service to potential buyers. In general, classified advertisements are more factual and brief. Display advertisements may contain facts about the goods but are intended to be more persuasive and attractive. It has been suggested that a display advertisement should achieve four purposes:

> attract *attention*,
> arouse *interest*,
> create *desire*,
> and lead to *action*.

Look at and listen to some ads, to see how far they seek to do all four things. In most modern advertisements the action part is left unstated.

Brochures are also an interesting example of advertising and publicity which are produced in a great variety of styles from almost all business organizations. We suggest you collect some and analyse them as pieces of communication.


## Advertising and persuasion

We have said that all advertising seeks to persuade the receiver of something. **Advertising wants to reinforce or shift attitudes and beliefs so that people will then behave differently.** For example, advertising might want us to believe that taking out certain kinds of insurance is a good thing. It might want us to feel positive about the image of some big company, and so perhaps to wish to buy their products.

There is plenty of evidence to show that advertising works in a general way for products and services but little evidence as to how it works. There is little evidence to prove one way or the other that advertising actually sells ideas (religion or politics).

The ways in which advertising may persuade us are much the same as those we use in everyday life when trying to persuade people to do something we want.

In particular advertising will communicate ideas of reward or punishment. There are various kinds of reward offered: material rewards like 20 per cent more soap powder free, fantasy rewards like the attention of women to go with the aftershave, moral rewards like the feeling of being a good mum for buying a certain sweet or candy for the kids. Punishment may go with the reward by implication: being a bad mum if you don't buy the candy; or it may be explicit, as when the deodorant advert suggests that one loses friends if one doesn't use the product.

A simple way of persuading people is through repetition. This is why a campaign is geared to saying the same thing many times across many media. It is why the same advertisements appear night after night on television. Advertisements may persuade us by arousing the desire to imitate what we read or view. This could mean imitating some famous person who is using the product, or it could mean imitating kinds of behaviour which we already approve of. For example we approve of going to have a good time with friends or of going on holiday. It could be that someone will order that kind of drink next time they are out with friends, imitating what they have seen.

This reminds one that a good way of persuading people is to tie your real message to another one about beliefs or values. If those values are things that the receiver already agrees with then they may agree with the advertising message as well. Everyone believes in romance and love so a lot of advertisements are tied in with these values.

Humour is another good persuader. If the communication makes people laugh it makes them feel good. If they feel good they feel OK about the product and they are more likely to buy it.

Most of all, because advertisers are communication people, they know that their messages have to recognize people's needs. We went into this at the beginning of this book. There we noted that it is often psychological needs of various kinds which motivate people most strongly. They want to be loved, they want to have friends, they want self-esteem. If an advertisement promises you these things you may be persuaded by it.

Look at some advertisements to see how the words and pictures may persuade in these various ways.

## Marketing

Advertising is now but a part of a broader approach to using persuasive communication. **Marketing plans to use a range of media to communicate particular views.** Marketing is about a whole strategy of persuasion, including devices of public relations. Its subjects may include the corporate image of companies such as Benetton or a collection of media products such as those sold under the Nike label. Marketing is about communication through many media on a national, even an international scale. It is as much about indirect and soft selling of products as about obvious direct appeals. You can sell Reeboks by getting famous sports stars to wear them in public places, as much as by taking out adverts in magazines. It is about taking a broad view of what it is you want to sell and how. Films are a good example because when a film is in preproduction and discussion the marketeers are right in there. They are thinking about selling the film on video and to television, as well as at the cinema. They are looking to the sales of spin-offs such as music albums, computer games and other merchandise such as toys. They are thinking about the image/persona of the stars, as much as the story. They are thinking about product placements – clothes and cars perhaps – in the film.

Most interesting of all, they will be thinking, like all marketeers, about the impressions and value messages given off by the film in its various versions in different media. They will ask questions such as, how will people feel before seeing this movie, and how will they feel afterwards? How can we generate these feelings? What rating will we get from the censors? What rating do we want? You can apply these questions and our comments to many films – *The Lost World: Jurassic Park* and *Men in Black* are current examples.

## 3.2 Visual communication

### Definitions

Many forms and media of communication are coded and decoded through the use of the eye, including writing.

But in practice, by visual communication we refer only to those means of communication which use clearly pictorial or graphic elements. However, it must be recognized that media can contain graphic elements even in their treatment of the printed words. For example, popular newspapers are certainly visual media, not only because of the high proportion of pictures in them, but also because of the intensely graphic treatment of print (banner headlines, varied typeface and type size and so on).

Having made these points, it is now possible **to divide visual communication broadly into representational and schematic modes**. Representational visuals purport to look like the thing they represent. Most magazine and news photographs are of this mode.

But schematic visuals, while they communicate visually, don't pretend to be anything but symbolic. A lot of what we think of as graphics are of this mode – bar charts, pie charts and the like.

This is a useful division. It will not fit every single case. And some examples could seem to be a bit of both. You should look around you at the enormous variety of visual communication in our environment (street signs for example), and make your own mind up about particular instances.

We want to concentrate here on representational and photographic images. This is because such images dominate the range of mass media, with the obvious exception of radio. Visual communication is a dominant experience in our culture. And, because representational images do look like the thing they stand for, they are absorbed into our consciousness with a kind of immediacy and force that the written or spoken word lacks.

This is not to claim that one form of communication is better than the other – merely different.

## Image reading

Images are composed of signs as much as any other form or medium. We learn to decode these signs when we learn to decode those other sound signs made by adults, called speech. Visual communication does not possess the precise sense of grammar and syntax that verbal communication does. But it does have conventions that for example predict the order of shots in a piece of film. We want to concentrate on the single image.

The signs through which we read images fall into three areas. First, there are the **position signs**. These are signs given by the placing of the camera (or artist's point of view). How close the camera is to what it depicts (proximity), and the angle that it takes, defines how we understand the image. This is about the meaning of the signs. The position of the camera defines our position as spectator. It becomes our position. For example, you will find that in many advertisements the camera actually directs attention to the product, though this may be a small part of the whole image. Or, if a woman is being used to sell the product, the camera directs attention to her sexuality. There is a fairly well known advertisement for a bath product in which we are positioned in a room behind a half naked woman in the foreground. The camera sign means, pay attention to this.

Next there are the **image structure signs**. These are elements from which the image is put together:

> *Composition* is about where items are placed in the frame.
> *Framing* is about the border, what it encloses, what it excludes.
> *Colour* is about overall hues, or the selective placing of colour within the frame.
> *Foregrounding* is about placing objects in the front of the frame, and so making them larger (this is also a sign of the supposed three-dimensionality of an image – a visual 'trick').
> *Middleground* and *background* is about placing objects in relation to foreground, and also saying something about their importance.

*Lighting* is about things like picking out or diminishing objects according to how well lit they are. It is also about ideas of style.

*Focus* is about what is made clear or unclear through choice and use of camera lens. This also may sign to us to direct our attention towards a certain object. Or it could sign something like, this is a dream or fantasy picture.

*Perspective devices* (relative size of objects – lines of ceiling or floor) are about the illusion of depth in an image. We learn to read such signs as 'depth'. An image, of course, has no depth.

Next, there are **image content signs**. These are simply the objects within the frame. In fact we have learnt to believe they are there because of various other signs that are part of the process of visual perception – shape, outline, hue, tone. But if we accept that they are so identified, then the objects themselves may sign to us, especially in combination. One visual cliché is the young girl and the apple, meant to sign health. This example is useful because it also reminds us that objects can become symbols in an image. In this case, there is an additional tinge of tease and sexuality because the two objects stand for more than just what they are. They also stand for the story of temptation in the Garden of Eden and all the associations that this has.

You may be able to add to these signs, and certainly to the examples. But the point about the three areas remains, as does the basic point that the meaning of the image is not natural, but is constructed by the image makers through the use of these signs. We understand the code. If we didn't we couldn't make sense of what we were looking at.

The overall meaning of the image is confirmed by our reference to all the signs. Two or three on their own may not be enough. In any case the meaning of most images is actually quite complex. It can take many words to explain a picture.

And the point of image reading is to get to the total possible meanings of the image. Often we are very careless about decoding images, either in not getting the full meaning or in not realizing that we are getting covert messages. It is commonly thought that pictures are 'easy to read'. This is questionable. But in any case, this doesn't mean to say that they are simple.

A visual medium like television can offer us multiple codes of communication – visual, non-verbal, written captions, the spoken word and so on. So there is a complex variety of signs giving us the message.

## Socialization and beliefs

**Images are especially powerful in offering messages about beliefs because they are a dominant channel of communication in the media.**

You should also refer back to what we said about the power of the mass media in general. For the same reasons they are also a powerful agent of socialization. Socialization describes the ways in which we are taught or learn to fit into society. This includes society in general, as well as particular parts of society. Obviously, for example, one's family is also an agent of socialization – we learn from our growing experience in the family. We learn ways of behaving, a way of looking at the world, sets of beliefs and values.

Images on television or in magazines are influential because they offer direct models. That is, we can see what we could look like, how we could behave, how we could relate to others – everything is illustrated for us. It is all there in the pictures. For example, there are certain pictures that say a lot to us about the importance of security. Insurance company advertisements are inclined to promote this value because their business is based on it. But one would also be able to find a wide variety of other media material which represented the security of the home, the security of having savings, the security of having long-term relationships.

The idea of socialization relates to the notion of security as follows. One sees images of social behaviour and social relationships, in which security figures. The insurance company advertisement may suggest that one is a good husband and a proper husband if one insures one's life, and the loving wife and family are there as a reward. DIY magazines present images of homes made more physically secure. Newspapers often represent disapprovingly those who appear to threaten security in the family or the work place or in society as a whole – strikers would be an obvious example here. 'Because ads are so pervasive and our reading of them so routine, we tend to take for granted the deep social assumptions embedded in adverts' (Goldman 1992).

## Denotation, connotation, anchorage

You may come across these three terms which are also used to help explain how images communicate and how we may analyse them. **Denotation** is about image content – see our 'Image reading' section above (pages 196–7). The idea is that one should look very carefully at everything that is in the image, and describe what it is and how it is treated. The idea is to stop one taking the quick and casual glance that we give to so many images around us – posters, for example.

**Connotation** is about image meaning. The idea is that one can then take the content carefully described, and work out the meaning of the parts and the whole. The meaning will result from personal and cultural associations and experiences which we more or less share. Once more, the intention is to get the whole meaning, not just a partial one: to get the covert messages as well as the overt ones.

**Anchorage** is about particular aspects of an image which help pin down (or anchor) its meaning. Newspaper photographs are anchored by their captions – these help pin down, for example, who a person is and what they are doing. Advertisements may be anchored by a logo, a slogan, or the presence of the product somewhere in the image. Try cutting out newspaper photographs without their captions. How do the meanings change? Then add your own captions. Now what are the connotations of the image as anchored by your words?

## 3.3 News

### Construction of reality

**News and current affairs material is crucial in constructing our view of the world.** This view is mainly a combination of information and beliefs. That is, what we think are the facts about the world we live in, and what beliefs and values we have which organize those facts. So we are talking about what we believe the world to be like. But our country, other countries, other ways of life, all look different depending on what point of view one starts from. The media help shape that point of view. For example, one could easily argue that western news machines represent Africa as a continent of war and disasters – war in Nigeria, starvation in Sudan, Aids epidemics in Kenya, civil conflict in Algeria. Of course there are peaceful happy places in that huge continent, but you wouldn't think so judging by news media.

Newspapers construct our view of what is going on and how we are meant to understand it in other ways. For example, the tabloids, or popular papers, are dominated by stories about personalities, the activities of media stars, by scandal and gossip. The so-called hard news of political and financial matters has little place in British tabloids. If you check on the news coverage on a given day comparing a tabloid with a quality paper, or broadsheet, sometimes you might think readers must be living on two different planets – or inhabiting two different realities. One can also look at this difference in terms of what is missed out in the tabloids. **What is absent is as significant as what is present.** Reality is selective.

### Selection and construction: gathering a story

These sections on news overlap to some extent, but they build up a picture of news as something which is made not found. Many news people tend to talk as if they are mining diamonds of truth 'out there' and bringing them back for the audience. This is not so. Some of those diamonds are entirely artificial, made-up stories, lies if you like, of the 'DJ ate my hamster' variety. But all the diamonds are cut and polished to suit the setting of the particular newspaper or news programme. Recently a story about a 30-year-old woman running away with a 14-year-old boy figured in all the tabloids, but did not make the front page of most of the broadsheet papers. Papers made different decisions about taking the story and about what they did with it.

The gathering of a news story like this one is an exercise in mediation (see 2.2) – the way in which the act of communication changes its subject. With the news machine especially, there are many points at which this mediation, the shaping, the selection of a story can happen. The stringer, the news agency, the reporter, the photographer are at an initial stage. But then there are the sub-editor and the editor also shaping material at later stages of production. What you read is a very mediated version of what actually happens. Following sections amplify questions of how and why news communication is shaped in the ways that it is.

The news is especially influential, not only because it comes through powerful media, but also because it is believed. And we believe television and radio news in particular because much of what is said is factually true, and because the news organizations have spent many years promoting their reputation for truthfulness and impartiality. However, given the necessary process of selection and construction which is part of news making, it is impossible for the news makers to provide the whole truth or a complete view of the world. They will interpret wars, disasters and affairs of state in the way that seems most truthful to them. This will be their view of the world. It is in effect offered to us and becomes part of our reality.

For example, members of some factions fighting in the Middle East have been referred to as 'terrorists' and the disapproving comments of politicians have been widely reported. But the news makers of some Middle Eastern countries have called those same people 'freedom fighters' and have quoted favourable comment. Neither view may be entirely right or wrong. But in both cases we are seeing views promoted, as much as facts reported. In each case, the view of the world believed by the news makers becomes part of the communication to the audience. And in each case, they are contributing a little more to each audience's sense of reality.

They are helping construct a reality which is made up of beliefs as well as facts.

## Agenda setting

This phrase means that **the news makers in various media promote a list of the more important news topics** (in the same way that an agenda of topics is set for a meeting). This list can be argued over in detail, but it certainly includes stories about political events, about disasters, about war, about the royal family and about popular public figures. You should also refer here to the next section on news values.

This list is of general topic headings. But the agenda is actually about particular events of the moment that will probably come under these headings. As we write this, stories on the agenda include a long-running miners' strike and an explosion on an oil tanker. With a little thought, you can provide your own agenda as you read this.

If you can do this – identify those stories which are dominating the news media in a given week – then you are also identifying what the news makers consider to be important. In effect, they are telling you what is important. They may or may not be right. We don't know or don't notice those items which are dropped or given little space or time. Indeed, in this way they are 'said' to be less important. But still, the fact is that, positively or negatively, we are 'told' what is on the news agenda for the week. The idea that newspapers and news programmes simply communicate what is happening does not hold up. Messages, even news messages, are shaped in particular ways for particular reasons.

So the idea of an agenda is useful because it helps us interpret news as communication. If we notice the pattern that is the agenda, then we may ask who sets the agenda and what effect this might have. These are questions about source and audience. In the first case, we notice that it is an editorial team, influenced by their ideas of news value. In the second case, we notice that the audience is affected once more in the sense that their view of the world is being defined by communication that they receive from others. None of this is to suggest that news makers conspire to set the agenda. The fact that there is an agenda of broadly similar items most weeks is a result of their own similar backgrounds and views of what is 'real' and 'important'. Also, news reporters and editors use the same news agency sources and continually look at what each other is presenting. For instance, radio and television editors always look at the newspapers first thing in the morning.

So, if the news does help construct our reality, we are finding out more about how and why this is done.

## News values

These values are accepted by the people who make the news. They are **beliefs about what topics make good news** and **beliefs about how those topics should be handled**.

The topics are those which we have already seen on the news agenda. The same sort of topics tend to appear every week in most media because people in news organizations believe that they are the right sort of topics to attract the audience into reading or watching. To a fair extent it seems that they are right. But we should also remember the point that, without trying alternatives, no one really knows what the audience might be interested in. Also, although there might be a kind of agreement about types of news story it is most important to present, this still doesn't prove that a particular story has to be chosen, or that it has to be treated in the way that news stories often are.

In fact, beliefs about the handling of topics are rather more important than beliefs about what is handled, we would suggest. 'It's not what you say, but the way that you say it.'

Dominantly, news stories are handled in terms of drama, conflict and visual qualities. **Dramatization** means that the creators of the story prefer something exciting, with a main character around whom the action revolves. So, in a disaster story in a popular newspaper, for example, one might get not only the drama of action as a fire is fought and people are rescued, but also a photograph and special story angle on the fireman hero who carried three children to safety. (Perhaps he was a hero, but then it is likely that so were some of his workmates who performed deeds with less emotional 'pull' than rescuing children.)

**Conflict** is introduced into stories by having two opposing sides, preferably villains to oppose the heroes. So, for example, many political stories on television are handled in terms of opposing views (as if there could not be more than two views on some event or issue). If the leader of one political party can be set up against the leader of another, so much the better.

The tendency to handle news in this way – a belief that it is right to handle it in this way – excludes shades of opinion. Its misleading effect needs to be seen in the light of the fact that relatively few people watch the current affairs programmes which might fill in the shades of opinion. If you look at news stories around you now, you will find various examples of this treatment – perhaps the police in conflict with some social group, for example. In this instance, it might well be demonstrators of some kind. Indeed, developing the old cliché that only bad news is good news, it could be said that peaceful demonstrations are bad news for the news people – there is neither drama nor conflict.

However, the third value of news handling might make a demonstration into a good story. It could provide lots of pictures. Television and popular newspapers have been made visual media, in a sense, because **there is a preference for using picture material**.

Television must have images of some sort, of course. But still, news makers will exploit this aspect of the medium by preferring stories with pictures and by sending out cameras to obtain picture material. Newspapers do a similar thing. As we have said, the story is put together, it doesn't just happen. Choices are made about how to handle it. And the use of a large picture of, for example, a personality arriving at an airport, with but a few words to say who and why, is definitely a choice. This choice represents a belief about what makes good news handling. This is the news value.

## Gatekeeping

Among the team making the news, it is the sub-editor who has most responsibility for upholding news values, whether of content or of treatment. This person has the job of taking the general run of news stories, deciding whether they are newsworthy or not and then cutting or rewriting them as necessary to suit the newspaper and its page or the broadcast and its time slot.

**People who handle information coming into an organization are called gatekeepers. The term also assumes that they have some power to decide who gets what information and sometimes to change some of it.** People like receptionists and secretaries can be gatekeepers.

In this case of the news, the point that is being made is indeed that newsworthy material can be and is filtered and changed to suit the policies of the paper or broadcasting organization – to suit their values.

Clearly many other people can have an effect on the final content and treatment of the news. The editor, or section editors like the features editor, can also be influential and do some gatekeeping. But still the point is to draw attention to the fact that there is one group of people who are very influential in the selection and treatment of messages – of the messages that we receive from the news programme or newspaper.

## Editorializing

This term describes **the ways in which the broad opinions or points of view of the news-making organization are expressed through the newspaper or programme**. Newspapers literally have an editorial – an article in which the editor expresses opinions on a number of news stories or issues raised by such stories. There is no question that newspapers do have a point of view. They have points of view defined in terms of their support for a political position or a political party. They may also have a position or attitudes towards matters that are not overtly political. For example, they may have particular attitudes towards conservation of the environment, or the outcome of a major legal case. So, newspapers cannot pretend to be unbiased. The kinds of bias or opinion that they have can be explored through investigation of covert messages revealed in patterns of content or treatment. For instance, it is generally acknowledged that the *Daily Mail* in the United Kingdom is angled towards an audience including a high proportion of females, and towards a position on the right of the political spectrum.

In the United Kingdom the case of broadcasting is rather different. News broadcasting does not editorialize in the way that a newspaper does. There are no editorials. Presentation of news items pays attention to the ideals of balance and impartiality. Points of view should not be expressed on things that have happened, or on issues raised, especially political issues. The Acts of Parliament that brought into being the BBC and the Independent Broadcasting systems actually require this neutrality. ITN news is paid for by the commercial contracting companies, but none of them actually owns it. It is not a commercial organization itself. Many countries also follow this line of 'telling the news like it is' in news broadcasting. However, perfect balance and impartiality is impossible to achieve. Someone has to make choices about what will be presented as news. There are reasons behind the choices that are made. These reasons are based on values and opinions.

So, we would argue that news broadcasting, not surprisingly, can editorialize covertly. The very notion of balance itself is a matter of opinion. It suggests the image of a weighing device called a balance. This has two sides. But we have already pointed out that many issues and arguments have more than two sides.

Certain news items, for example those to do with sensitive political or military matters, are likely not to be handled in a balanced way. One of the most obvious examples here in Britain relates to the situation in Northern Ireland, where British troops were fighting the Irish Republican Army. There is a long list of news items and current affairs programmes which have been censored by the government or by the executives in the news organizations because they would have represented a Republican point of view. Indeed there has been a ban on any members of that organization appearing on television. (Other books on news making provide fuller evidence of this case.) The point is that one cannot talk about balance if the views of one side are privileged and the other side suppressed. It may well be that many people would agree with this handling of the news in this case. But we should not pretend that it is balanced news. In an indirect and covert way the news broadcasters are actually editorializing. By leaving things out or by weighting picture time and interviews in such a news item, they can present a point of view or a way of looking at that situation.

## 3.4 New technology

The phrases 'new technology' and 'information technology' are often used to talk about the same things. These things are devices and systems based on the microprocessor, which is behind everything from computers to coffee machines. Many of the devices one might discuss have a lot to do with communication.

### Definitions

This section is concerned with **microelectronics and its effect on means of communication and systems of communication**. Sometimes old systems and means have been changed. Sometimes a new form or medium has been created.

The camera has been transformed as an object used to create visual communication: now it can set focus and exposure automatically. The telephone system has been transformed as new equipment controls the routing of electronic signals, passing via cables and satellites to most countries in the world, available from your home.

Communication devices like the video recorder are taken for granted. They have changed our lifestyles, our culture and our ability to send and receive communication.

We want to draw attention to some of these devices and systems because they are having a considerable effect on our patterns of work and leisure and because, in many instances, these effects are taken for granted.

For example, a watch is a device for measuring time. For hundreds of years it has communicated that measurement through the symbols of two hands circling a dial marked with numbers. Suddenly there is a new generation which no longer has to learn these symbols. The digital watch communicates through number alone. More to the point, new technology has made a watch so cheap that it is a throwaway object. Every child can have one.

A pocket calculator is a little more expensive. Yet its size and computing power would have made it a miracle even twenty years ago.

New technology has only just begun transforming our lives and our ability to communicate. Fresh surprises are round the corner, as scientists have begun creating objects such as the biochip that combines living tissue and electronics, and a computer that works with light rays instead of pulses of electricity.

## Effects on mass communication

**New technology has extended the range of many means of mass communication.**

It is now possible to talk to others around the world, from one's home. The development of the telephone system already referred to, the link-ups with satellites and new cable systems have made all this possible. And the most important development which has made it possible to connect these systems with each other and with computers has been the creation of technology that makes them all speak in the language of number – **digital information**.

For example, another extension is that of electronic mail services, which connect computer users across continents, exchanging electronic letters instantly and at any time. More dramatically, we now have the Internet and its subsidiary function, the Web. This spans the world, exploiting the explosion of cable and satellite links, and so far virtually uncontrollable by governments or corporations. It and electronic mail and fax systems are now fused into one world-wide communication system, based on computers. It is used to 'talk', to provide free information, sometimes to disseminate 'stolen' information, to sell houses, to link organizations globally. It supplies pictures as well as words. It is sharpening a new cultural divide between 'haves and have-nots'. For example, students who can access the Web can do their research globally from a chair. Those who cannot are hugely disadvantaged.

New technology has changed the production methods of many of the mass media in various ways. In general, it has made production quicker and cheaper and has improved the quality of what is produced.

For example, newspapers are now put together by a few people using a sophisticated kind of word processor instead of a number of people putting together pieces of metal. Colour pictures in magazines and books are now prepared with graphics programs that allow the printer to play around with the colours before deciding on the best version, instead of involving complicated efforts with photography and chemicals. Or a newspaper like the *Financial Times* (Europe) can be put together in Paris and the results sent along a wire to Frankfurt for printing.

New technology has brought new methods of distribution of material to the audience. In producers' terms, this means they can often get to a bigger market faster. For example, movies are now distributed through cable systems such as Ten in England or Home Box Office in the United States, or through satellite channels.

New technology has created new products that are mass-produced for large audiences. For example, video games are now being marketed on a huge scale. The technology for the present games and their computers did not exist even fifteen years ago.

The medium of television makes a good case study through which to describe the effects of new technology on the media. For example, the very production of cameras, televisions and the equipment of the industry depends on new technology. Then again, the functions of a modern television set – electronic tuning, Ceefax/Oracle facilities, remote control unit – also depend on the microprocessor. Many of the most imaginative television title sequences depend on computer graphics. Electronic news gathering (using video cameras) is now commonplace. The editing of news material, and indeed anything else that is produced through video cameras, uses electronic editing which itself relies on new technology.

## Information

**New technology has meant that systems of mass communication can handle more information faster than ever before.**

Business organizations and governments have made the most use of this expensive information technology because it helps them save money or find new ways of making money. But still, all this affects us, even indirectly. It certainly affects most people in their work – for example, shop checkout tills that can also keep track of what stock is being sold.

In the United States, communication corporations offer nationwide services to business users, allowing them to pass written and graphic information from one business centre to another, via satellites. There is less and less paper moving around.

Banking is computerized. Not only does this mean that customers can do things like take out money and check their accounts without going into a bank, but also it will soon mean that banks can stop moving paper cheques around altogether.

'Data processing' is now a commonly used phrase describing the ability of computer-based technology to store vast quantities of information about things like customers, stock and financial arrangements. This information can also be recovered quickly and moved around easily.

But here one should make at least some comment on the fact that such great changes in the communication of information have many effects, not all of them good. We are not going to make a lengthy analysis of social and economic effects, but two examples should indicate the scope of problems arising.

One point is that many people are losing jobs because of new technology. Apart from general production examples, like computerized lathes that can be 'taught' to operate without human hand, there is the loss of clerical jobs as files turn from the time-consuming paper systems to electronic stores. (Of course, new communications industries and jobs compensate for this situation to some extent.)

Another point could be the dangers of the computerized credit control agencies. These store information about many citizens, some of it personal and all related to their 'credit-worthiness'. At the moment it is impossible to control what is put on file and virtually impossible to see it and correct it. The power taken by those who operate new information systems is great, and the lack of checks on this power is worrying.

The issue of who gets to use and control new communication and information systems is a major one.

## Entertainment

**New technology has extended the range of mass-produced or mass-distributed entertainment.**

A number of examples already given help to prove this point. Entertainment is a big communications business. We pay for a lot of entertainment products. And as we have suggested already, this has other consequences when one considers the covert messages about values, or the reinforcement of culture and attitudes, that come with this entertainment. For instance, video games are often designed around notions of competition, violence, war and the like: they are orientated towards young males and the values conventionally offered to this group through other media such as comics. In another example we can see how new developments tend to extend the scope and the tendencies of existing technology.

Portable personal tape recorders and CD players do for the audio tape medium what portable radio did for that medium a generation ago. And all these extensions of entertainment are also an extension and diversification of the operation of existing media systems or media owners.

## Two issues

This brings us to the first of two issues with which new technology confronts us. **Are we going to get more of the same, or will we be offered something different?**

The immediate and regrettable answer is that, on the whole, new technology hasn't done much to change patterns of ownership, means of finance or the marketing of entertainment. In this sense, new developments tend to be absorbed by the existing systems and used in the way that they always have been. For instance, CD-ROMs are most successful as an integral part of computers and used as data stores (replacing the family encyclopaedia) or as games sources (existing dedicated games machines such as the Play Station). They are also beginning to move into the film player market (replacing videotapes); and similarly to provide music albums with pictures. In the last example they will take over from music CDs, which have themselves taken over from tapes and vinyl.

One other issue worth picking out is **the question of how much new technology will give us access to its new systems, or how much control we will have over what is offered to us**. Up to now we have been in a situation where mass-communications systems and products have been effectively directed or controlled by commercial organizations, with some intervention by government. In other words, the messages are framed and sent to us without our having that much say about who does this and how. Given the large, complex and expensive operation of systems like a national telephone or television service, this is not to suggest that everyone can have a direct part in running them or producing material. At the same time it is also worth pointing out that, for example, the city of Hull runs a good, independent telephone service. Dutch broadcasting manages a system that gives minority groups some right to air time. In the UK, it is admitted officially that there are some fifty illegal radio stations operating and serving particular areas or particular minority interests. Cheap technology makes it possible to run these operations on a shoestring.

So there are signs that rather more access and control for the audience or user is possible with new technology.

It is in the new cable systems and the applications of computers that one can see the best signs of this happening. Cables are being used to carry messages from the consumer as well as to them. For instance, in some areas of the United States and Britain it is possible to shop by cable, using a keyboard and display screen. Interactive learning systems allow a student to learn at his or her own pace. Information relevant to professions such as the law is on computer file to be retrieved by the professionals at work. It is now supposed that it will only be a matter of time before the whole of society is wired up and the population as a whole has the ability to get to more information more easily than ever.

Already many western countries are wired up with fibre optic cable both within and between their major cities. These cables can carry vast quantities of digital information. It is in the continuing nature of mass communication that governments and companies are investing billions of pounds in this process because they see the advantages of being part of an 'information world'. Business sees a lot of money to be made. The same mixture of profit motives and political controls which brought in media such as television is still at work. In some respects mass communication typically becomes cheaper, faster, more 'real' (e.g. videoconferencing). But it is also typically in a state of tension between real availability and consumer control (cheap video cameras and editing), and continuing dominance by international corporations which define what we get in terms of information and, especially, entertainment.

---

### Is this the age of the image?

Hint: how much time do you spend with words or with images in a week? Count it!

---

## Review

### 1 A MASS-COMMUNICATION SOCIETY

1.1   The word 'mass' refers to the volume, scale or speed of the system, product or audience.

1.2   The significance of mass production of communication is that it also means the mass repetition of messages. The messages are sometimes about ideas and beliefs. These may influence us because they are so often repeated.

1.3   The systems or organizations of mass communication are not directly within our control as individuals, unlike face-to-face communication.

1.4   Mass communication has enabled more sending and exchange of information. But we are not necessarily able to control who sends what to us or what they do with information.

1.5   Mass communication has increased the range of entertainment available to us. But the choice of types of entertainment is not as great as it might appear. And we don't have much say in what we get.

1.6   The various means of mass communication can be seen as extensions of ourselves and of our abilities to do things like speaking, listening, writing, reading.

1.7   The media are part of our society in general. They help build up a picture of that society.

1.8   The term 'institution' refers to various organizations, most of them commercial, which control and run various aspects of mass communication, especially the media.

1.9   The media have power and influence within society because of their ability to duplicate and repeat messages and because of their ability to get to us, even into our homes.


## 2 INTERPRETING THE MEDIA

2.1   All kinds of media material, including visuals, can be described as texts, and can be 'read' to make sense of them.

2.2   The idea of mediation refers to the way that material is changed by the workings of the media organizations. This is particularly relevant to media material that is about matters of fact.

2.3   Realism, in its various forms, is important to audiences. It is made up from conventions. There is no perfect realism.

2.4   Media language refers to specific critical and descriptive terms, as used in this book.

2.5   Narrative is a part of all media texts, especially fiction. It is about storytelling, about plot and drama, about devices used to help us make up the story in our heads.

2.6   Selection and construction refers to the way that any example of the media is the result of a process where items are picked, left out and put together in a certain way. One should then look at who does this, and why.

2.7   The idea of product refers to the fact that much media material is mass-produced, like cars, and packaged and sold, like breakfast cereal.

2.8   Ownership and finance refer to the source of media messages and to where they get the money from to pay for the operation. Ownership of the media tends to be dominated by relatively few organizations, mainly commercial interests. They are concerned with profitability above all and with increasing their dominant market position. In terms of finance, advertisers are especially dominant in influencing the kind of material we get, because they pay directly for a large proportion of media operations, even though the audience always pays in the end.

2.9 There are a variety of audiences for the various output of the media. These audiences are targeted and constructed by shaping material to suit particular tastes. Audiences are active, not passive, in the way that they 'use' material. It is suggested by the uses and gratifications theory that this use is often to satisfy needs within us. The characteristics (profile) and lifestyles of audiences are researched by the media, especially advertisers, when trying to attract and persuade those audiences.

2.10 Scheduling is a device used to attract and hold audiences. It applies mainly to television and involves placing certain types of programme for certain audiences at certain times of the day or the year.

2.11 The idea of overt and covert values refers to the fact that intentionally or unintentionally not all messages in media material are obvious at first. They may be hidden. And the important messages are about values – beliefs and opinions.

2.12 People, their behaviour and their beliefs are often represented in a simplified and misleading way in popular media material. They are easy to understand, but encourage prejudice and misunderstanding. Stereotypes are created through repetition of representation.

2.13 The idea of genres is that there are certain types of media material, often story types, which are also recognizable through repeated elements which go to make them up. Genres are popular. So one should look critically at covert messages that they may contain because they are also likely to be influential.

2.14 Most censorship of the British media is voluntary and run by the media industries themselves. The government influences media output in various ways, directly and indirectly. Any kind of censorship raises important issues about, for example, how far we should insist on the right of the public to know about things that organizations such as government do not wish them to know.

2.15 Effects of the media are much discussed, mostly in relation to sex and violence. But there is little or no clear evidence that the media have any specific effect on anyone.

2.16 Ideology is a view of the world whose values work in the interests of those who have power. The media tend to project that view because of their ownership and sources of finance, because they are 'in power'. When that view and those values are accepted as a matter of course by the audience, they are said to be naturalized.

## 3 THE MEDIA: PARTICULAR EXAMPLES

3.1   Advertising uses forms of communication in order to persuade. Marketing is about overall promotion; advertising is paid-for persuasive communication; publicity refers to promotion which is not paid for. Advertising uses and perpetuates stereotypes; contains covert messages and values; creates alternative realities for its products and services; is a use of communication and may be analysed through communication terms.

Advertising seeks to change behaviour by changing attitudes. The devices for persuasion through the media are the same in principle as those we use in everyday life. Examples of these are suggesting reward or punishment, using repetition, associating ideas with approved values, providing a context of humour, trading on people's needs.

3.2   Visual communication is a dominant means of communication in the mass media. In this sense it is mainly defined in terms of representational images, often the photograph. Images give meanings through signs which can be defined in terms of camera/viewer position, structure and content. Images socialize us into the system of beliefs and values that dominates our society by presenting that society to itself. Images can also be understood through terms like denotation, connotation and anchorage.

3.3   News is important, among other media material, because it brings us information about the world, which we use to construct our view of reality and truth. News makers set an agenda of topics which become the key issues and topics for us, the audience, at a given time. News makers have news values about what are important news topics and the 'right' ways to treat these topics. We tend to accept these values uncritically. The news machine illustrates the idea of gatekeeping in action, mainly through the selection and construction work done by sub-editors. News machines editorialize, overtly in newspapers, sometimes covertly in broadcasting: that is, they take positions on certain topics and issues. These points of view can represent kinds of political bias.

3.4   New technology, as defined through applications of microelectronics, is changing mass-communications systems, including the media and their products.

It has affected mass communication by extending its range, changing its production methods, bringing new distribution methods, extending access to the audience and creating new products. New technology has greatly increased our ability to exchange and store quantities of information. This has benefited government and commerce more than the general public. It has also raised issues such as the question of data control.

New technology has extended the range of mass entertainment. It has also raised many issues relating to media product, ownership and control. One crucial question is whether it can help bring us something different, or whether we will get more of the same. Another major question is whether or not we will have more access to use of communication systems as well as control of the material we get through them.

## Debates

### Where does one draw the line between mass communication and mass media?

- One point is that if there isn't any difference then perhaps that says a lot about new technology and its effects.
- Another point has to do with the nature of audiences for communication or of users of communications – if there is a difference.
- Another point has to do with whether there is any difference so far as ownership is concerned.

WHAT DO YOU THINK?

### Has mass communication taken over our lives?

- One related issue concerns whether we see ourselves as users or consumers, or possibly both.
- A similar issue has to do with control – whether we feel in control of communication technology and the media.
- Another issue turns on whether in fact we have simply assimilated mass communication into our lives – it is part of our life and what we want.
- This debate turns on how we live our lives, using communication. Also on whether we see mass communication as being constructive or destructive – and if so, in what ways.

WHAT DO YOU THINK?

### Is there too much power in too few hands where the media are concerned?

The matter of concentration of power in the media has been talked about in this chapter, to an extent. It is such an important matter to debate, that it is worth spending more time on the idea.

- You need to go back to the question of what kind of power.
- You need to go over the basics of media ownership – who owns how much in the different media industries.
- Then you need to consider the question of what 'too much' means. The main issue here probably relates to what is done or what may be done with that power.

WHAT DO YOU THINK?

**Is our culture too much dominated by advertising and marketing?**
This debate is also in one sense about power – financial power. But it also asks one to consider how, directly or indirectly, marketing may have taken over the hallmarks of our culture – our arts, our sports, even our religions.

- One point to consider is how far advertisements have become cultural artifacts in themselves.
- Another point is about how far marketability defines whether or not a media product is made in the first place.
- A further point is about the ways in which the practice of marketing affects what is being marketed – think about the presentation of football or of music groups.

WHAT DO YOU THINK?

**Should news people be stopped from investigating and reporting people's private lives?**
This debate focuses on one aspect of the power of press and broadcasting news makers. It is about freedom of speech conflicting with a right to privacy. It is sharpened by examples such as the circumstances surrounding the death of Diana, Princess of Wales.

- One problem would be to decide who should or should not be investigated.
- Another problem would be to decide who would stop such investigations, why and when.
- Another problem is to decide what should be public and what should be private when one is talking about people who hold public office (politicians).
- Another problem is to square this debate with other beliefs such as that of 'the public's right to know'.

WHAT DO YOU THINK?

## Assignments

## Assignment One

A leading Japanese company is going to market a three-dimensional image video system. This produces apparently real images in the space of a 70 cm cube. The company intends to sell the system like all previous ones, as a package, with a library of material on hologram discs. The discs play only. The company is also negotiating with broadcasters to make the 3D system available as a substitute for conventional TV.

To reinforce your knowledge of ownership, finance and control, answer the following questions about what would happen with such a 3D system.

(a)   who is likely to own the technology and the discs?
(b)   who is likely to control the broadcasting and sales of such a system?
(c)   how will the broadcast or the home versions be paid for?
(d)   who will make money out of it?
(e)   how might the player system be marketed?
(f)   what kind of material is likely to be put out through the broadcast or homeplay versions of this system?

Don't worry if you have more than one answer to each question.

## Assignment Two

Read this copy that might have come from a news agency such as Associated Press.

---

Coach Disaster – 14 killed                               (6.30 a.m., 27.8.98)

A holiday coach returning to Britain from the south of France crashed near Ampiegne in northern France in the early hours of this morning.

The coach skidded off the main highway, N21, and plunged down an embankment before overturning. 11 of the 53 passengers were killed outright as the upper half of the coach was crushed. A further 3 passengers died on the way to hospital. Another 27 are being detained in the regional hospital near Ampiegne. The extent of their injuries is not known as yet, though it is reported that a number are on the critical list. The coach driver was among those killed.

The cause of the accident has not yet been established. A local lorry driver at the scene reports that roads were slippery with rain after a long hot spell. The driver, M. Louis Gaspard, alerted French rescue and medical services through his CB cab radio. It is said that he saved the death toll from being even higher.

Mr Brian Ackroyd, a member of British embassy staff in Paris, has gone to Ampiegne. The French minister of transport, M. Patrick Furneaux, says there will be a full investigation into the causes of the crash, which is the worst of its kind for many years. However, there have been other accidents on this stretch of road.

The dead have not yet been named. One of the survivors, 3 year old Mandy Chalker, escaped by a miracle after being thrown through a skylight ripped from the roof of the coach. She landed in a bush only slightly bruised.

Questions are likely to be raised once again about the speed of the coach and about working conditions for drivers.

END

---

You may assume that the copy would be accompanied by a wire picture showing the crashed coach. For television there is also Visnews coverage, plus an interview with the French lorry driver. You may not change the facts as given. You may elaborate on them plausibly, edit, impose style and angle on the material.

(a)    Produce an article on the crash for page two of a popular daily tabloid newspaper.
(b)    Script an item for a main television news programme, running for one minute, twenty seconds, including film and graphics.

## Assignment Three: Case Study

You should refer to the promotional photograph of the group Damage to complete this assignment.

You are working with a PR and marketing consultancy that is making a pitch for business with this increasingly successful group. As part of your preparation you carry out the following tasks.

(a)    List the possible product spin-offs which could be used to market this group and its image.
(b)    List four magazines or programmes in which the group might like to get coverage.
(c)    List five public relations devices for promoting the group.

(d)    Design a press advertisement for the Damage EP, *Wonderful Tonight*. (The song 'Wonderful Tonight' is written by Eric Clapton and is copyright of Big Life Records (1994) Ltd.)

(e)    Storyboard a fifteen-second video that will be used as the introduction to a segment of a television programme on rising groups, and about Damage in particular.

## Suggested reading

Branston, G., and Stafford, R., *The Media Student's Book*.
Burton, Graeme, *More Than Meets the Eye*, 2nd edition.
Wall, P., and Walker, P., *Media Studies for GCSE*.
See also the resources list at the end of the book.

# Chapter 6

# Communication and media skills

Thorough planning is the key stone of making a good video . . . it still depends on human creativity and imagination to make a good video – and it always will.

John Hedgecoe, *Hedgecoe On Video, 1989*

This chapter provides a general framework for practical production using various media.

There are guidelines for developing skills in writing for different formats and purposes, for effective listening, for being assertive, for designing leaflets, for making presentations, for conducting interviews, for devising questionnaires, for storyboards, for producing audio tapes, tape–slide presentations, video tapes and mounting exhibitions and for using the Net.

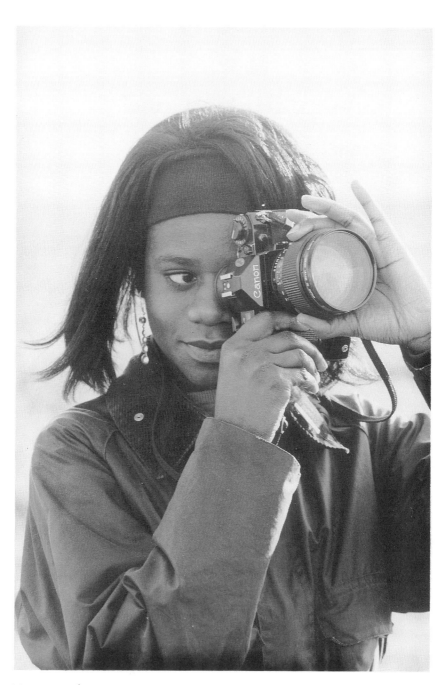

Never miss a photo opportunity

# 1 Getting started – general principles for approaching practical work

Every communication production of whatever length, complexity or simplicity is likely to come from two sources. One is the inner creative needs and visions which you have. The other is external forces – educational demands for you to make a communication project, or perhaps even because it is your job. This is a mixture of self-expression and desired outcomes from people or organizations who may have commissioned your production. You need to be well organized and clear about what you are trying to do.

If you are creating a communication project for GCSE or for A level, this remains true. You are expected to treat the activity as if you indeed have a job which depends on it. You have to develop a brief for your work, as would anyone who is working for a client. You have to keep a log evaluating what you are doing, especially in relation to your use of the medium, achievement of your aims and satisfaction of the needs of your audience. You have to research into your subject matter, the medium and the audience – to a greater or lesser degree, depending on what level you are working at.

Organization and preparation help successful communication and the process of creation. We recommend that you look at the chart summarizing guidelines for successful practical production (figure 43). The skills that you use are not just about the mechanics of designing a wallchart or using a video camera. There are other face-to-face skills used, for example, in interviewing people, explaining your work in progress, presenting your completed work to others. So in this chapter we are offering some coverage of interpersonal skills to supplement what we have written earlier.

Of course some examples of communication and audience are more or less creative and technically complicated than others. But remember that even writers of novels, for example, will do things like research their topics and background. They have a reader in their mind's eye. They block out sections of their novel so that they know in principle where the narrative is going. You will find that communication projects which focus on a particular audience with specific needs are usually the most effective in the end. The kind of project which is a 'guide to local clubs', for instance, often lapses into self-indulgence. If a local newspaper is going to publish an insert on this topic, the readers don't want a limited survey of what you get up to at the weekend. They want a range of real information, attractively presented.

So ask yourself questions like who wants to hear what I want to communicate about? What do they already know about the subject? What am I really trying to do through this communication – to inform, to warn, to entertain, to explain? It may be a mixture of these points, all of which form your aims. What is really the best medium for putting across my ideas?

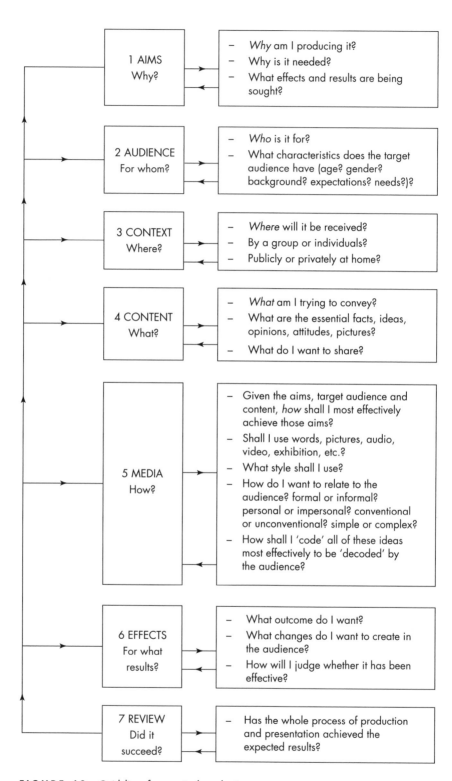

**FIGURE 43** Guidelines for practical production

Who would sponsor or pay for my communication, at least in principle? How would it actually get to the audience? You need to ask yourself both practical and creative questions – and never assume that you know the answers already!

## 2 Interpersonal skills

Chapters 2 and 3 contain information on a variety of interpersonal communication skills. These include using non-verbal communication, perceiving other people effectively and working in groups. You could refer back to these. This section develops other skills areas which should help you deal with other people.

## 2.1 Listening

All of us at some time must have accused other people of not listening to us. Since we spend virtually all of our waking hours listening (we cannot close our ears), it's worth learning to do it effectively. There is obviously more to listening than meets the ear. We listen not only with our ears, but also with our eyes and mind, using our experience and knowledge. In that sense we often do close our ears by not engaging our attention and our thinking.

**Hearing simply refers to our consciousness of sounds. Listening refers to our attempts to make sense of what we hear.** It is an active process that demands effort on our part. There has even been quite a lot said in recent years by various organizations about the importance of listening. The most famous of these has probably been the business which proclaims itself to be the 'listening bank'.

Successful listening and listening skills involve one in not only being seen to listen but in doing something about it. Try filling in the brief listening questionnaire that follows (figure 44). It should cause you to think about your own listening behaviour. This and the checklist chart (table 1) will help you realize that skilled listening to others requires action, such as giving non-verbal responses to show that you are paying attention; not shutting off when what is being said doesn't immediately grab your attention; asking for elaboration if necessary; not ignoring what people say simply because of who they are (or what you think of them!). It could be argued that not listening is a mixture of lack of skills and degrees of laziness and self-centredness.

We hope that you recognize that effective listening is something that you can control. It is as active as talking and it is something you can learn to do. There are ways you can develop your listening skills. The checklist may help.

Whatever the context, for example, a personal conversation, a group

WHEN YOU ARE TALKING TO OTHERS OR HAVING TO LISTEN TO A SPEAKER, HOW GOOD ARE YOU AT REALLY LISTENING?

Answer the following few questions – and then reflect on what your answers mean.

| | NEVER | SOMETIMES | OFTEN |
|---|---|---|---|
| Do you find yourself thinking about something else? | | | |
| Do you want to ask them questions? | | | |
| Do you interrupt them? | | | |
| Do you pretend to be listening? | | | |
| Do you think about what you want to say next? | | | |
| Do you talk a lot about the speaker's clothes and mannerisms afterwards? | | | |
| Do you talk about others being boring? | | | |
| Do you pick up on what the other person has been saying? | | | |

**FIGURE 44**  A questionnaire for listeners

meeting, a lecture, a radio or TV programme, these elements all apply. It is not easy to maintain concentration to listen effectively. It is tiring, because it calls for active attention and may demand a response.

A psychotherapist from the United States, Carl Rogers, devised a strategy for enabling people to check how effective their listening skills are. He suggested that the next time you are in an argument with someone, stop the discussion and try this experiment. Each person can speak up for him or her self only after he or she has first restated the ideas and feelings of the previous speaker accurately and to that person's satisfaction. If you try this, you may find that most of the time in our daily life we do not really listen to and understand what the other person has said to us. We have not really placed ourselves in their position in order to recognize what they feel or believe.

Being able to do this goes a long way to enabling us to be effective communicators. Our skills at receiving spoken messages from people from the media are as important communication skills as being able to present our own ideas.

## 2.2 Assertiveness

Being assertive comes into many situations where we communicate with others, not least when putting together a communication project. We want

Table 1 A guide to effective listening

| Key to effective listening | The poor listener | The good listener |
|---|---|---|
| 1 Find areas of interest | Switches off if the material seems dry or dull | Says 'what can I get out of this?' |
| 2 Concentrate on content, not delivery | Switches off if the delivery is poor | Judges content and ignores errors in delivery as far as possible |
| 3 Be patient | Tends to jump in and argue, or (mentally) disagree or reject ideas before hearing the speaker out | Doesn't judge until understanding is complete |
| 4 Listen for ideas | Listens only for facts even when the topic does not require this | Listens for central themes |
| 5 Be flexible | Takes intensive notes using only one system. Tries to write down every word | Takes few notes but uses 4–5 different systems, depending on the speaker |
| 6 Work at listening | Shows no energy output, any attention shown is faked, confuses 'hearing' with 'listening' | Works hard, exhibits active body state, engages with what is heard |
| 7 Resist distractions | Is easily distracted | Fights or avoids distractions, tolerates bad habits, knows how to concentrate |
| 8 Keep your mind open | Reacts to emotional or emotive words | Interprets or translates emotive words; does not get hung up on them |
| 9 Capitalize on the fact that thought is faster than speech | Tends to day-dream with slow speakers | Challenges, anticipates, mentally summarizes, weighs the evidence, listens between the lines to tone of voice, verbal give-aways, etc. |
| 10 Ask questions | Adopts a passive or bored attitude | Seeks to make sense of what is heard and to make clear what seems confused |

to open your mind to basic ideas about this topic, but recommend that you take on further reading if you are really interested. The main thing about being assertive is that it involves you in communicating clearly about what you want without being rude and without assuming that you will always get your own way. We think that assertiveness has a lot to do with effective interpersonal communication because it involves knowing what you want to say, saying it plainly, and not being evasive and manipulative in how you deal with others.

Assertiveness is very much related to what we have said about self, because it requires you to look at who you are and what you want in a given situation. It means that you stand up for your rights and beliefs without despising, ignoring or riding over the rights of others.

Assertiveness is often confused with aggression, especially where females are concerned. One common reason for this is that people, not least men, tend to assume that females should be submissive. One of the most common submission phrases which people use at the beginning of sentences (usually responses) is 'I'm sorry'. Often we have nothing to be sorry about and nothing to apologize for. Aggression is no better, of course. Telling someone to 'push off' if they ask you for something, even if it is unreasonable, is a good way to start an argument. If someone asks you to lend them money (and you don't want to) the best assertive response is to say briefly 'No, I don't want to'. If pressed, you might say, 'I really don't think I can afford it'. But after that, just keep on saying no. Be firm. Don't give in to attempts to blackmail you in some way. You have a right to say no, and you don't have to justify yourself. So to sum up, assertiveness skills are:

- deciding what you really want out of a given situation (particularly if it is to say no)
- saying what you want
- being brief and to the point
- using 'I' statements such as I want, I like, I think
- looking for ways round a potentially difficult situation if compromise is really OK for you – 'I can't lend you thirty pounds, but I'll lend you fifteen if you're able to pay it back next Monday'
- trying to find out what the other person wants – 'Is there something else I can help you with, if not the money?'
- being careful to sort out fact from opinion in the way that you talk. If you refuse an invitation to go to a club with a friend on the grounds that you think it is a boring place then that is not a fact. It is your opinion. So say so. Or it may be a fact that you were bored the last time that you went there.

## 2.3 Interviews

There are many books and leaflets which provide advice on how to be interviewed, especially in a job interview. The essential advice they all give is to be prepared and to anticipate as well as possible what you are likely to be asked and how you want to present yourself.

**An interview is best seen as a formal conversation; that is, it has a clear purpose and is approached systematically with a beginning, a middle and an end.**

This section is going to concentrate on how to conduct an interview rather than on how to be interviewed. Imagine that you need to interview someone to find out something he or she knows.

### Conducting an interview

#### PREPARATION

1   Be clear what you want from your interview.

2   Ensure the person to be interviewed is willing and has the information you want. If you are getting a news story, the person may not be willing to give the information he or she has. In this case, you have to use your persuasive powers and to spend more time developing their trust in you.

3   Devise likely questions in advance. Use open questions and avoid leading to a yes/no response. Always be clear and unambiguous in your questions. Try to anticipate the responses you will get.

4   Decide how you want to record the interview – written notes, audio tape, video tape, and maybe photographs.

5   Decide what you will do with the information afterwards.

6   Arrange the interview – clear date, time and place. Explain the purpose to the interviewee and how it will be recorded and used. Perhaps you might want to send questions in advance.

#### AT THE INTERVIEW

7   Introduce yourself and explain the purpose of the interview. Build up the trust and confidence of the interviewee.

8   Seek agreement on how it will be recorded and used (if you're using audio or video tape check that it is working properly).

9   Conduct the interview – clear questions, clear voice, use of non-verbal communication and layout of the room.

10  Conclude clearly, express your thanks and explain to the interviewee how the interview will be used.

11   Review the questions and answers.

12   Has it provided what you want? If not, do you need to return?

13   How can you now use it?

14   What have you learned about effective interviewing from this experience?

## 2.4 Making a presentation

'Have something to say and say it well . . . ' It sounds easy. But you may have memories of, or dread, the awful nerves when you have to stand in front of a group to give a talk. The most effective ways of dealing with nerves or fright are first to plan and prepare so you know what you are doing, second to practise giving the talk (the more you do the easier they become), and third, if necessary, use actors' techniques to relax and deal with stress. These might include testing your voice before you start; doing something totally different just before your talk to distract yourself from it; gently swinging your arms and rolling your neck to ease muscle tension; breathing deeply a few times, and thinking about the task and not thinking about yourself.

We suggest you review the early part of this chapter on getting started. All of the information there surrounding the questions of why, what, to whom, where, when and for what result, are important for making a presentation.

The following is a checklist of how you might set about giving a successful presentation.

## 1 Planning and preparing

1.1   Brainstorm for any ideas you may have on the topic. Make a list or a spider diagram with as many aspects as you can think of. Don't select or filter them at this stage.

1.2   Select and structure these jottings into the main ideas in an appropriate sequence. Think of 'hooks' for the audience's interest, decide on examples that you know will appeal to the intended audience.

1.3   Think of an interesting opening and a conclusion that your audience should remember. These could include some unusual fact, or an anecdote about something that happened to you.

1.4   Write up notes on one side of small cards, number each card and hold them together by punching a hole in the top left hand corner and using a treasury tag. There is nothing worse than dropping your notes in confusion. Avoid continuous sentences which you will read out. Make main headings, sub-headings, use numbers, use different coloured pens – anything that you think will be helpful in giving the talk.

1.5 Use visual aids such as slides for an overhead projector or a slide projector; use a flipchart, or use video or audio inserts. Keep your aids simple and try them out in the place beforehand. Pre-prepared overhead transparencies or flipchart sheets can be a great aid to the talk and a support to you. But don't use too many and do keep them simple and uncluttered. Where you can, use diagrams or pictures. If you want people to take specific information away prepare a handout which they can take with them.

1.6 Rehearse and practise for timing. This can help with nerves but overpractising the same speech can make it seem dull when you give it.

1.7 Think of your audience. Are the content, style and length of the presentation appropriate for the audience and the place?

## 2 Delivering your talk

2.1 Preparation is vital. Don't stand up and think, 'if only . . . ' Being well prepared gives you confidence and keeps down nerves.

2.2 Use the space that's available. Make sure you are visible and any aids you are using are visible. Think about the relationship you want to create with the audience.

2.3 Don't be afraid to over-act. What may seem very slow and overdramatic to you won't seem like that to the audience. Keep your expression, both in speech and in the way you present yourself, lively. Try to vary the speed and the pitch of your voice. Make sure everyone can hear you.

2.4 Use non-verbal communication, such as eye contact, smile at people, move about – but not too much, keep particular mannerisms in check. Try to be yourself and be natural. Other things which may help you are: looking just over people's heads if you are very nervous about eye contact; it is not helpful to sit behind a table, but if you are worried about standing, then it is OK to sit on the edge of the table – but avoid sitting on your hands; hands can be occupied with your check cards, but let them be free enough for use in emphasizing points.

2.5 Use audio-visual aids. They brighten up your talk and help explain things. Sometimes it is possible to use items such as a section of videotape by way of example. But the most common devices are overhead displays, flipchart displays and material which is handed out. Displays should be big and bold and brief. Remember the dangers of getting in the way of your checklist or diagram when standing near them. It is OK to use a pointer, if you need to draw attention to details. Switch off overhead projectors when not in use. If you use handout material by way of example then do decide what you want the audience to do with it. Point out what is relevant in the material and give the audience a little time to take it in. But then tell them firmly to leave the handout and that you are going on with the talk.

## 3 Reviewing the presentation

3.1  Seek feedback. You should be able to tell if people become bored or fall asleep! But ask people afterwards about your strengths and weaknesses.

3.2  Reflect on your successes and failures and analyse what went well or went badly. Had you prepared enough? Did you judge your audience accurately? Were your notes good enough? Did the aids you used work successfully? – and so on.

Some people may appear to be natural public speakers. But sometimes these people can seem to be doing it for themselves rather than for their audience. You may not feel like a natural public speaker, but through careful planning and practice you can gain these skills.

## 3 Writing skills

Many textbooks, especially for business communication, deal at length with conventions of letters, memos, notices, agendas for meetings, reports, press releases and so on. We are not going to repeat this information here; there are references at the end of this chapter and at the end of the book which you can follow up if you wish.

**The key to successful writing skills for communication is the appropriateness of what and how you write for the context and the audience. Be clear about what you want to say. Be clear about how it will be received.**

The great advantage of written communication is that it leaves a record. It stores the message for future reference. Writing does not necessarily depend on high technology, although written communication is now likely to be produced and reproduced through information technology. Using a word processor or a desk-top publishing system can ensure that whatever is produced is carefully prepared and designed for the effects you want.

Your style of writing – the choice of vocabulary, the length of sentences, the tone of language you adopt, all these reflect the relationship you want to create with your reader or readers. Often reading out loud what you have written can help capture the tone that you want. Tone is really about the relationship between you the writer and your reader. It comes out of the kind of voice that you can 'hear' when you read a piece of writing. This notion also helps define what is called style. If something is written in an ironic way or a serious way then this is evident in that voice.

## 3.1 Questionnaires

**A questionnaire is a set of written questions designed to collect information from individuals.** This information may include their personal attitudes. The questionnaire may be completed in the absence of the person who wishes to collect the data. A questionnaire can also be used as the basis for a face-to-face interview.

As always, be clear about what you want to achieve. Is a questionnaire the best way of obtaining the information you want? Make sure the questions do ask what you want to know. Make sure the results will be suitable to analyse and present. Are you asking the appropriate people?

Once you have decided to use a questionnaire, take care in designing it. Time spent in careful writing and layout and in piloting the questionnaire with a few people will save a lot of time later on. The way in which the information is collected will make a lot of difference to how easy it is to analyse and to summarize.

### Designing a questionnaire

#### 1 HEADINGS

Make clear at the top of the questionnaire where it is coming from. State who is conducting it. Make clear how the information will be used. You may want to guarantee people's anonymity and confirm that the information will not be published. State the purpose of the questionnaire.

#### 2 TYPES OF QUESTIONS

There are two types of questions: open and closed questions. An open question simply leaves the respondent to make a free statement in reply. For example, you might ask 'Why do you read a daily newspaper?' This leaves it free for the reply to cover whatever the person wishes.

There are various types of closed questions. These can lead the respondent to make a particular reply. They are much easier to analyse afterwards. There are five major types of closed questions as shown in the following examples:

(a)  *Tick one box*
     I feel that the news coverage of X was:
          biased in favour    ☐
          neutral             ☐
          biased against      ☐

(b)  *Yes–no*
     Did you find X helpful during the production?
         YES      NO
         ☐        ☐

(c)  *Rating*
     Did you find X helpful during the production?

| Very helpful | Helpful | Neutral | Not helpful | Not at all helpful |
|:---:|:---:|:---:|:---:|:---:|
| ☐ | ☐ | ☐ | ☐ | ☐ |

(d)  *Checklist*
     Tick as many boxes as necessary:
     What did you like about the project?
         More freedom than usual                ☐
         Being able to work on my own            ☐
         Being able to get on with my work       ☐
         Discussing my work with the teacher     ☐

(e)  *Ranking*
     The following statements have been suggested as relevant to project
     work. Put them in order of importance: put 1 alongside the statement
     you consider is most important, 2 alongside the next most important,
     etc.
         Improves practical skills               ☐
         Makes work more interesting             ☐
         Helps you become more independent       ☐
         Improves ability to work under pressure ☐

It is worth noting that open questions are quicker and easier to write, they
give more freedom in answering, and they do not have predetermined
answers. But they are more difficult to analyse, especially when you have a
large sample.


3 WRITING QUESTIONS

It is important that questions are:

     Easy to understand
     On one specific point
     Concise
     Clear and unambiguous
     Not in negative form
     Without bias

The instructions for completing the questionnaire must also be clear, concise and unambiguous. The layout must be open and attractive with plenty of room for replies. You should also make them easy to process and analyse afterwards.

### 4 TRIALLING

When you have drafted a questionnaire it is essential to test it out with a small sample of the target audience before you actually use it. You may find that questions you thought were clear, unambiguous and without bias were not. You may pick up useful hints for improving the questionnaire from the reactions of other people.

Although the responses you have may not be statistically valid, they can often provide you with useful information as part of producing a communication artifact.

### 5 COLLECTING AND PRESENTING THE RESULTS

When you draft the questions always keep in mind how you will bring together and present the responses. If you have a hundred or more responses it can be a big task.

With open questions you will need to summarize the general points and indicate how many of the total respondents agreed with the ideas.

With closed questions you will need to count the responses and convert to percentages, for example, 60 per cent said yes and 40 per cent said no. It is also useful to convert these percentages to a diagrammatic presentation with bar charts or pie charts.

## 3.2 Writing scripts (radio)

Before reading this section, try to find a radio and tune into your local commercial station. Listen to a selection of the advertisements.

What have you heard? We think you may have heard a mixture of music, some variety of voices, and some dialogue or drama. . . . You may have found the use of an accent or dialect or the selling tone of a voice annoying. The best radio advertisements are carefully scripted for maximum impact in thirty or sixty seconds. Words are chosen to create a quick positive impression and for ease of listening.

In the earlier section on listening skills (see pages 223–4) we concentrated on ways of improving listening skills. Here we shall say something about the skills of scripting which help people to stay listening attentively.

You may be preparing a script for reading or recording as part of a slide sequence, or as a voiceover on a video tape, or as an audio tape by itself.

## Checklist for writing a script

1  As always, be clear about what you want to say and how you want to say it. See figure 43. Look at the sample radio script (figure 45).

2  You are not writing an essay so the conventions of properly structured sentences and paragraphs with a beginning, a middle and an end don't apply.

3  Be direct, clear and simple. Write for a speaking voice. Use short sentences, natural speech rhythms and easily understood language. Obviously if it is a technical topic, you will have to use appropriate words to describe it. But only use jargon if you know that the target audience will understand it.

4  Keep paragraphs short.

5  Read out aloud as you write it.

6  Use more than one voice if possible. You can simply use a different reader, or you may be able to create some dialogue between two voices, or a conversation between more than two voices.

7  Use sound effects and/or music. Remember those radio adverts which you listened to. They may have crammed lots of different sound effects into just a few seconds.

8  Use vivid language. Stress the ideas you want to convey. Repeat main ideas to make sure people hear them.

9  Be prepared to leave gaps. You may want to use music to fill them.

10  Annotate your script with instructions on how you want it to be read or recorded. You can obtain published radio scripts or TV scripts which you can look at to see how they are set out. You can use your own notes for yourself so you know what you intended.

11  Record it and listen to it. Play it to one or more of the intended audience to get their response. Amend it in the light of their feedback.

As with all the communication skills we are discussing here, the more you practise it the easier it will become and the more effective you are likely to become at producing a script.

## 4 Design skills

In this section we are not attempting to provide an introduction to graphic design or desk-top publishing. We are simply seeking to provide a checklist of guidelines for producing formats such as booklets, leaflets or brochures. The resource list at the end of the book will indicate sources of information if you want to research further.

**The creation of a successful brochure requires the combination of words and pictures to form an attractive effect and to convey the ideas that are needed.** As always, being clear about your purpose, your target audience and how the brochure will be used is essential.

*(FADE UP EXTERIOR ACOUSTIC, SKYLARKS HEARD DISTANTLY. CLOSER TO, THE*
*RUSTLING OF BUSHES AS A MAN BREAKS THROUGH)*

| | |
|---|---|
| MAN: | *(Close to mike, pants heavily)* |
| JOHNSON: | *(A little away)* You're late. |
| MAN: | *(Sharp intake of breath)* |
| JOHNSON: | You are precisely two minutes and fifty seconds late. |
| MAN: | There was a hitch. The train was late. Where the devil . . . |

*(BUSHES RUSTLE AGAIN)*

| | |
|---|---|
| JOHNSON: | *(Approaching)* Right behind you. I was waiting. |
| MAN: | I told you, the train was delayed. I came as quickly as I could. |
| JOHNSON: | And the old lady? |
| MAN: | It's all right. She just caught it. |
| JOHNSON: | *Just* caught it? |
| MAN: | *(Wearily)* First-class compartment, three carriages from the front, corner seat facing the engine. A non-smoker, of course. Just as you said. |
| JOHNSON: | Good. |

*(A PAUSE)*

| | |
|---|---|
| MAN: | So what now? |
| JOHNSON: | So what now? That's all. You're finished. |
| MAN: | Finished? But I thought – |
| JOHNSON: | *(Softly)* I said, you're finished. |

*(A PISTOL FIRES CLOSE TO MIKE. CUT TO THE SCREAM OF A SIREN AS A DIESEL*
*TRAIN RUSHES PAST. CROSSFADE FROM CLATTERING WHEELS TO INTERIOR*
*OF TRAIN, A CLOSE ACOUSTIC IN WHICH TRAIN NOISE IS MINIMUM.*
*HOLD BRIEFLY TO ESTABLISH)*

| | |
|---|---|
| MISS TREE: | *(Gently, close to mike)* Young man. |
| YOUNG MAN: | I beg your pardon? . . . Oh, I see. |
| MISS TREE: | Thank you so much. But it is a non-smoker. I always make a point of insisting, you know. Trains nowadays are so dirty anyway, don't you think? |

**FIGURE 45**  Specimen page of a radio script (drama)

We suggest that you collect some leaflets and brochures from shops and offices and from community centres, and analyse what you believe are their successes and failures. Look at the typefaces and the lettering as well as the visuals and the general layout.

It is very useful to create **layout sheets** to help you visualize what the finished product will be like. Indeed these can be a part of your design package because however good your **mockup** is, it is unlikely that you can get it to professional printing standard. Layout sheets are usually bigger than the finished page size. This size is drawn on the sheet, and the space around the real page size lines can be used to put in notes. Areas of text and graphics are just sketched in outline on the page, so that their proportions and placing are clear. These blocks can be keyed by numbers (or letters for illustrations) to the writing and pictures which you have on other sheets. Big headings may be written out. The surrounding notes, perhaps with arrows pointing onto the page area, say things about intended final qualities such as, type face and size, use of colour, design of logo, details of graphic devices such as borders. This approach emphasizes the fact that you are designing, and do not necessarily have to have artistic or technical skills in order to communicate your vision of the particular print format.

## Checklist for brochures

1    Decide on the *content* including words, pictures and diagrams. These may have to be amended in the light of the practicalities and the cost of reproduction. But it is worth beginning with the impact you want to make. Try out rough scribbled versions to visualize how you want it to look. You may want it to be a formal, carefully laid out document or you may want it to be much more personal and quirky.

2    Decide on *the format and the layout*. These include the size of the page, the number of pages, how they will be folded or stapled. It's useful to try a mock-up with blank sheets to get the look of it and to get the page sequence right.

3    Be clear about *the front and the back*. Have some sort of introduction and some sort of conclusion. People want to know how to use it. In textbooks on advertising it's often suggested that an effective advertisement attracts attention, holds interest, creates desire and leads to action. It's often worth thinking what your brochure is doing to attract attention and what action you want from the people who have read it or seen it.

4    Decide *how it will be reproduced*. Will it be black and white or colour? How many will you print? Will you be able to print photographs effectively? There are a whole lot of practicalities to deal with. It is worth experimenting with your masters and a photocopier.

5    Be *sparing with colour* (maybe use coloured paper, which is cheaper than colour printing or copying).

6    Leave space around images or blocks of text, so that they stand out against the background colour, and do not crowd the page too much, especially at the borders.

7    Think how you will handle *the text on the page* – e.g. colours, type size, typeface, borders, etc.

8    *Create the final master*. Use one side of paper. Always use the same size of paper for the masters. Make sure the sequence is clear and leave wide margins especially where it may be stapled or folded.

9    Experiment with any photocopying that you want to do, especially to get material round the right way, and to get it facing properly if you are printing both sides of a sheet (as opposed to doing a straight pasteup).

10   Test a *pilot copy* of the brochure with your intended audience.

Desk-top publishing is revolutionizing our ability to lay out type and pictures. If you can get access to it, try out some experiments. The instruction manual will give you some help.

However you don't need a desk-top publisher to create an attractive brochure. Pen and paper and cut-and-paste can still lead to successful productions. You can cut out type from magazines, or you can buy sheets of transfer lettering from any stationer.

You can also use any basic word-processing package to print out text, even to arrange it, up to a point. You can then cut and paste what you have produced. The advantage of using word processing is that you can go on experimenting and printing until you get the size and the look of it as close as possible to what you want.

## 5  Storyboarding

Storyboards are sketches of picture sequences, perhaps with some written notes on the visuals and sound (see figure 46). They are relevant to creating items such as title sequences, adverts, action sequences, tape–slides. Storyboards come in two versions of detail. The looser is where the story-board frames illustrate key shots in a longish sequence. The tighter (and easier to handle) version is where every frame is a shot, or even two parts of an elaborate shot involving a moving camera. Professional film storyboards may have only the pictures for the sequence. But we recommend a version more like television storyboards, where you write notes on the shot and the scene to the right of the sketch frame (see figure 49).

This approach enables one to use words to make clear what the visuals intend. Of course it helps to be able to draw, but storyboarding – especially for communication/media courses – is about visualization and design. It is OK to draw stick people. If you can't sketch the right angle on a scene then describe it alongside. This brings us to visual language.

You do need to be able to use basic descriptive terms and abbreviations of these.

Everyone 'knows' this visual language because you see it happening every day – including in most comics. With your storyboard you should number every frame, explain how 'close' the shot is, explain the camera position/audience point of view if necessary, explain any camera movements, explain links between shots. The next sections describe these items.

The following sequence is from a film called *Clandestine Throes*, written and directed by Simon Dennis, which tells the story of three boys who follow a mysterious man they believe to be a hit-man on the way to one of his 'jobs'. These storyboards show the scene where one of the boys first sees the man.

1 Establishing wide shot (WS) of a Gents' toilet door inside a cinema. The camera slowly tracks in as tense, eerie music begins.

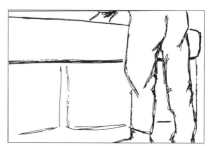

2 Int. toilets. Low angle mid shot (MS) of a man's legs in black trousers. We pan up . . .

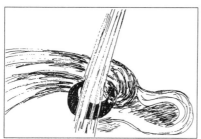

3  . . . to reveal the man dressed totally in black standing at a sink.

4 Close-up (CU) of man's belongings beside sink.

5 CU of blood being washed down sink.

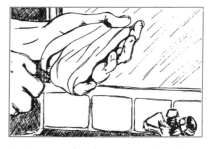

6 CU as man bandages his bleeding hand.

7 MS of reflection in mirror of man clenching fist. Pan up and pull out of focus to . . .

8 . . . man's blurred face as he turns his head. We hear the door opening.

**FIGURE 46** An example of a storyboard

## Proximity/framing

Extreme close-up (ECU) – eyes
Close-up (CU) – head
Medium close-up (MCU) – head and shoulders
Medium shot (MS)
Medium long shot (MLS)
Long Shot (LS)

## Shot types

**Establishing shot** – shows a scene/location and establishes where characters are within the scene.

**Cutaway shot** – shows some significant detail off to one side of the main scene, like the face at the window behind a character.

**Two shot** – describes a conventional framing of two characters, probably in conversation.

**Subjective shot** – is one where the viewer believes they are seeing what a characters sees.

## Camera position

Is about the angle of the camera on a scene and the point of view (POV) of the viewer/camera. Usually this is commented on only when it is quite dramatic. So if the POV is from a balcony down into a square then it could be described either as, e.g., Evita's POV from balcony to crowd below, or as high camera angle past balcony and down on to crowd.

## Camera movements

**Pull in/pull out** (also **zoom**) – strictly the lenses moving, not the camera. Brings the subject closer or further away.

**Track in/track out, track sideways** (also **dolly**) – the camera moving on a trolley and rails. Gives different effect from zooms and pans.

**Tilt up/down** – the camera pivots vertically up or down something like a skyscraper.

**Pan right/left** – the camera pivots horizontally across a scene.

**Crane shot** – the camera is on a crane, and so – 'camera cranes across square and into hotel window'.

## Shot links

These terms are in effect about editing. Professionally it is assumed that there is a cut between shots unless it says otherwise. You can write your instructions between one frame and another. Electronic video allows one to do many complicated changes such as when one picture zooms towards us out of the middle of the previous one. But the basic repertoire of links are these:

> **Cut to** – the sequence 'jumps' from one picture to another.
> **Dissolve/mix** – one picture merges into another.
> **Fade in/out** – the picture goes slowly to white or black, and the next
> one comes in.

You can learn a lot about storyboards from watching adverts and titles on TV. But basically we would advise you to learn to vary your proximity and angle: it is boring to watch a whole sequence of medium shots.

## 6 Taking photographs

If you are taking a Communication or Media Studies course you are more than likely to be using a stills camera of some sort – perhaps to produce some slides for a tape–slide presentation. This section aims to give you a brief guide to using a 35mm (Single Lens Reflex) camera (SLR), as well as talking about flashguns, compact cameras and different techniques for taking photographs (for example, how to take professional-looking portraits).

### 6.1 The camera

Unless you have your own camera, it is likely that you will use a college one. There are so many different cameras available on the market today, that it is impossible in this book to explain how to use each of them in detail. There will probably be an instruction manual available with the college camera, so if in doubt consult that. This section will teach you in general terms how to use an SLR camera.

First, here are a few technical terms that you may find useful.

**Aperture**: A series of blades inside the *lens* that open and close to let in different amounts of light. The size of the hole in the middle of the aperture governs the *depth of field*. The aperture is measured in *f*-stops; typically *f*1.8 to *f*22. The higher the number, the smaller the hole.

**Depth of field**: The range of things in focus, governed by the size of the *aperture*. For example, if you focus a *wide-angle* 28mm *lens* at one metre, and set the *aperture* at *f*8, the zone of focus will be from 0.8 metres to 1.5 metres – everything in between those two distances will be in focus. With the same lens's aperture set at *f*22, everything from 0.6 metres to ∞ (infinity) will be in focus; virtually everything in the *frame* will be sharply defined.

**Film**: There are three main types of film: colour print, colour slide and black and white print. Your choice of film depends on what you want the end result to look like. For example a slide film is imperative for a tape–slide presentation, while colour print film is good for staging an exhibition on display boards. Black and white film is good for 'atmospheric' shots, and is easy to develop yourself.

**Film speed**: Measured in ASA or ISO (which give the same figure), the film speed is written on the outside of the film box. The range of film commonly available has an ASA rating from about 25 ASA to 3200 ASA. The higher the number, the more sensitive the film is to light; however, the faster the film, the harsher the 'grain'. Basically, grain is the number of 'dots' that make up the film. With faster films (ASA rating of more than about 1000), the dots become bigger, and therefore more obtrusive. Generally speaking you should use a 100 ASA for outdoors shooting in the summer, 200 ASA for outdoors shooting in the winter, and 400 ASA for indoors.

**Flashgun**: A portable light source that usually sits on top of the camera to provide a short burst of light, to illuminate an indoor or night scene that would be too dark to photograph otherwise. There are several different types of flashgun that will be covered in detail later.

**Frame**: On an SLR camera what you see is what you get; you are actually looking through the *lens*. The *frame* is the area that will be shown on the final uncropped photograph.

**Lens**: The series of glass elements that focuses light onto the film. With an SLR camera these are interchangeable. There are four main types of lens: the wide-angle, standard, telephoto and zoom. The *standard lens* is the one that you will use most. It approximates the view of the human eye, and has a focal length of 50mm. The *telephoto* lens gives a narrow angle of view, and due to its magnification power is good for taking subjects that are far away. It has a focal length from 85mm to 2000mm – the larger the number, the greater the magnification. The *wide-angle lens* gives a broad angle of view, so is useful when you want to include a lot in a photograph, but are unable to stand back too far. It ranges typically from 20mm to 35mm; the one you are most likely to have in a college SLR kit is a 28mm. A *zoom lens* is useful as it has a variable focal length, thereby making it effectively several lenses in one. There are two types: the wide-angle zoom, that ranges from about 28 to 70mm, and the telephoto zoom, which ranges from 70 to 210mm. These two lenses are really all you need for most photography, although because their *apertures* do not let in so much light (due to the lens's construction), they are not well suited for taking pictures in dark conditions.

**Tripod**: Camera support with three legs to keep the camera steady.

**The four main different types of SLR camera:**

1   *The all-manual version* (e.g. Pentax K1000, Praktica MTL50). With this camera, you have to alter the shutter speed dial and aperture ring in order to provide the correct exposure for the lighting conditions. Inside the viewfinder there are either two needles that you have to align to achieve correct exposure, or a series of lights that serve a similar purpose. The lights are normally a green one showing correct exposure, with two red + and – signs either side indicating over or underexposure.

2   *The semi-automatic* (e.g. Olympus OM10, Minolta X300, Canon AE1). With the semi-automatic camera, half the work is done for you. There are two types: shutter priority and aperture priority. With aperture priority you set the aperture you want, and the camera will select the shutter speed necessary for correct exposure. Shutter priority works on a similar principle, although this time you select the shutter speed you require. The semi-automatic is a good camera to use for quick shots, as you only have one function to worry about. With the aperture-priority camera, you are in full control of depth of field.

3   *The program camera* (e.g. Minolta X700, Pentax P30n, Canon AE1 Program). This camera sets both the shutter speed and aperture for you, according to the light level. This allows you to concentrate on composing the photograph. The main drawback is that you lose control of the aperture and shutter speeds; but most program cameras have an aperture/shutter-priority mode as well, so you have the best of both worlds. Program mode is very useful for shooting quick moving action, as you only have to focus.

4   *The autofocus program* (e.g. Canon EOS600, Minolta Dynax 7000i, Nikon F401). These cameras have lenses that focus themselves automatically. They usually have semi-automatic and program modes, thus allowing you to concentrate on the framing of the picture. However, they are fairly expensive to buy, so your college may not have one of these.

## 6.2 Taking the picture

After familiarizing yourself with the camera you are going to use, you are ready to take your first pictures. Here's a brief checklist before you start:

1   Is there a film loaded?
2   Is it the right sort for what I want to do? (See page 241 'Film'.)
3   If you have to set the film speed (ASA) manually (you do on most of the cameras listed above), then remember to set it at the right setting. If you don't your pictures will either be over or underexposed.
4   Is the lens focused?

5   Have I got the right lens on for the picture I want to take? (A rough guide follows below.)

6   How much depth of field do I want? (See page 240 for details.)

7   Is the camera set on the right setting (e.g. manual, semi-automatic, etc.)?

Rather than influence your picture-taking technique directly, we would like to suggest a few good practices for successful picture taking.

Make sure that the frame is filled. One of the most common problems with 'bad' photographs is that the main subject is just a small object bang in the middle of the picture; there is too much wasted space around the sides of the frame. Whenever possible move in close to your subject, and if this is not feasible, fit a telephoto lens to make the subject bigger in the frame.

Good exposure is necessary for all photographs, but with slide film it has to be especially accurate because the film has less exposure latitude. One of the main problems occurs when there is an especially dark or light object occupying a large part of the frame. The camera's built-in exposure system reads too much from the light or dark subject, and the result can be disappointing. An example of this is when there is a large amount of sky in a picture. The camera takes a reading from the sky, so the ground (which is more than likely to have the main subject on it) comes out too dark. The best way to remedy this is to go right up to your subject, and set the camera's exposure by taking a reading right next to it. You can then reframe your shot (making sure not to alter the exposure), and the resulting picture will be much better exposed. If you are unable to approach the subject, then take a reading from something that looks similar – the ground nearby, or even your hand.

Do not be afraid to tilt the camera upright or even diagonally. A set of photographs that are all horizontal can look very boring after a while – do not be afraid to experiment with different ways of tilting the camera. Try crouching on the floor, standing on a chair or even trying a new angle from a step-ladder when taking a photograph of something. The different angle could make the difference between an interesting and an outstanding image. One possible suggestion to get you started is to use a wide-angle lens, and shoot your subject from a very low angle. This will make virtually anything dramatic.

One of the main things that can ruin a picture very easily is camera shake. This is caused when the camera is not being held steady, and the result is a blurred, out of focus print. There is a very simple rule that will eliminate camera shake: never use a shutter speed lower than the focal length of the lens. For example, if you are using 135mm telephoto, do not use a shutter speed of less than 1/125 second. If you do then you are in danger of camera shake. If you cannot have a faster shutter speed than 1/60 second, and the aperture is at its widest setting (i.e. the smallest number on the aperture scale), then you have three choices: use a faster film, put the camera on a tripod or use a flashgun.

## 6.3 The flashgun

If you do a lot of photography indoors or when it is quite dark, then a flashgun becomes a necessity. Most flashguns are powered by batteries, so if you are going to be taking a lot of photographs with flash, remember to check the batteries before shooting, and ideally take a spare set. There are three main types of flashgun:

1   *Manual units*: with these, you have to set the aperture on the lens according to the distance the subject is away from the camera. There should be a chart on the back of the flashgun where you can read off the distance and, according to the film speed, set the aperture as written. The camera also has to be set at its flash synchronization shutter speed (normally highlighted by a little lightning bolt symbol, or the letter 'X' next to it). The most common speed is 1/60 second.

2   *Semi-automatic units*: there should be two settings on the back of the flashgun, that encompass a certain distance range, for example: 0.6 metres to 3 metres, and perhaps 3 metres to 8 metres. Each one of these two settings has its own specific aperture. For example, $f8$ for the first setting, and $f5.6$ for the second. There is a sensor built into the front of the flashgun, and as long as the subject is within the distance range, and the aperture is correctly set, then the subject will be correctly exposed. Some semi-automatic flashes set the camera sync. speed for you (you can generally tell that they do if a lightning bolt symbol shows up in the camera viewfinder), but if not, you will have to set it yourself.

3   *Program flashguns*: these flashguns are the most easy to use, as they work out all the exposure details for you. When you push the camera shutter button down, the flashgun emits a small infra-red impulse that the flashgun uses to work out exposure. The details are processed in milliseconds, so all you have to do is point and shoot; no calculations or settings are necessary. These flashes only work with program cameras however.

## 6.4 Specific techniques for certain types of photography

It is more than likely that you will have to take certain types of pictures during your course, and this section aims to give you a few hints towards taking professional-looking shots.

*Portraits.* You will probably be trying to make the portrait as flattering as possible, so the first thing is to select the best lens for the job. If you want to shoot a head and shoulders portrait, then the telephoto (or a telephoto zoom) lens is best, because it flattens perspective. Although you may be standing quite a way away from your subject, rest assured that this is the best lens for the job. Another good practice is to concentrate on the subject by blurring the background out of focus using depth of field. This means using the widest aperture (smallest number) possible.

If you want a full length or sitting down portrait, then use a 50mm lens. This allows you to get everything in without having to stand too far away. Again use depth of field to blur the background, and do not be frightened to shoot from a higher position than your subject; this can result in an interesting image. Two golden rules in portrait photography are to ensure that the subject's eyes are in focus and turn the camera vertically to get the best frame-filling results.

*Landscapes/buildings.* The main bit of advice here is fill the frame. Many people say that you can only photograph landscapes with wide-angle lenses, but this is untrue. Telephoto lenses are good for landscapes, as they allow you to isolate a particular part of the subject. Zoom telephotos are especially good, as they allow you to crop the image as you like by altering the focal length. Remember to be careful of the exposure if there is a large expanse of sky in the picture.

*Sport/action.* With action photographs, you will probably want to freeze the action still. This can be done by using as fast a shutter speed as possible. With an aperture-priority camera this can be done by selecting the widest aperture the lens will allow. To get in close to the action, you will have to use a telephoto lens, so a fast film (say 400 ASA) would be advisable. During the darker winter months, a film like Kodak Ektar 1000 may be necessary.

As well as freezing action, you can pan to create an interesting image. Panning (like a video camera) is where you follow the subject, but with an SLR camera you use a slowish shutter speed (like 1/60 second) to blur the background. This technique may require some experimentation, but the results can be spectacular.

*General photography.* If you are not really sure what you will be shooting, then you will need to be adequately prepared for virtually any situation. A good lens to use would be either the wide-angle zoom, or just a simple wide-angle prime lens. This allows you to fill the frame without having to move too far away. Set the camera ready for use, so that you can take pictures as quickly as possible. With a manual camera, this is not very easy; but with an aperture priority you can set the aperture to about $f5.6$, which allows reasonable depth of field. A program camera is ever-ready.

## 6.5 The compact camera

This final section briefly talks about the compact camera, which has recently become a worthy alternative to some SLR cameras. Most compact cameras have autofocus, a built-in flash and automatic film advance. This allows the user simply to 'point and shoot', thereby making them very quick to use, but you cannot change the lenses on a compact camera, so they are not as versatile as the SLR. Nevertheless, for most general situations, the compact camera is quite good enough.

Because on most compact cameras everything is done for you, there are only two main things to remember when using an autofocus compact:

1   Ensure that the focus circle (always in the middle of the frame) is on the subject you want to be in focus. If you have an off-centre subject, remember to do a 'focus lock' on it before taking the shot (a focus lock is where you push the shutter button half-way down to lock the focus at a certain distance, before reframing the shot).

2   Remember not to put your finger over the flash or the lens itself. With an autofocus compact, you are not actually looking through the lens (as you would with an SLR), so you must be sure that nothing is obscuring it.

## 6.6 Electronic cameras

It is worth knowing that these cameras – like the Quiktake – are increasingly available and being bought by educational institutions. They are very easy to use and there is not much to go wrong. Because they record visual information digitally, they have to be linked to a computer to screen the pictures and to a printer to make a hard copy. There are definite limits to quality compared with ordinary cameras (unless you have a really expensive professional version). But then once in the computer, and with a program like Photoshop, you can manipulate the images fairly easily. It is possible to change a picture, add things to it, put it in with text.

There seems to be little doubt that domestic quality will go up and prices will come down, eventually to the point where existing conventional cameras will disappear. This has already largely happened in the image reprographics industry.

At this time of writing we have opted not to go into further details of the use of the camera (dead simple) or the relevant programs (more complicated). But if you can get hold of one of these cameras, can use an Apple computer system, and get a copy of the book *Mac for Dummies* (Pogue 1994), then you could learn a lot about image manipulation and desk-top publishing. Certainly the authors' students in further education are doing this as a matter of course. And all degree-level communication and media courses have moved this way, or will have to soon.

# 7 Audio-visual production

Here, what we are seeking to do is to give you guidelines for creating your own productions. One of the main reasons for producing materials as a student of communication is to experiment with equipment and to experiment with conventions of communication. For example, if you and a group decided to produce a news magazine or some advertisements you might 'naturally' follow broadcast conventions. But you might want to seek to challenge those conventions and to create your own individual style of presentation.

Technical limitations may cramp your style. What is important is your creative planning and individual ideas. Access to the means of home production is now greater than ever before. Most schools and colleges can now give access to audio and video recording equipment. In our experience, there are usually frustrations between the ideas we want to create and the limitations of technical equipment and our abilities in using it. This does not prevent the whole practical production from being great fun and enabling us to learn a good deal about how mass-media products are created.

This section is not going to give technical details about a range of equipment. You can obtain that elsewhere, indeed from equipment manuals. We aim to provide some basic checklists that will help you to use audio-visual equipment more successfully.

## 7.1 Producing audio tapes

To produce an audio tape you obviously need a cassette recorder and a microphone. It helps a great deal if you have a second direct-link cassette player to record from tape to tape and also a remote mike.

Let us imagine you are going to produce ten minutes of sound about the area where you live for people who may be thinking of moving into your locality. If the tape turns out well, you might be able to sell it to a local estate agent who can lend it to customers to play on their car cassette players. Figure 47 provides a flow chart of how you might go about producing this sound tape.

Listening to pre-prepared cassettes and radio broadcasts, particularly from local radio stations, will provide you with ideas of how to produce your own. You may, of course, seek to do it differently from the broadcasts.

If you have access to a sound studio and/or mixing equipment it is much easier to combine sounds, music and voice-overs, but you can still do this with one or two cassette recorders. For example, you can play music and speak over it so that both are picked up by a simple recording mike.

As with all of these audio-visual production skills, keep experimenting and trying out ideas.

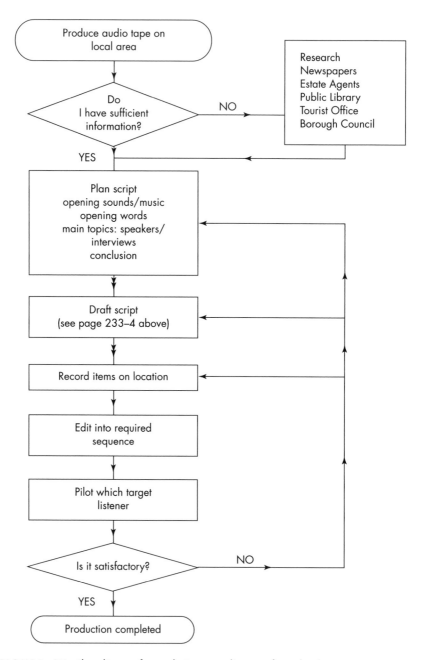

**FIGURE 47** Flow diagram for producing an audio tape of your local area

## Practical checklist

Check your batteries
Check your microphone before you record for real
Check the record button is engaged
Avoid outside noises

## 7.2 Producing a tape–slide sequence

If you visit tourist centres, museums and galleries, or historic sites, you will probably have seen professionally produced tape–slide sequences. These often use several stacked projectors which are electronically controlled for precise fading and picture build-up, with stereo sound and orchestrated light shows to create an all-embracing environment. Examples of these sorts of productions can be seen at the exhibition centre for the Thames Barrier in London, at the Clovelly Experience in Cornwall, England, or indeed at a whole range of general exhibitions. Try to visit places where you can see fully professional productions.

There is a tendency to consider that video film has replaced the still image and the sound tape, but this still provides a presentation that is effective and comparatively easy to produce. Tape–slide has the advantage that you can update individual slides and sound track without a complete revision of the whole production.

### Guidelines for producing a tape–slide sequence

In this section we shall confine ourselves to a single projector and tape production.

1   **Consider the general treatment** which you are seeking. Decide on your overall conception of what you want to say and how you want to say it. All of this is in the context of your target audience and how the production will be used. Will it be viewed individually or in a group? With this in mind, begin your research.

2   **Research**
    *Visual research*: whatever the topic, the quality of the images is a crucial factor for final success. Before you set off with camera in hand (or commission someone else to take the photographs for you), you need to list the sort of images you want. These are likely to include people, groups of people, places, objects, documents, maps, cartoons and so on. Be as varied as possible in your collection of images. You don't want to create a sequence that looks like a collection of holiday slides, all landscapes and personal snapshots. Think about camera angles. Think about different ways of using long shots or close-ups of the same places or

objects. Remember the frame of the slides is what you will get back. You cannot crop it like a photo print.

*Sound research*: obviously the quality and content of the script is the other crucial factor for final success. See pages 233–4 for ideas on writing a script. Whenever appropriate, you should also seek to record music and sound effects and 'real voices' to associate with the topic. Your research should lead you to a variety of audio and visual impressions.

3    **Planning**: the planning of the sequence with a clear beginning, middle and end for any time-based production goes hand in hand with the research. You will now want to take stock of the materials you have assembled and assess what you still need in order to realize your over-all treatment. Only when you feel you have sufficient raw material should you begin scripting and assembling the slides for the final version.

4    **Storyboard**: look at what we have said in section 5 above. Figure 48 provides an example of a storyboard blank sheet on which you can make sketches and explain the basics of visuals and sound.

5    **Script**: when the storyboard is completed to show the general shape of the programme, you can begin detailed scripting using the chosen images and approximate allocations of time per slide. Whilst the script is likely to be a voice-over commentary for most tape–slide sequences, use dialogue, interviews and sound effects whenever available. Depending on the purpose of the sequence it's also possible to pro-duce one that has no verbal script, that simply uses music and sound effects for the whole of the sound input. Remember to make the sound overlap slides as much as possible – this helps the continuity of the production.

Figure 49 gives an example of an all-purpose outline script. In this case the slide shots are held for a relatively long time because of the mechanics of slide changing and to allow for the voice-over [VO]. An advert sequence would run much faster – maybe twenty-two seconds altogether. It is possible to extend the boxes to put in all the narration or dialogue. But usually it is easier to make another script version for examples like documentary and tape–slide, where there may be a lot of narration. In this case you would mark the slide shot numbers (and therefore changes) over the narrator's words.

6    **Recording**: the successful effect of a tape–slide sequence depends on the creative combination of images and sound, so time spent ensuring these complement each other is time well spent. The script must be recorded with the slides in view and you may find the planned time allocations in your storyboard need revising in the light of the actual

| | | |
|---|---|---|
| Programme title: | Individual /group: | Sheet of |

| Shot No. ☐ | Length of shot (Secs) ☐ | Shot description | Action |
| | | | _____ |
| | | | _____ |
| | | | _____ |
| | | | _____ |
| | | Camera angle/ movement | Sound/ Script in/out |
| | | | _____ |
| | | | _____ |
| | | | _____ |
| | | | _____ |
| Transition to next shot ☐ | | | _____ |

| Shot No. ☐ | Length of shot (Secs) ☐ | Shot description | Action |
| | | | _____ |
| | | | _____ |
| | | | _____ |
| | | | _____ |
| | | Camera angle/ movement | Sound/ Script in/out |
| | | | _____ |
| | | | _____ |
| | | | _____ |
| | | | _____ |
| Transition to next shot ☐ | | | _____ |

| Shot No. ☐ | Length of shot (Secs) ☐ | Shot description | Action |
| | | | _____ |
| | | | _____ |
| | | | _____ |
| | | | _____ |
| | | Camera angle/ movement | Sound/ Script in/out |
| | | | _____ |
| | | | _____ |
| | | | _____ |
| | | | _____ |
| Transition to next shot ☐ | | | _____ |

| Shot No. ☐ | Length of shot (Secs) ☐ | Shot description | Action |
| | | | _____ |
| | | | _____ |
| | | | _____ |
| | | | _____ |
| | | Camera angle/ movement | Sound/ Script in/out |
| | | | _____ |
| | | | _____ |
| | | | _____ |
| | | | _____ |
| Transition to next shot ☐ | | | _____ |

FIGURE 48   Sample storyboard blank

| SLIDE | TIME | VISUAL IMAGE | SOUND |
|-------|------|--------------|-------|
| 1 | 7 seconds | Long shot of school buildings | Fade in children's voices from playground |
| 2 | 6 seconds | Close-up on children in science lab. | Voices and music |
| 3 | 6 seconds | Children in art lesson | Voices and music |
| 4 | 6 seconds | Children on sports field | Voices and music |
| 5 | 15 seconds | School assembly | Script – welcome to Newton school, etc. |
| 6 | 10 seconds | Close-up on school choir | Commentary on assembly music, school community |
| 7 | 10 seconds | Shot of school open evening | Commentary on parents and school |

**FIGURE 49**   Script for tape–slide production

time and your sound script. Only by viewing the whole thing can you assess the appropriate length of time on screen. For some slides ten seconds may be too short if there is a lot of detail to discuss; for some slides ten seconds may be too long if you want a rapid sequence to create interest. Viewers can take in a lot of visual detail in two to three seconds. But you also need to remember that slides take time to change – they cannot cut like film or video.

If you have access to a slide machine, with a cassette built in which can record on tape and record a pulse to change the slide automatically, this is a great help. If you do not have this machine for pulsing the tape, you need a cue script for the presenter to be able to change the slides at the required point.

7   **Presentation**: as with all productions seek to test it before you finally complete it. Seeking feedback from the target audience is crucial to ensure that you are meeting their needs.

## 7.3 Mounting an exhibition

An exhibition provides a permanent or temporary presentation for large numbers of people in a variety of locations. It does not necessarily depend on access to technology for its use and it can have good visual impact as well as providing verbal information.

Here we shall confine ourselves to the design of a few easy to handle panels. However, professional exhibitions may be the creation of a complete environment in, say, a museum, a gallery or a trade exhibition where a stand may consist of a complete room using a whole range of technical inputs.

Any exhibition requires the design of images and words and the design of a physical layout and space to engage the attention and participation of visitors. An exhibition can include posters, photographs, cartoons, diagrams, text, slides, sound, video input, computer data display, leaflets or question-naires to take away, people to talk to, food to taste and so on. There is almost no limit to what can be provided if resources allow it.

With these ideas in mind, the producer of an exhibition needs to address the following issues:

1   **The stand itself**: size, weight, location for display, the materials it is to be made of, whether it is self-sufficient or needs people to manage it and display it. Use arrows or layout to show people how they should follow the items.

2   **Text**: keep words to the minimum; capture key ideas; these should be carefully written and use eyecatching graphic layout to create interest. Type size is obviously crucial and will vary according to the scale and location of the stand.

3   **Pictures**: photos (not small snapshots), captions, cartoons and line diagrams all need to be bold and eyecatching at the right scale. You need to think about how far away people will be when they view it. You may be able to build in a slide projector or video player as part of the stand.

4   **Sound**: use of pre-prepared tape with sound, music or voices is useful to capture attention. Be wary of using voices, however, since the stand is likely to be surrounded by noise anyway.

5   **Things to take away or things to do**: a summary leaflet may be useful; a questionnaire could be appropriate; you could have a game or quiz, or you may have free samples. All of this will depend on the nature of the exhibition and the impact you want to have after the exhibition has gone.

6   **Layout in exhibition space**: it is useful to make a ground plan so that

you can experiment with what goes where. Think about where people come in and what they first see – probably a display that explains the whole exhibition and which directs them in some way. Think about the space needed for people to circulate around safely and comfortably. Think about giving people enough room to stand back from a display board and to see things properly. Think about the direction or sequence that you may want visitors to take. This can help to stop crowding in a confined space. It may be about making sense of the whole thing.

In producing exhibition boards, your access to large-scale printing or photo-copying will dictate the possibilities.

Since people will be moving around the exhibition, the issue of safety is important. You must make sure if someone touches it or knocks it, it will not fall down.

The overall theme for mounting an exhibition should be to keep it uncluttered. Think of exhibitions or displays that have made an impact on you. Probably they were simple and direct with a few key ideas well expressed, with strong images and strong use of lettering. Detailed text is best put on a sheet for people to pick up.

## 7.4 Making video tapes

This section assumes you have access to one portable video camera and to an editing facility with two video recorders. However most of the ideas here can be done with one single camera, especially if you are fully prepared to 'edit' shots in camera as you take them using the pause button. We are interested in helping you to produce video tapes from a communication point of view. We are not seeking to introduce technical jargon or to cover video production at anything like a professional level. In the resource list at the end of this book, you will find several sources of information to take video-making further.

Producing videos can be great fun and good for experimenting with interesting ways of presenting material. But video productions can also be very disappointing when what gets recorded on tape bears little relationship to what you intended. This may be a result of your own lack of experience, the limitations of the equipment, or your need to manage other people more effectively when you need their help. The interpersonal and group skills required for producing video productions should not be underestimated.

A successful production depends on detailed planning and careful preparation at every stage as well as a range of technical and social skills. The most important single piece of advice is to be well organized.

The following is a checklist of steps that will help you towards the final production you hope for.

1    **Get to know how to use your equipment.** The basic quality of picture and sound determines the final outcome. Use your instruction manual and have lots of practice. Make sure that you carry out a quick check before you go out. Check that batteries in the video camera, the audio recorder and the neck of an external microphone are there and charged. Have spare batteries with you if at all possible. Check that the camera is set up – until you get confident, put all the relevant switches on auto or leave them alone. In particular, if your camera has an SVHS switch then leave it off the SVHS setting unless you know that you can use SVHS kit. If you are using a separate recorder as part of your shoot, then do a voice check to make sure it is working. If you are plugging a separate microphone into the camera, then try taping it firmly to a strong bamboo garden cane – this gives you an instant boom mike! If your camera has an edit pause switch (usually at the back of the camera), then put it on. This means that your stops and starts come out as clean cuts on screen (see 5 below).

2    **Experiment with using the camera** in a range of shots, for example, long shots and close-ups on people. Try a range of angles, at eye level for example and from a high or low angle. Try techniques of panning (sideways movements of the camera) and tilting (up and down movement). Observe the effect on the viewer when you review your camera work; if you are using a low angle it probably suggests some sort of looking up to authority. In early days with the camera, there is a tendency to move it around as if it were a hose pipe: such an effect on the viewer can be irritating. Think about the frame of your picture and what you are putting into the shot. When you are filming for real, use a tripod if at all possible. No one has a totally steady hand. Run through each shot in terms of zoom or pans and framing, before the take. Note that zoom is the [W]ide–[T]ight rocker switch on your camera. Make your camera movements in what you think is slow motion – it will look fine on screen.

3    **Experiment with lighting.** Get to know the effect of different light direction. Basically keep your light sources behind the camera unless you want special effects. This means that you should never shoot people against the sky or a window because they come out as black silhouettes.

4    **Experiment with sound** through the camera and, if you have them, through different sorts of microphone. Remember that the inbuilt camera mike is only good for sounds up to about two metres away. This is why it is good to have a separate mike plugged in. The camera mike is not bad for a half body shot on someone talking. But further than

this and it 'chooses' to pick up other sounds around that you may not want. With some cameras you can plug in headphones to monitor the sound that you are getting. If you can, use these. If you can borrow a rifle mike you will find this is excellent for selecting sound in a certain direction and from a distance – very useful for voices.

5  **If you have access to editing equipment again practise with the equipment.** If you have only in-camera editing you will have to choose the order and length of your shots within a sequence very carefully in advance. Similarly, experiment with sound editing and dubbing (putting new sound over the visual image) if you can. If you don't want to or can't do in-camera editing but will use an edit suite, then allow over-run at the end of each shot, and preferably put a few seconds of blank tape between each shot. When you use a camera in 'standard mode' and start it again after a pause (especially if it has gone to standby) then it runs back over the last three seconds of tape and wipes it. This could mean losing the end of the previous shot.

6  Once you have some confidence in using your equipment and you know its capabilities, **then you can think about producing a 'programme' or a film story.** All we have said elsewhere about getting started (see pages 221–3) and about using storyboards and scripts also applies to video productions. Ideally you need three people to shoot video: camera operator, sound person probably holding external mike and production assistant to log everything that is recorded (what it is and how long).

The essential sequence of planning and producing a programme is likely to include:

- Brainstorming for ideas and discussing them with other people
- Carrying out research on topics, people, places for filming, possible sequences and a variety of visual and sound input
- Using a storyboard to visualize the total sequence
- Preparing an outline script
- Preparing a plan for producing the whole sequence which will include dates, times, places and people involved
- Producing final scripts with any necessary titles or captions as well as sources of material
- Logging (recording and noting) everything that you have recorded: timing, shot numbers, tape numbers, shot/location description
- Editing recordings: this is a very time-consuming activity
- Dubbing sound recording onto your finished tape where appropriate

# 8 Into the Net

This section is a brief account of some basic features of the Internet. In terms of the hands-on skills of accessing it and using it, you would be wise to get some first-hand advice or demonstration. The Net isn't at all difficult to use. We want to raise its profile in students' minds now that most schools and colleges have access to it, and that it has become a useful source of information.

To access the Net, you need a telephone connection, a computer, a modem to link the last two, a user deal to access the Net and have an e-mail address, and programs [cheap, such as *Netscape*] to access and search it. All you have to do is to get your new program to work through the modem and dial into the Net. Then you can look for 'places' to go.

These places – called websites and bulletin boards – are electronic locations where someone has displayed lists of information or pictures or even software which in many cases you can access and print out. For a student a major use of the Net is to research topics. You can send and receive electronic mail. You can also simply explore, literally around the world – the famous 'surfing'.

For many bulletin boards and all e-mail addresses you may need a 'code' to get to it. These are easy to get from other users. Once you have found a useful board or site you can store it on your machine (ours are called 'bookmarks'), giving it your own name. So the next time you want to visit that site, all you have to do is to click on your bookmark. You can collect these under headings, like news. You will also find sites where someone has already done that for you. It is also possible to 'jump' from one address to another – your screen will show you 'hot' hypertext links. Although commercial organizations are increasingly using the Net to seek publicity and make contact with customers, there are a lot of private users and educational institutions that are generous with their material. To be fair to them, organizations like radio stations and TV companies are also generous in providing information about their businesses.

Although we may not have imparted many specific skills in this last section, we hope that we have encouraged readers to see why they should acquire them. It is easy to get overexcited about new technology. But it is simply a matter of fact that this is an area where communication students need to be competent – like using the telephone. Tomorrow has become today.

## Assignment: Case Study

---

NATIONAL SOCIETY FOR ROAD SAFETY
Barnham House
Colwell Terrace
London NW16 5NM

Tel: 0171 – 5827966

Press Release: immediate

30 June 1997

CARMAGEDDON: Computer game

This game has been referred to the Society for comment. It has been the subject of much discussion in the press. Players drive simulated cars at high speeds and gain points for knocking down people and animals.

The Society regrets that the Video Standards Council has awarded this game a 15 plus certificate. We find the game disturbing. It is not an appropriate message to be sending out. People endure much pain and grief because of reckless driving. Glorifying such behaviour can deliver a dangerous signal to future and current drivers who use the game.

END

Contact: The Press Secretary

---

You should refer to the press release from the National Society for Road Safety, to complete these tasks.

You are a researcher/production assistant for an 'issues'-based radio programme entitled *Now Britain*. The producer has decided to run an edition on sex, violence and sexism in computer games.

You obtain an interview with the marketing manager of the company selling the game *Carmageddon*. He says of the graphics and game victims, 'We have made slight cosmetic changes ... giving the characters zombie-white faces and red eyes. When they are hit they emit a green gunk as opposed to blood ... we are not trying to offend people ... the idea of cars deliberately hitting people is not new: it was aired by the film *Death Race 2000*.'

You also interview the editor of *PC Magazine*, who says, 'We liked it. Mowing down pedestrians clearly isn't something we would like to encourage but it is so obviously over the top as to be pure fantasy. It may not be morally correct but it is fun. There is no question that it will sell well.'

Now complete the following tasks.

(a) List who else you might interview in the course of your research, and why.

(b) Draft a blurb to go in one of the listings magazines such as *Radio Times*, describing this programme edition.

(c) Script the voice piece introducing the edition. You may use sound from the game and an interview clip. The piece should not run over thirty seconds.

(d) Write a draft for a script segment to be used by the programme presenter, which puts forward arguments for and against censorship of video games – to last no more than one minute.

(e) Script a radio advert for *Carmageddon*, lasting fifteen to twenty seconds.

## Suggested reading

Dimbleby, R., Dimbleby, N., and Whittington, K., *Practical Media: a guide to production techniques*.

For further information on practical communication and media skills, see the section on practical communication resources on page 269.

# Glossary of communication terms

This list provides a brief definition of how some important terms are used in communication studies. We also suggest you consult the Index of this book. For further references and information see *Key Concepts in Communication* by T. O'Sullivan, J. Hartley, D. Saunders and J. Fiske (2nd edition); and *A Dictionary of Communication and Media Studies* by J. Watson and A. Hill (2nd edition).

**Agenda setting** refers to the process by which the news media define which topics (the agenda) should be of main interest to the audience. Hence the media have a significant influence on issues for public discussion.

**Assertiveness** refers to skills through which the communicator asserts her/his needs without imposing on others.

**Audience** Those persons who are the receivers of a message, particularly of a mass-media message. (Also called **receiver** or **destination**.)

**Barriers to communication** Factors in the communication process that impede open communication between source and destination. (Also called **filters** or **noise**.) They exist within individuals (psychological filters), within the sign/message (semantic filters) and within the context (mechanical filters).

**Channel** The means of communication through which messages flow from source to destination. Most examples of the communication process include multiple channels.

**Code** A system of signs bound by conventions. The English language is a primary code (see also the notion of secondary codes, page 29).

    **Encoding** refers to the process of translating ideas, feelings, opinions into signs following the conventions of a code (e.g. speaking or writing).

    **Decoding** refers to the understanding and interpreting of signs (e.g. listening or reading).

**Communication** The process of creating and sharing meaning through the transmission and exchange of signs. This process requires interaction within oneself, between people, or between people and machines.

**Communication skills** are about the ability to control various means of communication in order to produce effective communication. Skills are to do with managing social interaction successfully, rather than to do with technical expertise.

**Consensus** refers to the centre ground of beliefs and values agreed within a society. These are broadly held and proposed by the mass media. As expressed by the media consensus tends to exclude the notion of alternative or multiple views of a given topic or issue.

**Context** is the environment or surroundings in which communication takes place. Contexts may be physical or social/cultural.

**Conventions** are rules defining how signs are used within codes and how these signs, collectively, may be understood.

**Culture** A collection of beliefs, values and behaviours distinctive to a large group of people and expressed through various forms of communication. It is common to identify culture in terms of nation (e.g. French), or area (e.g. European), or race and religion (e.g. Jewish). Culture is represented through dress, religion and art forms in particular, as well as through language.

> **Popular culture** generally refers to popular and commercial forms of art and media entertainment.

> **High culture** generally refers to the culture of an educated and dominant class.

> **Folk culture** generally refers to the culture which is created by people for themselves. It usually relies on oral traditions.

> **Mass culture** generally refers to the popular culture shared by a mass media/consumer audience.

**Discourse** is a term which is used in a variety of contexts to describe how certain kinds of understanding are created and perpetuated within various institutions in society. These discourses are about ideas and meanings which are made apparent through the use of communication. Whilst the word originally referred to patterns of speech, it is now used to refer to patterns of communication processes in education, the mass media or television or a particular type of television, such as news.

> **Discourse analysis** refers to the ways of trying to identify the elements in the communication processes of a particular medium. It is usually used to refer to the analysis of the output of mass media and how the audience interacts with that output.

**Feedback** is communication in response to a previous message. It includes the idea that the sender adjusts his or her communication style in response to feedback. Feedback is continuous in conversation. It may be a deliberate response (e.g. a spoken reply) or an unintentional response (e.g. some non-verbal behaviours).

**Gatekeeper** refers to an individual within an organization who has some power to control and direct the flow of information into and out of that organization. This power may include the right to select information or even to interpret it (e.g. a news sub-editor).

**Genre** A term describing a recognizable body of work with common characteristics (e.g. science fiction). Genres are thus usually recognized within popular narrative fiction and art forms.

**Ideology** is a term for describing a particular view of the world constructed from certain sets of values. The twentieth century has been much influenced by a conflict of two ideologies, capitalism and communism, not to mention those ideologies which we call religions. There is usually a **dominant ideology** in a given culture. The values and beliefs of this dominant ideology come to us through major agencies of socialization – family, school and the media. The value messages concerned are contained in media texts. From one view these messages are 'packaged up under topic headings' such as family, or crime, and can be called **discourses**. These messages/meanings often come across implicitly, through the ways that the media text puts things across, as much as through what it obviously says.

**Image** A picture, as seen in a photograph or single frame of film. In literary criticism an image is an extended metaphor. More broadly image can refer to a mental conception of a person, place or thing (e.g. a brand image of a particular consumer product).

**Information** refers in the first place to factual communication, including verifiable and objective facts about the world. More broadly the term can include anything which adds to our sum of knowledge about the world and people. In this case, beliefs and opinions given and received could be described as information. Information serves to reduce uncertainty – you know more than you did before gaining the information.

**Institution** describes a great range of organizations, usually commercial, which own and control media industries. Most obviously, one is talking about businesses like Carlton Communications. But Reuters news agency or Microsoft could also be described as institutions.

**Internet** describes the world-wide network of communication based on computers and existing cables and satellite links. The Web, which is what most people use, is a system which uses the network. The Net, or the Web, is unique in that no company owns it. It lives through its users. Some companies (e.g. Demon or Virgin) can make money selling you a connection to it and an e-mail address, and others by owning particular websites with things for sale.

**Language** is a widely used term referring to a system/code for organizing signs according to conventions. Learning how to use our native language is fundamental to becoming a social being. We use language for personal purposes (to think, organize our ideas and perceptions, and to imagine), for social purposes (to exchange messages with one another) and for cultural purposes (to record the past and to transmit ideas and values to the future).

**Meaning** What is signified by a message conveyed through the signs that we give or receive. The meanings of messages are in our heads, not in their words or pictures. What a sender means by the signs offered may be different from what the receiver understands by the signs received. Levels of meaning are often distinguished in signs: for example, a sign serves to **denote** a generally agreed basic meaning within a culture and it also serves to **connote** broader personal and cultural associations (e.g. words like *slim*, *slender*, *thin*, *lean*, *skinny* have similar basic denotations but also suggest different connotations).

**Medium/media** A channel or means of communicating. A medium usually comprises more than one form of communication. The word **media** has now come to refer to mass media.

> **Mediation** refers to the process of selection and interpretation which transforms material passing through the media.

**Message** A unit of information, whether of fact or of opinion, passed via a channel. In most examples of the communication process more than one message is passed. It is the **content** of a piece of communication.

> **Overt messages** are those which are apparent and obvious.
>
> **Covert messages** are those which are concealed, intentionally or otherwise. They may well be messages about beliefs, opinions and attitudes .

**Model of communication** is a consciously simplified description of a communication process which is usually expressed in graphic form as a diagram showing the elements of the process and how they relate to each other.

**Narrative** describes the story functions which exist in most media material. It covers aspects such as the unfolding of the storyline (plot) and the treatment of the story (drama). The term most obviously relates to items such a radio drama or a novel. But the news or a magazine travel feature, for example, also has narrative.

**NVB** Abbreviation for **non-verbal behaviour**. This phrase refers to all the actions people display, apart from speech, from which other people may draw meanings.

**NVC** Abbreviation for **non-verbal communication**. That is, the means of communication which includes body language, paralanguage and dress.

**Perception** refers to the process by which we make sense of the world and other people. It involves selecting, organizing and interpreting what we receive through our senses to create our own mental reality. Perception is a fundamental aspect of decoding meanings and depends on our knowledge, beliefs and experience.

**Process** refers to the act of communication, including the various factors which contribute to communication. Examples may be taken within any one of the four categories of communication (i.e. intrapersonal, interpersonal, group, mass). Communication is described as a process because it is not static.

**Realism** refers to the quality of real-ness in a media text. This quality is the result of our reading certain conventions from the text. There are different kinds of realism, some described by titles such as documentary or fiction.

**Representation** is the act of re-presenting something through the media. Generally, one could have representations of anything – London, family life. In particular the term is often applied to representations of groups/types of people. It does lead one to the study of stereotyping, but this is not all that it is about.

**Role** A part played by an individual within a given group and situation. This part includes selected personality traits and kinds of behaviour which help define that person's relationship with other people in a group (e.g. work roles or family roles).

**Semiology** The discipline or area of study that examines signs and their meanings.

**Sign** A single unit of communication which conveys a meaning (or meanings) that is learnt through education or socialization. Most examples of communication include a flow of signs, perhaps through more than one channel, all of which interact. Anything which we can say has a meaning may be defined as a sign, whether it be a word or an object.

**Socialization** The process through which we learn the dominant beliefs, values and behaviour acceptable within our society. So it is also concerned with learning to communicate. The family, work, school and the media are significant agents of socialization.

**Stereotype** A simplified depiction of a person or group, in writing or in a picture, usually represented in the media. The type has a few dominant characteristics that make it easily identified (e.g. the nutty professor).

**Strategy** A piece of communication with a purpose. The term usually refers to interpersonal communication in which we use strategies, learnt through experience, to achieve a purpose such as the breaking-off of conversation.

**Sub-culture** A cultural group within a dominant larger culture. The subculture nevertheless has its own distinctive characteristics and behaviour and beliefs (e.g. West Indian communities in Britain, Hell's Angels).

**Text** describes any piece of media material using any form of communication. TV programmes, newspaper articles, computer games are all texts.

    **Textual analysis** is the process of looking into a text to see what messages are in it. The most important messages are to do with values and beliefs – ideology.

**Transaction** A communication exchange, usually with functional connotations (e.g. withdrawing money from a bank). Two or more people agree to deal with one another (interact) to develop a relationship that will enable the exchange of meanings.

# Resources list for Communication Studies

This selected resources list is arranged in three sections: books, other resources and addresses. (S) denotes a book that is accessible to college or senior school students. (G) denotes a book that is accessible to GCSE level students. It includes books referred to in the text.

## Books

### General communication, including theory and language

Baker, Larry, *Communication*, New York, Prentice Hall, 1988 – a US textbook providing basic introduction (S).

De Vito, Joseph A., *Human Communication: the basic course*, New York, Harper & Row, 3rd edn, 1985 – another useful general US textbook (S).

Ellis, Richard, and McClintock, Ann, *If You Take My Meaning: theory into practice in human communication*, London, Edward Arnold, 2nd edn, 1996 (S).

Fiske, J., *Introduction to Communication Studies*, London, Methuen, 2nd edn, 1990 – useful coverage of the communication process. Strong on linguistic approach. Has a great deal to say about semiotic approaches (S).

Gill, David, and Adams, Bridget, *ABC of Communication Studies*, Basingstoke, Macmillan, 1989 (S).

Gration, Geoff, Reilly, John, and Titford, John, *Communication and Media Studies: an introductory coursebook*, London, Macmillan, 1988 – aimed at A-level students, well illustrated and practical information (S) (G).

McKeown, Neil, *Case Studies and Projects in Communication*, London, Methuen, 1982 – strong on working approach to case studies and projects: also an introduction to concepts. Discusses method from experience and examples (S).

McQuail, Denis, and Windahl, Sven, *Communication Models for the Study of Mass Communications*, London, Longman, 1981 – discusses purposes of 'modelling' and reproduces many different mass-communication models (S).

Montgomery, Martin, *Introduction to Language and Society*, London, Routledge, 1986 – readable introduction to sociolinguistics (S).

Morgan, John, and Welton, Peter, *See What I Mean: an introduction to visual communication*, London, Edward Arnold, 1986 (S) (G).

O'Sullivan, Tim, Hartley, J., Saunders, D., and Fiske, J., *Key Concepts in Communication*, London, Methuen, 1983 – reference book with definitions and descriptions of terms used in communication studies (S).

Watson, James, *What is Communication Studies?*, London, Edward Arnold, 1985 – concise introduction to aspects of studying communication (S).

Watson, James, and Hill, Anne, *Dictionary of Communication and Media Studies*, London, Edward Arnold, 2nd edn, 1989 – contains entries on a large number of words and phrases. Useful source of reference (S) (G).

## Interpersonal and group communication

Argyle, Michael, *The Psychology of Interpersonal Behaviour*, Harmondsworth, Penguin, 3rd edn, 1978 (S).

Argyle, Michael, *Social Interaction*, London, Methuen, 1969 – Argyle's books deal clearly with aspects of non-verbal communication and the processes of personal and group interactions.

Argyle, Michael, *The Social Psychology of Everyday Life*, London, Routledge, 1992 (S).

Berne, Eric, *What Do You Say After You Say Hello?*, London, Corgi, 1975 – transactional analysis (TA) approach to social interaction (S).

Burton, Graeme, and Dimbleby, Richard, *Between Ourselves: an introduction to interpersonal communication*, London, Edward Arnold, 1988 – readable survey of social psychology aspects of communication (S).

Douglas, Tom, *Groups: understanding people gathered together*, London, Tavistock, 1983 – detailed study of 'natural' and other groups.

Gahagan, Judy, *Social Interaction and its Management*, London, Routledge, 1984 – readable account of communication between people and groups.

Goffman, Erving, *The Presentation of Self in Everyday Life*, Harmondsworth, Pelican, 1959 – classic study of personal interaction in social institutions.

Hartley, Peter, *Interpersonal Communication*, London, Routledge, 1993 (S).

Honey, Peter, *Face to Face Skills*, Aldershot, Gower, 1990 (G).

Honey, Peter, *Improve Your People Skills*, London Institute of Personnel, 1988 – an alphabetical list of skills from acquiescence to worry (S).

Marsh, Peter, *Eye to Eye: your relationships and how they work*, London, Sidgwick and Jackson, 1988 (S) (G). This is a generously illustrated work with useful concise text and a great range of topics.

Morris, Desmond, *Manwatching*, St Albans, Triad Panther, 1978 – popular, brightly illustrated approach to non-verbal communication, including some cross-cultural perspectives. In an abridged edition too (S) (G).

Myers, G.E., and Myers, M.T., *Dynamics of Human Communication*, New York, McGraw-Hill, 4th edn, 1985 – American textbook for courses in speech communication, but also deals with important areas of self-concept, non-verbal communication, perception, language and interpersonal skills. Readable, clearly laid out, with ideas for practical work (S).

Patton, B., and Giffin, K., *Interpersonal Communication in Action*, New York, Harper and Row, 2nd edn, 1977 – readable account of processes and concepts of interpersonal communication. Summaries of other authors and helpful diagrams/models (S).

## Communication in business and organizations

Chambers, Ian (ed.), *Business Studies*, David Hall, Richard Jones and Carlo Raffo, Ormskirk, Causeway Press, 1996 (S).

Evans, Desmond W., *People, Communication and Organizations*, London, Pitman, 2nd edn, 1986 – summary of communication structures and conventions in 'business communication' (S).

Myers, M.T., and Myers, G.E., *Managing by Communication: an organizational approach*, New York, McGraw-Hill, 1982 – written for students of business and management in the USA, it contains communication theory and practical work. Lots of case studies, assignments and simulations.

Sallis, Edward, and Sallis, Kate, *People in Organizations*, 2nd edn, London, Macmillan, 1990 – readable and practical guide to business communications (S).

Stanton, Nicki, *Communication*, London, Macmillan, 1990 – readable account of the processes and forms of communication in business. It includes useful exercises and case study materials (S) (G).

## Mass media

Alvarado, Manuel, Gutch, Robin, and Wollen, Tana, *Learning the Media: an introduction to media teaching*, London, Macmillan, 1987 – organized around several major themes in media education.

Alvarado, Manuel, and Thompson, John O., *The Media Reader*, London, British Film Institute, 1991 – an anthology of writings from the 1980s.

Bazalgette, Cary, *Media Education*, London, Hodder & Stoughton, 1991 – brief guide to key concepts in media education and how they can be used in the curriculum.

Berger, John, *Ways of Seeing*, Harmondsworth, Pelican, 1972 – this and the BBC programmes (for hire) are still provocative essays on perception and the visual arts. In particular Berger presents original and well argued ideas about how we have learnt to see advertising images and images of women (S).

Branston, Gill, and Stafford, Roy, *The Media Student's Book*, London, Routledge, 1996 (S).

British Film Institute Television Monographs – booklets on television: note especially *Nationwide*, Television News, Structures of Television, Broadcasting and Accountability (S).

Burton, Graeme, *More Than Meets the Eye: an introduction to media studies*, London, Edward Arnold, 2nd edn, 1997 – readable introduction to the major theories of media education with useful examples and material for students (S).

Clarke, Mike, *Teaching Popular Television*, London, Heinemann, 1987 – a chapter on each major programme genre.

Crisell, Andrew, *Understanding Radio*, London, Routledge, 1987 – useful introduction to radio as a medium (S).

Curran, J., and Seaton, J., *Power Without Responsibility: the press and broadcasting in Britain*, London, Methuen, 4th edn, 1991 – useful comprehensive coverage of the development of the press, radio and television. It takes a critical view of ownership, control and the encouragement of consensus views (S).

Dutton, Brian, *Media Studies: an introduction*, Harlow, Longman, 2nd edn, 1995 – a lot of basic information and well illustrated for students (S) (G).

Dyer, Gillian, *Advertising as Communication*, London, Methuen, 1982 – study of advertising as a form of communication including cultural and semiological approaches (S).

Glasgow University Media Group, *Bad News*, London, Routledge & Kegan Paul, 1976 – 'Bad News', 'More Bad News', 'Really Bad News' – all carefully documented studies of TV news. Broadcasters contest the conclusions.

Goldman, Robert, *Reading Ads Socially*, London, Routledge, 1992 (S).

Gunter, Barrie, *Television and the Fear of Crime*, London, John Libbey, 1987 (S).

Hart, Andrew, *Making the Real World: a study of a television series*, Cambridge, Cambridge University Press, 1989 – a book that is part of a teaching pack to take you behind the making of science programmes (S).

Hartley, John, *Understanding News*, London, Methuen, 1982 – comprehensive study of news collection, news values and news presentation as communication (S).

Lusted, David (ed.), *The Media Studies Book: a guide for teachers*, London, Routledge, 1991 – collection of articles of major issues of media education.

Masterman, Len, *Teaching about Television*, London, Macmillan, 1980 – source of philosophy and practice for all teachers of television studies.

Myers, Kathy, *Understains: the sense and seduction of advertising*, London, Methuen, 1986 – one of the best analyses of advertising and its effects.

O'Sullivan, Tim, Dutton, Brian, and Rayner, Philip, *Studying the Media: an introduction*, London, Edward Arnold, 1994 (S).

Tunstall, Jeremy, *The Media in Britain*, London, Constable, 1983 – contains a good deal of background factual material about British media since 1945 (S).

Wall, Peter, and Walker, Paul, *Media Studies for GCSE*, London, Harper Collins, 1994 (G).

## Practical communication

Bowkett, John, *Communicate with Video*, Nottingham, Kore Publications, West Bridgford, NG2 7DR, 1978 – practical step by step guide to making video programmes (S).

Dimbleby, Richard, Dimbleby, Nick, and Whittington, Ken, *Practical Media: a guide to production techniques*, London, Hodder & Stoughton, 1994 – a clear and useful account of a range of media equipment and how to use it, with accessible and relevant tasks.

Evans, Harold, *Editing and Design*, London, Heinemann, 5 vols, 1972–8, especially *Newsman's English* (1972) and *Pictures on a Page* (1978) – readable, entertaining, well illustrated books by an experienced journalist (S).

Fawbert, Fred, *Video Handbook 1990*, Cambridge, National Extension College Trust Ltd – practical guide (S).

Hedgecoe, John, *Hedgecoe on Video: a complete creative and technical guide to making videos*, London, Pyramid Books, 1989 – a series of video tasks, lots of excellent illustrations (S) (G). See also *Hedgecoe on Photography*.

McCann, Richard, *Graphics Handbook*, Cambridge, National Extension College Trust Ltd, 1990 – practical guide (S).

Morrissey, Peter, and Warr, Sue, *Media Communication and Production*, Oxford, Heinemann, 1997 – designed for advanced GNVQ Media courses, but packed full of useful practical tasks, not only for using equipment but also for carrying out work such as audience research (G).

Pogue, David, *Macs for Dummies*, Foster City, CA, IDG Books Worldwide, 1994 – one of a set of books on using computers which is actually user-friendly (G) (S).

Turk, Christopher, *Effective Speaking*, London, Spon, 1985 – a comprehensive account of how to make an oral presentation (S).

Zeitlyn, Jonathan, *Effective Publicity and Design: a do-it-yourself guide to getting your message across*, London, Interchange Books, 1988 – practical aspects of designing posters, leaflets and exhibitions (S).

## Other resources

### Audio-visual materials

Addresses where these materials can be obtained are in the address list.

Barker, Peter, and Clarke, Mike, *Talking Pictures: an introduction to media studies* – filmstrip collection plus cassette commentary and printed teachers' notes. Section 1 deals with reading of images; section 2 deals with genres in film and television; section 3 investigates the presentation of news. From Mary Glasgow Publications Ltd.

*Reading Pictures and Selling Pictures* – photo sheets, teacher's book, slides. Intended for 14–15 year-olds to introduce the analysis of meaning in photographic images as 'representations of reality'. From the British Film Institute (BFI) Education Department. The BFI also produces many other slide collections and documentation for film analysis. Also available are film and video extracts (e.g. *Boys from the Blackstuff, Coronation Street*).

*Choosing the News, Teachers' Protest, The Market, The Station, The Visit* – simulations and exercises using photographs and printed material. From Society for Education in Film and Television (SEFT).

*Media Education: an introduction* (1992) – a pack containing workbook, video tape, audio tape, 36 slides and a course reader with extracts from key documents, published by BFI Education and The Open University.

*Media at Work* by Team Video includes videos of 'Making News' and 'The British Media'.

*The Music Business*, a teaching pack with audio tape, T. Blanchard, S. Greenleaf, J. Sefton-Green, Hodder & Stoughton – a pack of information materials and educational activities interrogating the commercial nature and values of the pop music industry.

*The Newspaper File*, D. Grey and A. Hayhoe, Cambridge University Press – a resource pack which enables the user to look at aspects of the industry and the content and treatment of newspapers. Not very critical.

*Stop Press*, J. Hulley and D. Martin, Macmillan – an activity pack which deals with newspaper composition and treatment.

*The Television Programme* – Sheffield Media Unit, c/o Central Library, Surrey Street, Sheffield, S1 1XC – a photocopiable resource pack aimed at a basic level, dealing with common aspects of television study.

### Simulations

*Interplay* – a collection of case studies, articles and simulations for group work. Other collections are available on communication and psychology. From Longman Group Ltd, Resources Unit, 33–5 Tanner Row, York, YO1 1JP.

*Practising the Media* – activity pack covering news, genre and programme-making simulation from W.R. Chambers, Annandale Street, Edinburgh, EH7 4AZ.

*Radio Covingham, Front Page, The Dolphin Project* – a series of role play games from European Schoolbooks Ltd.

## Booklets and files

*Advertising Matters*, The Advertising Association – a most useful pack full of information about advertising and the media. The Association provides a list of other materials published, including *The Advertising Business: a guide for students and teachers.*

Banks, Tom, and Weston, Jane, *The Communications Kit*, Cambridge, Cambridge University Press, 1989 – a loose-leaf ring file with photocopiable masters, primarily designed for A-level students.

*Communication Skills Guide* including Letter writing, Report writing, Effective speaking, Interviews, published by the Industrial Society, Peter Runge House, 3 Carlton House Terrace, London, SW1Y 5DG.

Cuts, Martin, and Maher, Chrissie, *Writing Plain English*, 1980, published by the Plain English Campaign.

Film Education booklets – this organization has gone from strength to strength in organizing film screenings, producing booklets on films, and producing excellent booklets on topics such as genre and ideology, as well as offering a quarterly newsletter.

## Magazines and journals

For communication studies all newspapers and magazines can provide a source of materials for linguistic and image analysis, but this section contains a brief list of magazines that contain frequent articles on aspects of communication.

| | |
|---|---|
| *Audio Visual* | (monthly) |
| *Broadcast* | (weekly) |
| *Campaign* | (weekly) |
| *Marketing* | (monthly) |
| *Media, Culture and Society* | (quarterly) |
| *Media Education Journal* | (quarterly) |
| *Private Eye* | (fortnightly) |
| *Sight and Sound* | (quarterly) |
| *Spectrum* | (quarterly) |
| *Spectator* | (weekly) |
| *Time Out* | (weekly) |
| *UK Press Gazette* | (weekly) |

Addresses and other information for these journals can be found in the current edition of *Willings Press Guide*.

## Addresses

The following organizations provide materials of interest to the student of communication such as free leaflets, handbooks, reports, publicity brochures, film hire, educational packages and courses.

Advertising Association, Abford House, 15 Wilton Road, London, SW1V 1NJ.

Advertising Standards Authority Limited, 15/17 Ridgmount Street, London, WC1E 7AW.

Association for Media Education, Scotland (AMES), c/o The Scottish Film Council, 74 Victoria Crescent Road, Glasgow, G12 9JN.

Audio-visual Productions, Hocker Hill House, Chepstow, Gwent, NP6 5ER.

BBC, Broadcasting House, Portland Place, London, W1.

Birmingham Film and Video Workshop, 2nd floor, Pitman Buildings, 161 Corporation Street, Birmingham, B4 6PT.

British Film Institute, Education Department, 21 Stephen Street, London, W1P 1PL.

Campaign for Press and Broadcasting Freedom, 9 Poland Street, London, W1.

Central Film Library, Chalfont Grove, Gerrards Cross, Bucks, SL9 8TN.

Centre for Contemporary Cultural Studies, University of Birmingham, PO Box 363, Birmingham 15.

Engineering Careers Information Service, Engineering Industry Training Board, Clarendon Road, Watford.

English and Media Centre, 136 Chalton St, London NW1 1RX.

European Schoolbooks Limited, Croft Street, Cheltenham, Gloucestershire, GL53 0HX.

Film Education, 41–2 Berners Street, London, W1P 3AA.

Guild Organization Limited, Guild House, Oundle Road, Peterborough, PE2 9PZ (library of BBC, ITV and Open University films for sale and hire).

Independent Television Commission, 70 Brompton Road, London, SW3 1EY.

Industrial Society, Peter Runge House, 3 Carlton House Terrace, London, SW1Y 5DG.

Institute of Practitioners in Advertising, 44 Belgrave Square, London, SW1X 8QS.

Local Radio Workshop, 12 Praed Mews, London, W1.

Mary Glasgow Publications Limited, Brookhampton Lane, Kineton, Warwick, CV35 0BR.

MOMI Education, Museum of the Moving Image, South Bank, London, SE1 8XT.

National Museum of Film, Photography and Television (Education Department), Princes View, Bradford, BD5 0TR.

Plain English Campaign, 131 College Road, Manchester, M16 0AA.

Rank Aldis, PO Box 70, Great West Road, Brentford, Middlesex, TW8 9HR.

Video Arts Limited, Dumbarton House, 68 Oxford Street, London, W1N 9LA.

# Index